TOLERATING INTOLERANCE

Tolerating Intolerance

THE PRICE OF PROTECTING EXTREMISM

Amos N. Guiora

OXFORD
UNIVERSITY PRESS

Oxford University Press is a department of the University of Oxford. It furthers the University's objective of excellence in research, scholarship, and education by publishing worldwide.

Oxford   New York
Auckland   Cape Town   Dar es Salaam   Hong Kong   Karachi   Kuala Lumpur   Madrid
Melbourne   Mexico City   Nairobi   New Delhi   Shanghai   Taipei   Toronto

With offices in
Argentina   Austria   Brazil   Chile   Czech Republic   France   Greece   Guatemala   Hungary
Italy   Japan   Poland   Portugal   Singapore   South Korea   Switzerland   Thailand
Turkey   Ukraine   Vietnam

Oxford is a registered trade mark of Oxford University Press in the UK and certain other countries.

Published in the United States of America by
Oxford University Press
198 Madison Avenue, New York, NY 10016

Library of Congress Cataloging-in-Publication Data

Guiora, Amos N., 1957-
  Tolerating intolerance : the price of protecting extremism / Amos N. Guiora.
    pages cm—(Terrorism and global justice series)
  Includes bibliographical references and index.
  ISBN 978-0-19-933182-6 ((hardback) : alk. paper)
1. Minorities—Civil rights. 2. Political rights. 3. Radicalism.
4. National security—Law and legislation. I. Title.
  K3242.G85 2014
  303.48'4—dc23   2013017235

9 8 7 6 5 4 3 2 1

Printed in the United States of America on acid-free paper

Note to Readers
This publication is designed to provide accurate and authoritative information in regard to
the subject matter covered. It is based upon sources believed to be accurate and reliable and is
intended to be current as of the time it was written. It is sold with the understanding that the
publisher is not engaged in rendering legal, accounting, or other professional services. If legal
advice or other expert assistance is required, the services of a competent professional person
should be sought. Also, to confirm that the information has not been affected or changed by
recent developments, traditional legal research techniques should be used, including checking
primary sources where appropriate.

*(Based on the Declaration of Principles jointly adopted by a Committee of the
American Bar Association and a Committee of Publishers and Associations.)*

You may order this or any other Oxford University Press publication
by visiting the Oxford University Press website at www.oup.com.

While writing this book I trained for my first marathon, the Salt Lake City Marathon: I would like to thank family and friends who encouraged me, ran with me, trained me, answered all my questions, and were full participants in the process. To all, my deep appreciation.

Contents

Preface

A BOOK OF this nature is, obviously, a significant undertaking; to my immense gratitude I have been extraordinarily fortunate in calling upon many friends and colleagues, new and old alike. This book was born when my then editor, Kevin Pendergast, suggested a follow-up to *Freedom from Religion: Rights and National Security*. Although I was engrossed with the idea, the combination of existing obligations and uncertainty regarding secular extremism caused me to doubt the *plausibility* of the project Kevin envisoned. However, after a number of conversations with Kevin and others I decided to undertake the project. In doing so, I was convinced that in-country interviews would be essential to truly understand extremism in the context of a comparative analysis.

In that vein, I was very fortunate to receive a grant from the Earhart Family Foundation (Ann Arbor, Michigan); without their generosity and support this book would not have seen the light of day. Similarly, the Stuart Family Foundation (Chicago, Illinois) provided generous support enabling earlier travel and research in the Netherlands. Finally, the very gracious research stipend provided by the S.J. Quinney College of Law, University of Utah was, as always, invaluable and deeply appreciated.

The support, encouragement, and friendship provided by Dean Hiram E. Chodosh has proven, again, to be an inherent part of my scholarship. Hiram, who has accepted the Presidency of Claremont-McKenna College, will be sorely missed; this is the time and place to wish him the best of luck in his new capacity.

Because of the generous support provided by the Earhart Foundation, Stuart Foundation, and University of Utah Law School I was able to travel to Israel, the

Netherlands, Norway, and the United Kingdom. In spending time in each country (including, obviously, the United States) I was able to interview a significant number of experts in each country. There is no substitute for meeting with experts; although other forms of communication are very effective, personal meetings are invaluable. I was very fortunate that in each country experts, literally and figuratively, opened their doors to me.

Not only were they willing to meet with me but they often took the "extra step" of introducing me to colleagues and others they thought I should talk with. The age-old Israeli expression, "friend brings a friend," is wholly applicable to the research that provided much of the rich material presented in this book. To all those with whom I met, many thanks; this book is in many ways a reflection of your graciousness, generosity, and honesty. Because of the large number of people with whom I met or communicated via email or telephone I will refrain from mentioning all specifically. In addition, as is understandable in a book of this nature, a number of people must remain anonymous. However, records of all meetings are in my notes.

Yet, a number of individuals must be named; in doing so, I intend no offense to others; I trust this will be understood.

My friend, college roommate, and trusted advisor, The Reverend Dr. John C. Lentz, JR, pastor of the Forest Hills Presbyterian Church (Cleveland, Ohio) was, as always, a remarkably cogent commentator on previous drafts. In addition, John convinced a group of terrifically thoughtful subject matter experts in Cleveland to meet with me and to comment on earlier drafts. I am eternally grateful to John.

My friend and colleague, Professor Paul Cliteur, Professor of Jurisprudence, University of Leiden, read previous drafts and was an invaluable sounding board throughout the research and writing process. In addition, Paul very generously provided speaking and research opportunities for me in the Netherlands that significantly contributed to the final product. Because of Paul, Leiden has literally become a third home for me.

Two University of Utah law students agreed to the task of working with me on this book: during the academic year 2011–2012 Kennedy Nate (JD, 2012; designated a Quinney Scholar by the Law School) worked tirelessly with me both in the initial research and writing stages; thanks to a smooth handoff, Griffin Weaver (JD expected, 2014) effortlessly stepped into the large shoes Kennedy left. Griffin's efforts and dedication to this project were invaluable. I am, therefore, deeply appreciative of both Kennedy and Griffin for their significant contributions to this book.

Although I am in the debt of many people ultimate responsibility, obviously, rests with me. However, although that is, unequivocally, the case I must reiterate my enormous gratitude to all those—literally hundreds of individuals in six different countries—who agreed to help me better understand extremism. Your individual and collective willingness to take hours out of your busy schedules is both inspiring and humbling. Please know you have my deepest gratitude.

I close with a personal note: I lead a complicated life, regularly commuting between Salt Lake City and Tel Aviv (my family and I live outside of Jerusalem) and traveling extensively on a regular basis. This arrangement (now in its ninth year) is made possible through the efforts of many people. In particular, I would like to thank—and publicly acknowledge—the unstinting efforts of a wonderful group of people at the S.J. Quinney College of Law, University of Utah: Virginia Beane, Kathy Christiansen, Baiba Hicks, Lynette Saccomanno, Pam Pannier, Margaret Spight, and Mary Wheeler.

Introduction

I TRAVEL A great deal, domestically and internationally. Like anyone who spends significant time on planes (250,000 miles in 2011) it is my preference to tune out the world, particularly the person next to me; I do so thanks to BOSE headphones, listening to music my kids have gathered for me (I would not know how to download music if my life depended on it), and reading, working, or looking out the window. Sometimes, however, the person seated next to me seems particularly interesting, and relying on instinct I engage in conversation. If I am truly lucky, such a conversation can be extraordinarily engaging and thought provoking. This happened on a flight from Atlanta, Georgia, to Augusta, Georgia. My partner in row 1 was a physician with a busy private practice in Augusta. After a quick exchange of pleasantries we, somehow, made our way to discussing religion and extremism.

I told him about my previous book, *Freedom from Religion*, and about this book project. He was clearly intrigued and shared with me that he and his wife adopted a child because of their faith; he explained that as they have means it is their duty to share with others less fortunate than them. In his own words, he is an evangelical Christian and faith is the most important guide in both his professional and personal life. I asked him how he resolves his deep evangelical faith with modern medicine; his response was a total surprise for me. Simply put, he does not believe in evolution, viewing it as physiologically impossible.

For him, creationism is the only possibility, and all efforts to explain evolution are nonstarters. I asked him how he resolves the tension, perhaps intellectual disconnect and profound contradiction are better terms, between modern science and creationism. His response was simple and clear: my job is to save peoples' lives, and evolution plays no role in what I do. Simply put, it is God who decides. When I shared this conversation with physician friends, their reactions ranged from bewilderment to apoplexy; many expressed regret they did not have the chance to directly engage him in a science-based conversation—something I am thoroughly incapable and incompetent to do.

The second part of our conversation related to his family and homosexuality. He shared with me that he and his wife have six children. One of his children is a bachelor in his mid-20s regarding whom we had the following exchange based on a hypothetical—akin to a law school exam—that his son is a homosexual:

ANG: What would you do if that child were to inform you that he is a homosexual?

MD: My wife and I would seek to talk him out of it.

ANG: What would you do if your child wanted to bring his homosexual partner home?

MD: The partner would never step into our house.

ANG: Would you attend your son's homosexual wedding?

MD: (After looking wistfully into space for a few seconds) No, my wife and I would not attend, and we would request that our other children also not attend.

ANG: But I thought you loved your son more than anything in the world.

MD: I do, but I love the Bible more than I love my son.

I found the conversation extraordinarily enlightening, perhaps painful, and certainly candid. After discussing it with friends and colleagues, and wrestling with what is the appropriate forum for sharing this exchange, I decided it is a relevant and powerful opening to this book. I do so carefully because the conversation was private; however given the rawness of its emotions and what it conveys regarding the depth of religious belief, I decided to include it. There was one last exchange, which, for me, was of extraordinary importance.

ANG: Listening to you reminds me of conversations with deeply religious Jews and Moslems, for both are convinced of the absolute rightness and truth of their faith and path.

MD: Correct, but there is a difference.

ANG: What is the difference?

MD: I know the truth.

ANG: Funny, because that is what they say.

MD: I know, but I am right.

Perhaps, more than any other dialogue this last exchange neatly summarizes how a person of deep religious faith articulates his or her worldview. I would not define this individual as an extremist;[1] however, his conviction that his truth is the absolute truth places him—whether he agrees or not—in the same camp as religious extremists. Although I assume my seatmate was not a man of violence, his refusal to accept that others may also believe they "know the truth" and that their faith is as valid as his suggests that this educated physician is a religious extremist. Not violent, but unrelenting in absolute conviction of the rightness of "my truth" and the total dismissal of others. In particular, I was struck by his conviction that he and his family not attend his son's hypothetical wedding. Whether this is akin to "hate the sin, love the sinner" in that he is proving his love to his son by not participating in the son's celebration is a valid question. Regardless of the answer, the father's faith trumps the son's hypothetical decision. This type of extremism, though, is not unique to religion and can also be found in the political arena. An example of this is seen in the defeat of six-term Senator Lugar in the Indiana Republican Party Senate Primary. In a statement shortly after his loss he explained what he believed caused it:

> Unfortunately, we have an increasing number of legislators in both parties who have adopted an unrelenting partisan viewpoint. This shows up in countless vote studies that find diminishing intersections between Democrat and Republican positions. Partisans at both ends of the political spectrum are dominating the political debate in our country. And partisan groups, including outside groups that spent millions against me in this race, are determined to see that this continues. They have worked to make it as difficult as possible for a legislator of either party to hold independent views or engage in constructive compromise. If that attitude prevails in American politics, our government will remain mired in the dysfunction we have witnessed during the last several years.[2]

Much like the stranger on the plane, it seems this extremism or conviction of rightness at the complete dismissal of other viewpoints has led to an ignoring of what is best for the public and entertaining only what fits a particular ideology.

This conversation, along with Senator's Lugar's words, is a most appropriate background for the issues this book explores: religious and secular extremism in a number of countries. Six nations—Germany, Israel, the Netherlands, Norway, the United Kingdom, and the United States—will be surveyed by examining specific examples from each country. The book focuses on a myriad of issues including the US civil rights movement, child endangerment in the context of religious extremism, soccer hooliganism, public demonstrations against women singing, unbridled religious extremist incitement, violent neo-Nazism, extreme right-wing actions, multiculturalism, the limits of free speech,

---

[1] An issue discussed at length in this book.

[2] Mike Zapler, *Lugar Unloads on "Unrelenting" Partisanship*, POLITICO BLOG (May 9, 2012, 7:48 AM), http://www.politico.com/blogs/on-congress/2012/05/lugar-unloads-on-unrelenting-partisanship-122891.html.

tolerating intolerance, and the social compact. The theme of "tolerating intolerance" is essential to this book.

Dean (then professor) Martha Minow's article,[3] "Tolerance in an Age of Terror," is the intellectual background for the discussion ahead. No other law review article has so significantly shaped my thinking; I have read it innumerable times and include it in my seminar "Global Justice." After all, in discussing extremism, the key questions are: to whom is a duty owed, and what are the limits of intolerance that are to be tolerated?

Answering these questions requires examining limits and rights; analyzing them in the context of extremism is the "core" of this book. Although freedom of speech and freedom of religion are vital to democracies, these freedoms are not unlimited. Where to draw the line between permissible and impermissible is complicated. Doing so in the extremist paradigm significantly exacerbates that complexity; lines are starkly drawn because extremists and extremism pose threats, yet the public must determine to what extent it protects itself from extremists while ensuring that extremists' rights are not violated. Addressing this tension is essential; it is, to coin a phrase, where the book is "going." The basic theme that will be woven is that religious and secular extremists pose dangers to society and individuals alike; the question I will seek to answer is to what extent should, and does, society protect itself against a readily identifiable threat. The threat is readily identifiable because extremists do not hide; their visibility is undeniable. Whether society chooses to "see" that threat is essential to the discussion; why the threat is minimized, at best, and ignored at worst is a classic example of history repeating itself.

Undertaking this examination requires balancing rights and limits; complicating the analysis is the "sacred veil" that protects religion and hinders candid discourse regarding dangers posed by religious extremism. Addressing the immunity oftentimes granted religion can pierce that veil, if not lift it. Secular extremism does not enjoy similar protection; nevertheless, line drawing between protected and illegal secular conduct is no less complicated than tackling the dilemma regarding religious extremism. In addressing the dangers posed by religious and secular extremism, I hope to highlight the dangers both pose to society and individuals alike. Furthermore, the book includes recommendations for specific measures that will facilitate the nation-state's ability to protect itself while ensuring protection of those posing a danger to the state. That is, to what extent does the nation-state protect freedom of religion and freedom of speech to those who would minimize freedoms for and of others?

2012[4] marks 17 years since the Murrah Federal Building bombing, 11 years since 9/11, four years since the coordinated attacks in Mumbai, and one year since the tragic attack in Norway that killed 77 Norwegians. Each serves as a tragic reminder of the extraordinary power of extremism, religious and secular alike. Clearly, extremism is not a new

---

[3] *See* Martha Minow, *Tolerance in an Age of Terror*, 16 U.S.C. INTER. L.J. 453 (2007).

[4] When these lines are written.

phenomenon; however, because it continuously confronts society on a daily basis it is essential to study, understand, and define it. Narrowly defining extremism is essential; otherwise the danger of recklessly castigating, much less punishing for mere thought alone is a distinct possibility.

One of the specific goals of this book is to propose a narrow, carefully crafted definition of extremism. Arthur Miller's powerful play *The Crucible*[5] brilliantly articulates the dangers of extremism when used to justify harming otherwise innocent individuals. It must be recalled that *The Crucible* depicts the horrors of the Salem Witchcraft Trials while analogizing to the "darkness at noon"[6] of McCarthyism.

To that end, both the iconic phrase "round up the usual suspects" made famous in *Casablanca* and Justice Jackson's seminal warning regarding the "unfettered executive"[7] serve as powerful reminders of the requirement to balance legitimate individual rights with equally legitimate national security rights. Although extremism poses a danger to society there is equal danger in casting an arbitrary, capricious net in an effort to protect society. The responsibility and burden confronting decision-makers regarding this tension is, literally, overwhelming and fraught with danger. One of this project's goals is to address the tension candidly and to recommend mechanisms facilitating resolving its seemingly intractable conundrum.

There is an interesting paradox to be noted: although history is replete with examples of overreaction in the face of crisis, contemporary society has demonstrated a startling inability to clearly recognize an obvious threat. In addressing extremism from the balancing perspective, the primary question is whose rights are to be protected and how the tension between individual rights and national security rights is to be resolved. In addressing this core question the assumption is that both are legitimate and must be protected.

Clearly extremism is not a new phenomenon; any effort to limit its scope and impact must be done with sensitivity and respect for otherwise guaranteed rights. After all, the right to free speech is essential to democratic societies and culture. That said, the extremism confronting contemporary society is exacerbated both by the tone of the current political climate and the power, speed, and reach of the Internet. The blogosphere, social network, and Internet dramatically impact how the message of extremism is conveyed. One of the great challenges confronting decision-makers is how to respond to the Internet's facilitation of extremism while respecting individual and civil rights.

In other words, the challenge is determining what degree of extremism can be tolerated—in the context of freedom of speech—before determining that extremists pose a clear and present danger.

A research project of this scope significantly benefits from direct outreach to a broad range of experts, commentators, and observers; to that end, a questionnaire was sent

---

[5] *See generally* Arthur Miller, The Crucible (Dramatists 1952).

[6] *See generally* Arthur Koestler, Darkness at Noon (Scribner 1968).

[7] Youngstown Sheet & Tube Co. v. Sawyer, 343 U.S. 579 (1952).

to academics, security officials, policy makers, thought leaders, and religious leaders in Germany, Israel, the Netherlands, Norway, the United Kingdom, and the United States. Given the dangers posed by extremism and its ramifications for society and individuals alike, wide spectrums of society must participate in the discussion regarding extremism.

Respondents to the questionnaire were asked to address the following issues:

a. The definition of the term "extremism";
b. The dangers extremism poses to society;
c. The differences between secular extremism and religious extremism;
d. The causes/motivations for extremist movements (secular and religious);
e. The role of religion in fomenting/encouraging extremism (historically and currently);
f. The power of the Internet and social media in facilitating extremist movements and ideas;
g. The contemporary social tensions (i.e., economic crises, breakdown of traditional family structure);
h. The measures and methods to minimize reach/power of extremism/extremist leaders (both secular and religious);
i. The power of "hate speech" and what, if any, limits should be imposed on free speech in the context of extremism.

The book "tracks" these questions as reflected in the chapter headings. That is, the book's flow largely mirrors the questions posed in the questionnaire. Interspersed throughout the book are specific examples that highlight a particular issue. As an example, the trial of Dutch Member of Parliament, Geert Wilders, acquitted of five counts of hate speech and discrimination,[8] is an important "case study" addressing whose speech should be protected in the context of public discussion regarding religious extremism. As was made clear in the Wilders case, *how* to resolve this complex dilemma raises profoundly important questions regarding values and principles of contemporary society.

With respect to the chapters: there is, as readers of earlier manuscripts noted, an imbalance in their tone and content. The chapters, individually and collectively, are based on scholarship from different disciplines including law, sociology, religion, and political science; analysis of court cases from different jurisdictions; and significant in-country research. The in-country research, proceeded by significant study intended to enhance familiarization with the six surveyed countries, emphasized conversations with subject matter experts from distinct fields including national security experts,

---

[8] *Geert Wilders Acquitted on Hate Speech Charges*, Telegraph, June 23, 2011, http://www.telegraph.co.uk/news/worldnews/europe/netherlands/8593559/Geert-Wilders-acquitted-on-hate-speech-charges.html.

academics, faith leaders, people of faith, politicians, individuals previously convicted of extremist-related crimes, members of the media (traditional and non-traditional), and thought leaders. Rigorous effort was made to ensure that the book not reflect one of the disturbing, if not frightening, characteristics of extremism: the echo chamber. That is, I met with a wide range of experts representing and articulating disparate viewpoints on issues relevant to this book.

As to the imbalance in the chapters: some are "descriptive heavy," others reflect significant legal analysis, whereas others incorporate sociological and penal data. The free speech discussion (Chapter Seven) incorporates judicial decisions from a number of jurisdictions; the comparative approach is necessary to best understand the tension between free speech and its limits. Because of my belief that limiting the power of the inciter is essential to countering extremism, the freedom of speech discussion has magnified importance in this book. For that reason, Chapter Seven is particularly long; given the importance I attach to considering limiting free speech in minimizing the impact of extremism, the discussion must be detailed in its analysis of judicial rulings. That does not minimize the importance of the other chapters, quite the opposite. Because of the book's interdisciplinary and comparative approach, there is a clear need to explain, in depth, the relevant social, political, religious, and cultural paradigms pertinent to each surveyed country regarding extremism.

Although this is not a "travel-book," examining extremism from a comparative perspective requires understanding local culture, mores, and norms. To that end, there is a need for a descriptive discussion to better understand extremism in each country. The detailed discussion regarding a wide array of subjects is necessary both to enhance understanding extremism and to facilitate means to minimize its impact and dangers. The "how to minimize" discussion is both legal and nonlegal. The former focuses (as mentioned above) on limiting freedom of speech of inciters, the latter on a range of issues including education and employment.

One reader of an earlier draft commented that the book has innumerable spin-off possibilities primarily because it is very difficult to fit extremism into a one, unitary category. By its very nature it is interdisciplinary; that was consistently reinforced in meetings with thoughtful subject matter experts representing distinct disciplines. To that end, this book is painted on a wide canvas while focusing on specific issues; that is, addressing what is extremism and what dangers it poses requires a two-step process. The first step is the larger picture; the second step is a narrower focus. In that sense, spin-offs are a correct suggestion because of the large number of issues deserving further treatment, whether from the perspective of the law or from a distinct approach.

Defining extremism and determining the limits of tolerable extremism is essential to framing the discussion that drives this book. Although some might suggest definitions are problematic, the need to determine limits of lawful, tolerable behavior outweighs concern that definitions contribute, directly or indirectly, to limits on free speech. Undoubtedly that is a valid concern; nevertheless, the limits of lawful conduct must be candidly discussed.

Arguably the broad philosophical approach that "one man's terrorist is another man's freedom fighter"[9] would be preferred by those who shy away from definitions and the inevitable limits they impose on individual liberty and freedom. However, respecting the rights of individuals to articulate principles seemingly "outside the box" while ensuring speech stay within boundaries society can tolerate justifies defining relevant terms. In *Freedom from Religion: Rights and National Security*,[10] I chose not to define religion while proffering a definition of religious extremism. This decision—criticized by some—reflects my belief, after consulting with respected theologians and academics engaged in the study of religion, that defining religion is, frankly, all but impossible. It is, in many ways, whatever an individual chooses it to be; in other words, to quote the colloquialism, "whatever works for you."

However, although defining religion is an issue that I chose to shy away from, narrowly defining religious extremism was necessary. The reasons are twofold: because the harm religious extremists potentially cause is significant, and measures implemented by the nation-state to minimize the impact of religious extremism potentially impact civil and political rights. Religion, when practiced by people of moderate, mainstream faith, is largely concerned with man's relationship with God and provides positive social and faith exchanges for people either on an intra- or interfaith basis.

For that reason, moderate, mainstream religion does not pose a threat to civil, democratic society; accordingly, the state need not engage in a discussion on how to limit faith. That is in direct contrast to religious extremism that entails, as defined in *Freedom from Religion*, a willingness to harm another individual in order to bring glory to God. That reality—*the very real possibility of harm*—justifies government-imposed limits on the practice of extremist religion because the primary responsibility of government is to protect the civilian population, specifically children,[11] from harm, whether external or internal. That obligation imposes on government the responsibility—and the right—to impose limits on how religious extremism is *practiced*; similarly, it justifies imposing limits on the *free speech* of religious extremists. By extension, then, the same principle applies to secular extremism.

Nevertheless a "yellow card" is in order: there is danger in identifying threats to society. History has repeatedly shown that casting aspersions and collective punishment can have tragic results. However, the danger to society in not clearly defining potential threats—and failing to take pro-active measures to minimize possible harm—is no less.

The wide-ranging responses to the questionnaire question "how do you define extremism" reflect an extraordinary lack of uniformity and agreement; nevertheless there are

---

[9] GERALD SEYMOUR, HARRY'S GAME 62 (1975).

[10] AMOS GUIORA, FREEDOM FROM RELIGION: RIGHTS AND NATIONAL SECURITY (2009) (second edition forthcoming 2013, Oxford University Press).

[11] Amos N. Guiora, *Protecting the Unprotected: Religious Extremism and Child Endangerment*, 12 J.L. & FAM. STUD. 391 (2010).

certain basic similarities in the definitions offered. What, in broad strokes, the definitions suggest is that extremism is an explicit rejection of existing societal norms and mores. The extremist in addition to taking the law into his own hands unequivocally rejects restrictions and limitations imposed by society that are intended to preserve civil and social order.

That reasonable minds can reasonably disagree is one of the most treasured values and principles of democratic society; in many ways, it defines liberal society where discussion and debate represent an ideal. Highlighting extremism, then, potentially paints those who 'think outside the box"—punishing those deemed unconventional, free spirits who push the envelope while living on the edge. Those qualities, perhaps causing discomfort, do not, inherently, pose a danger to society. The human race has undoubtedly benefited from the contributions of individuals deemed extremist by their societies' mores, norms, and conditions.

The litany of such individuals is lengthy; obvious examples include Jesus, Newton, Copernicus, and Galileo. Conversely, others *also* considered extremists have caused unimaginable harm both to their own people and to the larger international community. The roster whose short list includes Hitler, Stalin, Pol Pot, and Mao reflects the true evil of unbridled extremism facilitated by what Daniel Goldhagen correctly identified as "willing executioners."[12]

There is, then, risk in highlighting extremism; some individuals, defined as extremists, have made extraordinary contributions to mankind. However, given the polarized age in which we live, failure to both address extremism and explore how to effectively, yet legally, curtail the influence of extremists is more dangerous. The burden, then, is to engage in a narrow discussion regarding individuals who directly threaten both society (in general) and vulnerable group-particular or individual-specific members of society while neither unduly nor unjustifiably limiting rights of those who push society within the bounds of the law. Hyperbole is the great danger in this discussion, both from the perspective of those who argue that limiting freedom of speech is inherently unlawful, and those who argue that broadly limiting free speech is justified in the face of nonconformity.

Mere thoughts cannot—and should not—be subject to limitation; however, words and actions must be subject to scrutiny in order to determine whether they pose a threat. Without doubt, the margin for error demands this demarcation line be clear; otherwise, basic rights will be violated in an arbitrary and capricious manner devoid of due process. However, although society must be protected against potential harm, determining whether it is ephemeral or concrete requires careful examination. Otherwise, striking a balance between individual rights and government obligation to protect the public is exceptionally difficult.

---

[12] *See* Daniel Jonah Goldhagen, Hitler's Willing Executioners: Ordinary Germans and the Holocaust (1996).

Nevertheless, ignoring threats is akin to "putting one's head in the sand"; it is a risk society cannot tolerate. Deliberately denying or underestimating risks posed to society because of concerns ranging from political correctness to minimizing otherwise protected rights to inexplicably ignoring harm are unacceptable alternatives. Equally dangerous, as the pages of history make clear, is overreaction, collective punishment, and unjustified violations of civil and political rights.

These contours serve as our guide in examining extremism in six different countries; although the bookends are, perhaps, clear the gray zone is just that—amorphous, vague, and complicated. However, because of the danger posed by extremism and the concomitant combination of overreaction and under-reaction in the face of risk, this uncomfortable discussion is essential. Perhaps that, more than anything else, drives this book. In that vein these insightful words are of particular importance: "the narrower question of the relationship between religious liberty and national security has only rarely been explored."[13]

---

[13] Samuel Rascoff, *Establishing Official Islam? The Law and Strategy of Counter-Radicalization*, 64 STAN. L. REV. 125 (2012).

THE COMPLEXITIES DEFINING EXTREMISM

I. Defining Extremism in Civil Society

What is extremism? Many have commented, written, spoken, and pontificated on this question. The answer, undoubtedly vague, depends on one's particular perspective, milieu, and culture. However, definition is critical to the issue this book addresses. After all, how can we limit something if we do not fully know what it is? Responses to the questionnaire regarding definitions of extremism were varied; the range of proposed definitions highlights its complexity and nuance. It is important to note that respondents did not have difficulty offering a definition of the term; rather, their struggle was in articulating a narrow and circumspect definition that avoids unnecessarily infringing on individual rights.

The tension is obvious; a broad and unwieldy definition both casts too wide a net and imposes limits on otherwise guaranteed rights whereas a narrow definition potentially harms members of society.[1] The magical word is *balance*: balancing legitimate individual rights with equally legitimate national security rights is, arguably, the most complicated

---

[1] The term "society" is used to incorporate both the population at large and specific groups and individuals targeted from within and without.

question confronting civil democratic society. Dean Minow addressed the balancing discussion in her law review article, "Tolerance in the Age of Terrorism":[2]

> A single nation may seem to or actually produce both intolerance and too much tolerance, generating both overreactions and under-reactions to terrorism. Because the United States and European nations each have pursued policies that threaten civil liberties and indicate intolerance of immigrants and dissenters, a detailed assessment is necessary—and so is analysis of the rhetorical arguments about over-reaction and under-reaction. Moreover, tolerance can be a feature of personal ethics, or national character, or public policy, and the connections between tolerance and anti-terrorism can take complex forms at each of these levels.[3]

In light of this need for a "detailed assessment" it is important to explore definitions from multiple sources and varying perspectives in order to best understand extremism. Although far from complete, some of the proposed definitions suggested by questionnaire respondents are highlighted below.

Extremism = violence in the absence of reason, or rather, the belief that committing an act of violence will produce benefits that outweigh the cost of human life. Violent extremism is homicide, genocide, fratricide, and, yes, it can also be terrorism.[4]

Single-mindedness, lack of empathy or tolerance for differing points of view.

Political extremism is the approval of violence as a means to achieve political goals.[5]

Extremism is a term used to describe either ideas or actions thought by critics to be hyperbolic and unwarranted. In terms of ideas, the term extremism is often used to label political ideology that is far outside the political center of a society.

Extremism is often used to identify aggressive or violent methodologies used in an attempt to cause political or social change.

---

[2] Martha Minow, *Tolerance in an Age of Terror*, 16 USC INTER. L.J. 453 (2007).

[3] *Id.* at 454.

[4] *See generally* Jon Mroz, *Lone Wolf Attacks and the Difference between Violent Extremism and Terrorism*, EASTWEST INST. (Apr. 24, 2009, 1:32 PM), http://www.ewi.info/lone-wolf-attacks-and-difference-between-violent-extremism-and-terrorism.

[5] James Vega, *What Is "Right-Wing Extremism?"*, DEMOCRATIC STRATEGIST, Apr. 30 2009, http://www.thedemocraticstrategist.org/strategist/2009/04/part_i_what_is_rightwing_extre.php.

Taking any idea and distorting it beyond the parameters of the idea generally accepted by the group or groups to which the idea applies.

I know you've discussed extremism as involving the threat/use of violence, but some observers also see the possibility of non-violent extremism (in the sense of radical views about society that do not espouse the use of violence to achieve that society), so that will be an issue to address (but may already be included in your initial bullet point about defining extremism).

Extremism is a relational term. Therefore, what we consider extreme behavior in contemporary times may have been normative in the past and, whereas, today do we view such behavior as extremist (e.g. Hassidim, "Ultra"-Orthodox).

One need to distinguish, I believe, between extremism as a matter of weltanschauung or personal life style as opposed to extremism as a matter of tactics to achieve a particular goal—political or otherwise. Are they the same?
I don't think so. (If a lawyer refuses to compromise and litigates it out—is he an extremist? Is that necessarily bad? Why do we admire the tough lawyers of Boston Legal, et al?)

Extremism nurtures a mindset of intolerance, permitting the faithful to "curse" and act violently towards the non-faithful.

The snippets above are but samples of definitions proposed by questionnaire respondents; reviewing the proposed definitions reinforces the complexity in proffering a definition. Some respondents suggested extremism implies violence; others proposed that nonviolent behavior and language are also manifestations of extremism. In suggesting that extremists are not empathetic, respondents articulated an important point: extremists are absolutists, and to that end are locked in on their particular viewpoint, largely incapable of understanding, if not intolerant, of other perspectives for their ideology is invariably "the truth" to be defended at all costs.

In addition, a common theme among the proposed definitions was that extremists sought to radically change existing norms and mores. Not all members of society view change as a positive; after all, change can "upset the apple cart" impacting preexisting manners and ways. Whether that is a negative or positive depends, in large part, on a variety of factors. Those factors include perceived self-interest, preexisting values and principles, and the extent to which proposed change directly, or indirectly, affects one's station in life and the manner in which change occurs.

As suggested by participants in a round-table conversation discussing this book, how change is perceived is akin to "beauty being in the eye of the beholder." By example: the end of Jim Crow[6] was perceived by many[7] as beneficial to American society while others[8] believed that Jim Crow represented stability and established clear lines between the races. In the language of the times, Jim Crow guaranteed that African Americans living in the South "knew their place." That, of course, was a euphemism for racism, and denial of full rights, privileges, and protections to African Americans.

The difficulty is determining what value to attach to extremism; although some view the civil rights movement in its entirety as extremist, I suggest it was a positive whereas others would argue it was a negative. Whether extremism is positive or negative depends, then, on one's perspective and interests. Change can occur in distinct manners: some violent, others through traditional democratic means. Rearticulated, do certain dire social, political, and economic conditions justify extreme measures in an effort to protect victims of injustice and brutality and mitigate their suffering? Dr. Martin Luther King, Jr. answered that question in the negative; Huey Newton and others in the Black Panthers answered that question affirmatively. After all, as Barry Goldwater famously said, "extremism in the defense of liberty is no vice."[9]

The answer is, in many ways, in the question; in certain paradigms change demands dramatic measures rather than acceptable working-within-the-system approaches. By example: although Rosa Parks was not an extremist, her simple human action of refusing to give up her seat and move to the back of the bus[10] was instrumental to the civil rights movement. Although the decision to choose Rosa Parks was not happenstance, for it was carefully considered and weighed by leaders of the nascent civil rights movement,[11] her actions, ultimately, spoke loudly for rights and freedom.

There are three distinct paradigms relevant to examining extremism: secular, social movements; religious extremism; and movements that combine secular and religious themes drawing on both in articulating their reason d'être. In examining the three it is essential to understand both the existential and practical social structures that impel individuals to articulate, lead, and act in a manner that fundamentally challenges existing mores and norms.

---

[6] "Jim Crow was the name of the racial caste system which operated primarily, but not exclusively in southern and border states, between 1877 and the mid-1960s...Under Jim Crow, African Americans were relegated to the status of second class citizens. Jim Crow represented the legitimization of anti-Black racism." Ferris State Univ., What Was Jim Crow (Sept. 2000), http://www.ferris.edu/jimcrow/what.htm.

7 See Sen. James Eastland (D-Miss): "In fact, segregation is desired and supported by the vast majority of the members of both races in the South, who dwell side by side under harmonious conditions." http://www.spartacus.schoolnet.co.uk/USAjimcrow.htm.

8 For a website discussing Jim Crow laws: *see* Ferris, *supra* note 6.

[9] Barry Goldwater, *Goldwater's 1964 Acceptance Speech*, WASH. POST, http://www.washingtonpost.com/wp-srv/politics/daily/may98/goldwaterspeech.htm (last visited Nov. 3, 2012).

[10] *The Story behind the Bus*, THE HENRY FORD, http://www.hfmgv.org/exhibits/rosaparks/story.asp (last visited Nov. 3, 2012).

[11] *See* Jannell McGrew, *An Interview with Rosa Parks* (Dec. 1, 2000), http://www.montgomeryboycott.com/book/

In doing so, both violent and nonviolent behavior is relevant; although some[12] suggest extremism must be understood to imply violence, there is little doubt that extremism can also be nonviolent. The most obvious example of the latter is speech; the adage "words kill" is particularly relevant to this discussion. After all, hatred articulated by an individual identified as a leader—whether secular or religious—undoubtedly has the ability to compel *others* to act even though the message, purportedly, was not explicitly violent. Important to recall that words are *also* violent in the atmosphere they create and actions they facilitate. Whereas belief is a private matter, the complexity is in regulating and possibly prosecuting conduct (including speech); the difficulty is in the gray area, particularly determining when speech incites to violence. In this vein, ascertaining when speech compels others to act cannot be defined as black/white; rather, determining whether the speaker's words resulted in actions by another depends on various conditions and circumstances.

The dilemma with respect to the gray area is significant. Broadly defining permissible speech can directly contribute to unwarranted limitation of freedom of speech; narrowly defining impermissible speech may cause harm either to specifically targeted individuals or to random victims of extremists. Striking a balance that protects constitutional rights while protecting public and individual safety is simultaneously complicated and essential. In assessing whether the speech has the potential to compel another to act requires determining a number of factors, including the relationship between the speaker and the audience, the speaker's intent, the specificity of the speech, and the relevant time frame between the speech and the action. Although "words kill" is, indeed, the common refrain, not all words kill. Determining which words either have the potential to cause harm or caused actual harm requires sensitivity to both the principles of freedom of speech and the state's obligation to protect the public and individuals.

By example: some voices in the Netherlands suggested that Theo van Gogh was an inciter whose words had the potential to cause harm; others perceived van Gogh as a provocateur whose words could not cause harm. The distinction is significant: if the former, then van Gogh could have been liable for prosecution, whereas the latter falls under the category of protected speech. The same argument can be made with respect to US radio personalities including Rush Limbaugh and Glenn Beck: the question is ascertaining when the speech has crossed from protected to incitement. In the context of Justice Holmes's famous phrase "shouting fire in a crowded theater," the question regarding extremism is whether the fire has not already started and to what extent the theater is burning. Geert Wilders would argue that the theater is burning and his voice is the one that should not be muzzled.

---

[12] *See, e.g.,* Eugene Abov, *Interview with New Russian Presidential Advisor Mikhail Fedotov*, Dec. 1, 2010, http://www.telegraph.co.uk/sponsored/russianow/politics/8174053/Interview-with-new-Russian-presidential-advisor-Mikhail-Fedotov.html.

Moving from the theoretical to the practical: although differences of opinion are inevitable in a discussion of this nature, I propose extremism be defined as "conviction" that tenets of a given belief system—secular or religious—justify violence against others. In discussing religious extremism, Professor Pascal Boyer suggests "extremism is simply an excessive form of religious adherence."[13]

Although the liberal, democratic ethos advocates maximum rights of and for the individual, the danger posed by extremism requires reexamining that premise. The burden is persuading the reader both as to the necessity of limiting otherwise protected rights and providing a roadmap for decision-makers and the public on how to implement this limitation within the cointours of the law. That same conviction, in essence absolutism,[14] representing the extreme manifestation of religious faith that leads people of extreme faith to harm believers and nonbelievers alike, is equally applicable to secular extremists.[15] The physician referenced in the introduction would view *his* absolutism as justified given his conviction that his truth is absolute. He would, therefore, view negatively the absolute conviction of devout Jews or Moslems that their truth is *the* truth. From a secular perspective, absolutism practiced by religious extremists creates dangers because of the obligation it imposes. Religious extremists believe it their responsibility to bring glory onto God; if their faith leader implies (directly or indirectly) that glory requires violence, then absolutism poses a danger.

The absolute conviction of the "rightness" of a particular cause, whether religious or secular, and the determination that violence, actual or verbal, is justified characterizes secular and religious extremism alike. Timothy McVeigh and Anders Behring Breivik were no less convinced of the legitimacy and rightness of their extreme secular worldview than was Osama Bin Laden. Although McVeigh and Breivik were not motivated by religion their convictions and beliefs were no less absolute and violent than Bin Laden.[16] In other words, they had different motivations with similar results.[17]

---

[13] PASCAL BOYER, RELIGION EXPLAINED: THE EVOLUTIONARY ORIGINS OF RELIGIOUS THOUGHT 292 (2001).

[14] Absolutism is defined as "a political theory that absolute power should be vested in one or more rulers" Merriam-Webster Online, http://www.merriam-webster.com/dictionary/absolutism; Absolutism emerged as a form of government following the religious wars that dominated much of 16th-century Europe. In essence, absolutism was based on the theory that a strong central government could prevent anarchy. J.P. Sommerville, *Absolutism and the Divine Right of Kings*, http://history.wisc.edu/sommerville/351/351-172.htm (last visited Nov. 3, 2012).

[15] A prime example of secular extremism was the actions taken by Anders Breivik, who claimed that immigration was "ruining his country." *See* David Wilkes, *Did Schoolboy Row Turn Anders Breivik into Migrant Hating Monster?*, DAILYMAIL.CO.UK, July 26, 2011, *available at* http://www.dailymail.co.uk/news/article-2018758/Anders-Behring-Breivik-Did-schoolboy-row-turn-migrant-hating-monster.html.

[16] *See* Paul Cliteur, *Cultural Counter-terrorism, in* TERRORISM, IDEOLOGY, LAW, AND POLICY 457, 483 (Gelijn Molier, Afshin Ellian & David Suurland eds., Republic of Letters Pub. 2011).

[17] McVeigh's bombing killed 168, Breivik's rampage killed 76 while Bin Laden's attacks spanning approximately 27 years killed thousands. *See Osama bin Laden: A Chronology of His Political Life*, PBS.ORG, http://www.pbs.org/wgbh/pages/frontline/shows/binladen/etc/cron.html (last visited Nov. 3, 2012).

It is that conviction coupled with violent action—whether self-imposed or externally articulated and subsequently internalized—that most accurately depicts extremism. However, and the caveat is essential to truly understand the power of extremism, the act is based on a belief system (secular or religious) that has, in many cases, been articulated by someone other than the actor. For that reason, extremism should not be understood in the narrow context of action exclusively; doing so unnecessarily and dangerously grants the speaker unwarranted and unjustified immunity.

Membership and participation in civil democratic society explicitly demands citizens acknowledge the supremacy of the rule of law. Rousseau argued that as citizens we are all signatories to the grand social contract.[18] In essence, we have given up absolute rights in exchange for the safety and comfort that a government/village can provide. In other words, indiviudals have agreed to be subject to laws and regulations that protect them while limiting their rights. That is the essence of the social contract that establishes boundaries of acceptable behavior between the individual and the state. Extremists undermine the social contract; their actions cause harm to individuals (victims) and society alike.

In articulating, and subsequently implementing responses to extremism, the state must determine what factors have contributed, directly and indirectly, to individuals uniting for the purpose of committing acts undermining society. This is of the utmost importance both in developing policy that minimizes the impact of a particular group and preventing additional groups from seeking to undermine society's stability.

Although extremists challenge, if not undermine, the fragile social structure that describes civil, democratic society, the nation-state is limited in its response. After all, limited state power defines democratic society; unrestrained measures and responses describe either totalitarian regimes or democratic states engaged in "panic response."

However, unlike individuals who commit crimes[19] associated with the traditional criminal law paradigm, the actions of extremists (regardless of their motivation) are intended to directly impact the social fabric that defines civil society. For that reason the danger posed by extremists—violent and nonviolent alike—extends dramatically beyond the specific act they commit. In the criminal law paradigm the impact is most dramatically felt by the victim and his or her immediate family; in the extremist paradigm the intended audience extends far beyond the victims and their families.

Although in both paradigms the victim *may* be randomly chosen, more so in extremism, one of the principle differences between the two is that the extremist actor is focused on sending a message to society whereas the criminal is focused almost exclusively on his/her personal needs (e.g., money for drugs, personal revenge).

---

[18] Christopher Bertram, Routledge Philosophy Guidebook to Rousseau and the Social Contract 74–75 (2004).

[19] For purposes of this book, "crimes" refers to actions the state has deemed violate the relevant Criminal Code.

II. The Civil Rights Movement

Defining extremism and its subsequent practical application requires extraordinary sensitivity and caution for governmental overreach, and undue exaggerated response is, inevitably, a legitimate concern. The FBI's unceasing focus on Dr. Martin Luther King, Jr. raises deeply disturbing and pertinent questions.[20] Was King an extremist, and did he pose a threat to society in a manner that would endanger members of society? There is little doubt that King was an extraordinary figure whose rhetorical brilliance and sheer force of personality combined with his unique ability to capture the moment and articulate basic demands were, literally, unparalleled. King preached and practiced nonviolence, subjecting himself to pain, suffering, and humiliation on behalf of his cause. Others, similarly, truly placed themselves in harm's way: Freedom Riders who challenged segregation laws in the South,[21] those who sought to ensure African Americans have the right to vote,[22] and those who participated in demonstrations against the institutionalized segregation and racism of the American Deep South.[23]

The civil rights movement to which King dedicated his life challenged basic norms and mores of American society in the 1950s and 1960s; in innumerable ways, it changed America. Obviously, for millions of Americans that was extraordinarily unsettling, if not threatening; one has only to listen to the speeches of George Wallace and Lester Maddox and to see pictures from Birmingham, Alabama, to viscerally feel the pure hatred and unadulterated racism that defined how much of White America in both the North and South reacted to King's message. Conversely, the hope and promise that King expressed for millions of Black Americans who believed, as he preached, that "one day…little black boys and black girls will be able to join hands with little white boys and white girls as sisters and brothers"[24] is equally powerful and compelling.

The FBI, under J. Edgar Hoover, was unceasing in its efforts regarding King; the incessant wiretapping, monitoring, and harassing reflected an unmitigated obsession,

---

[20] Jen Christensen, *FBI Tracked King's Every Move*, CNN (Mar. 31, 2008), http://articles.cnn.com/2008-03-31/us/mlk.fbi.conspiracy_1_dream-speech-david-garrow-civil-rights?_s=PM:US; Richard Powers, *Martin Luther King Jr.: FBI's Campaign to Discredit the Civil Rights Leader*, HISTORYNET.COM (June 12, 2006), http://www.historynet.com/martin-luther-king-jr-fbis-campaign-to-discredit-the-civil-rights-leader.htm.

[21] *See generally Freedom Riders*, PBS, http://www.pbs.org/wgbh/americanexperience/freedomriders/ (last visited Nov. 3, 2012).

[22] *See* the killing (in Mississippi) of civil rights' activists James Chaney, Andrew Goodman, and Michael Schwerner, http://law2.umkc.edu/faculty/projects/ftrials/price&bowers/price&bowers.htm; their killing was depicted in the movie *Mississippi Burning*, http://www.imdb.com/title/tt0095647/.

[23] *See generally*, DIANE MCWHORTER, CARRY ME HOME (2001); TAYLOR BRANCH, PARTING THE WATERS: AMERICA IN THE KING YEARS 1954–63 (1988); TAYLOR BRANCH, PILLAR OF FIRE: AMERICA IN THE KING YEARS 1963–65 (1988); TAYLOR BRANCH, AT CANAAN'S EDGE: AMERICA IN THE KING YEARS 1965–68 (2006); NAN ELIZABETH WOODRUFF, AMERICAN CONGO: THE AFRICAN AMERICAN FREEDOM STRUGGLE IN THE DELTA (2003).

[24] Martin Luther King Jr., *I Have a Dream Speech*, HUFFINGTON POST (Jan. 17, 2011) (transcript available at http://www.huffingtonpost.com/2011/01/17/i-have-a-dream-speech-text_n_809993.html).

bordering on seeming irrationality. The unremitting efforts reflecting consistent violations of civil liberties and rights were extraordinary; it was as if Hoover were convinced that King posed a grave danger to US public safety and security.

Actually, as available documents suggest, that is *exactly* what Hoover believed.[25] Assessing whether Hoover's efforts reflected objective and somber analysis regarding threats King and the civil rights movement posed, or were a manifestation of unbridled efforts to reign in a challenge to mainstream America, depends on one's perspective. It also depends on how threat and extremism are defined; clearly Hoover defined both broadly, which directly led to excess in seeking to curtail King. However, the efforts to discredit King and the civil rights movement were not restricted to FBI wiretapping; they also included extraordinary violations of civil and political rights of American citizens by local law enforcement officials, sometimes cooperating with private citizens. Bull Connor,[26] *Mississippi Burning*,[27] and the police dogs of Birmingham, Alabama, have come to represent the abuses the civil rights movement was subjected to in its effort to ensure rights and freedoms for African Americans living in the Deep South. Important to recall is the degree to which racism was both institutionalized and internalized; lynchings, after all, were widely attended events often with parents bringing their children.[28]

Parents—sometimes observing a Sunday lynching after attending church that morning—undoubtedly would gainsay that their actions were akin to extremism; nevertheless the suggestion is not far-fetched. Although they themselves were not active participants, their willful attendance, regardless of its passive nature, raises legitimate questions regarding the significance and impact of acquiescing behavior of the bystander. This is not an abstract question: passive conduct is essential to understanding extremism and how it is facilitated.

Thus, an analysis of extremism must not be restricted exclusively to those most clearly partaking in a particular activity. The conduct of both facilitators and observers must

---

[25] Christensen, *supra* note 20 (quoting FBI memo calling "King the most dangerous and effective Negro leader in the country"). *See also* BRANCH, PARTING THE WATERS, *supra* note 23; BRANCH, PILLAR OF FIRE, *supra* note 23; BRANCH, AT CANAAN'S EDGE, *supra* note 23.

[26] "Eugene "Bull" Connor was Birmingham's Commissioner of Public Safety in 1961 when the Freedom Riders came to town. Connor was an ultra-segregationist with close ties to the KKK who encouraged the violence that met the CORE Freedom Riders at the Birmingham Trailways Bus by promising local Klansmen that, 'He would see to it that 15 or 20 minutes would elapse before the police arrived.'" *Freedom Riders, supra* note 21.

[27] "Two FBI agents investigating the murder of civil rights workers during the 60s seek to breach the conspiracy of silence in a small Southern town where segregation divides black and white. The younger agent trained in FBI school runs up against the small town ways of his former Sheriff partner." MISSISSIPPI BURNING (Orion Pictures 1986) http://www.imdb.com/title/tt0095647/ (last visited Nov. 3, 2012).

[28] Photographs depicting these lynchings can be found at http://executions.justsickshit.com/?s=executions&paged=2

be considered to fully appreciate extremism in the context of community and group behavior. That is, the issue of extremism—to be understood at its most potent and dangerous—requires a broad examination extending beyond the readily identifiable and visible specific actor. To focus exclusively on *that* actor is to underestimate the importance of additional participants in the extremism paradigm.[29]

However, to cast an unduly wide net is similarly dangerous; although King clearly challenged conventional American norms and mores of the 1950s and 1960s, nonviolence was the essence of the civil rights movement he led. That is in direct contrast to those African Anerican leaders who followed, particularly Stokely Carmichael,[30] H. Rap Brown,[31] and Huey Newton.[32] Although it has been suggested that King's power and prestige was on the wane when he was killed,[33] his impact on American culture and politics was extraordinary. Arguably, his "I Have Been to the Mountaintop"[34] speech is one of the most powerful and important in American history. The words conveying his hope for a different, better America were a remarkable clarion call for all Americans. However, and the caveat is essential, the speech—undeniably stirring and challenging—did not invoke violence. That is in marked distinction to the open calls for violence that characterized the words and actions of the Black Panthers; the distinction between King and Newton, Brown and Carmichael is like night and day. Similarly, King's "Letter from a Birmingham Jail" written after he was incarcerated (1963) brilliantly articulates the justness of the civil rights movement, compellingly distinguishing between its inherent moderate principles and the extremism he rejected:

> We know through painful experience that freedom is never voluntarily given by the oppressor; it must be demanded by the oppressed. Frankly, I have yet to engage in a direct action campaign that was "well timed" in the view of those who have not suffered unduly from the disease of segregation. For years now I have heard the word

---

[29] Daniel Jonah Goldhagen, *The Evil of Banality*, 207(3–4) New Republic 49 (July 15, 1992) (reviewing Christopher R. Browning, Ordinary Men: Reserve Police Battalion 101 and the Final Solution in Poland (1992). In the Afterword of the 1998 reissue of his book, Browning tries to refute Goldhagen's argument. *See* Christopher R. Browning, Ordinary Men: Reserve Police Battalion 101 and the Final Solution in Poland 191–223 (reissued 1st ed. Harper Perennial, 1998) (1992)

[30] Stokely Carmichael participated in the Freedom Rides and later became one of the leading voices for the Black Power movement. He would go on to serve as the chairman for the Student Nonviolent Coordinating Committee (SNCC) starting in 1966 and an honorary prime minister of the Black Panther Party. *Freedom Riders, supra* note 21.

[31] Former member of the SNCC who was sentenced to life in prison in 2009 for killing a sheriff's deputy. *Life for 60's Radical H. Rap Brown*, CBSNews (Feb. 11, 2009, 9:12 PM), http://www.cbsnews.com/stories/2002/03/13/national/main503687.shtml.

[32] Co-founder of the Black Panther Party. Eyes on the Prize, PBS, http://www.pbs.org/wgbh/amex/eyesontheprize/profiles/26_newton.html (last visited Nov. 3, 2012).

[33] April 4, 1968.

[34] Martin Luther King Jr., Address at the Mason Temple: I've Been to the Mountain Top (Apr. 3, 1968), *available at* http://www.drmartinlutherkingjr.com/ivebeentothemountaintop.htm.

"Wait!" It rings in the ear of every Negro with piercing familiarity. This "Wait" has almost always meant "Never." We must come to see, with one of our distinguished jurists, that "justice too long delayed is justice denied."

We have waited for more than 340 years for our constitutional and God given rights. The nations of Asia and Africa are moving with jet like speed toward gaining political independence, but we still creep at horse and buggy pace toward gaining a cup of coffee at a lunch counter. Perhaps it is easy for those who have never felt the stinging darts of segregation to say, "Wait." But when you have seen vicious mobs lynch your mothers and fathers at will and drown your sisters and brothers at whim; when you have seen hate filled policemen curse, kick and even kill your black brothers and sisters; when you see the vast majority of your twenty million Negro brothers smothering in an airtight cage of poverty in the midst of an affluent society; when you suddenly find your tongue twisted and your speech stammering as you seek to explain to your six year old daughter why she can't go to the public amusement park that has just been advertised on television, and see tears welling up in her eyes when she is told that Funtown is closed to colored children, and see ominous clouds of inferiority beginning to form in her little mental sky, and see her beginning to distort her personality by developing an unconscious bitterness toward white people; when you have to concoct an answer for a five year old son who is asking: "Daddy, why do white people treat colored people so mean?"; when you take a cross county drive and find it necessary to sleep night after night in the uncomfortable corners of your automobile because no motel will accept you; when you are humiliated day in and day out by nagging signs reading "white" and "colored"; when your first name becomes "nigger," your middle name becomes "boy" (however old you are) and your last name becomes "John," and your wife and mother are never given the respected title "Mrs."; when you are harried by day and haunted by night by the fact that you are a Negro, living constantly at tip-toe stance, never quite knowing what to expect next, and are plagued with inner fears and outer resentments; when you are forever fighting a degenerating sense of "nobodiness"—then you will understand why we find it difficult to wait. There comes a time when the cup of endurance runs over, and men are no longer willing to be plunged into the abyss of despair. I hope, sirs, you can understand our legitimate and unavoidable impatience. You express a great deal of anxiety over our willingness to break laws. This is certainly a legitimate concern. Since we so diligently urge people to obey the Supreme Court's decision of 1954 outlawing segregation in the public schools, at first glance it may seem rather paradoxical for us consciously to break laws. One may well ask: "How can you advocate breaking some laws and obeying others?" The answer lies in the fact that there are two types of laws: just and unjust. I would be the first to advocate obeying just laws. One has not only a legal but a moral responsibility to obey just laws. Conversely, one has a moral responsibility to disobey unjust laws. I would agree with St. Augustine that "an unjust law is no law at all."

Now, what is the difference between the two? How does one determine whether a law is just or unjust? A just law is a man made code that squares with the moral law or the law of God. An unjust law is a code that is out of harmony with the moral law. To put it in the terms of St. Thomas Aquinas: An unjust law is a human law that is not rooted in eternal law and natural law. Any law that uplifts human personality is just. Any law that degrades human personality is unjust. All segregation statutes are unjust because segregation distorts the soul and damages the personality. It gives the segregator a false sense of superiority and the segregated a false sense of inferiority. Segregation, to use the terminology of the Jewish philosopher Martin Buber, substitutes an "I it" relationship for an "I thou" relationship and ends up relegating persons to the status of things. Hence segregation is not only politically, economically and sociologically unsound, it is morally wrong and sinful. Paul Tillich has said that sin is separation. Is not segregation an existential expression of man's tragic separation, his awful estrangement, his terrible sinfulness? Thus it is that I can urge men to obey the 1954 decision of the Supreme Court, for it is morally right; and I can urge them to disobey segregation ordinances, for they are morally wrong.[35]

Nevertheless, for the FBI King *was* a danger to American society, justifying blatant violations of his civil and political rights. Herein lies the critical question: is one who challenges conventional thinking an extremist? If so, does that justify actions and measures akin to those used by the FBI in the 1950s and 1960s? Those questions are essential to understanding the limits of civil discourse and the extent to which society tolerates dissent, criticism, and free speech. These are, obviously, not abstract questions; the answers define society, its relationship with the individual, and the extent to which voices calling for change challenging society will be tolerated.

Healthy civil society brooks dissent and tolerates challenging voices; however, society need not tolerate calls for violence that *may* lead to harm and place innocent individuals at risk. The lines are not necessarily broad and clear; oftentimes, they are subtle and subject to interpretation. When clear, marking boundaries is greatly facilitated; when blurred, overreaction is a distinct possibility, with troubling consequences both for the individual and society. Analyzing whether society is overreacting requires examining context and circumstances. Determining whether actions and words are, indeed, extremist cannot be divorced from the relevant political, social, economic, and cultural reality.

---

[35] Martin Luther King, Jr., "Letter From Birmingham Jail," *in* THE NORTON ANTHOLOGY OF AFRICAN AMERICAN LITERATURE 1854–66 (Henry Louis Gates, Jr. & Nellie Y. McKay eds., Norton 1997) (1963), *available at* http://www.africa.upenn.edu/Articles_Gen/Letter_Birmingham.html.

III. History of Limiting Speech

Hate speech is a hotly contested area of First Amendment debate.[36] Unlike fighting words, or true threats, hate speech is a broad category that encompasses both protected and unprotected speech. To the extent that hate speech constitutes a true threat or fighting words, it is unprotected; to the extent it does not reach the level of a true threat or fighting words it is protected.

During the 1980s and early 1990s more than 350 public colleges and universities sought to combat discrimination and harassment on campuses through the use of so-called speech codes.[37] Proponents of the codes contend existing First Amendment jurisprudence must be reversed because the marketplace of ideas does not adequately protect minorities. They claim hate speech subjugates minority voices and prevents people from exercising their First Amendment rights. Similarly, proponents posit that hate speech is akin to fighting words, a category of expression that should not receive First Amendment protection. In doing so, proponents cite the Supreme Court's holding in *Chaplinsky* that they (fighting words) "are no essential part of any exposition of ideas, and are of such slight social value as a step to the truth that any benefit that may be derived from them is clearly outweighed by the social interest in order and morality."[38]

However, speech codes that have been challenged in court have not fared well; though no case has been brought before the Supreme Court on this question, lower courts have struck down these policies as either overbroad or vague. The District Court for the Eastern District of Wisconsin in the University of Wisconsin school code case articulated the reasoning behind the codes' lack of constitutional muster:

This commitment to free expression must be unwavering, because there exist many situations where, in the short run, it appears advantageous to limit speech to solve pressing social problems, such as discriminatory harassment. If a balancing approach is applied, these pressing and tangible short run concerns are likely to outweigh the more amorphous and long run benefits of free speech. However, the suppression of speech, even where the speech's content appears to have little value and great costs, amounts to governmental thought control.[39]

---

[36] *See* Virginia v. Black, 538 U.S. 343 (2003); R.A.V. v. City of St. Paul, Minn., 505 U.S. 377 (1992); Nat'l Socialist Party of Am. v. Vill. of Skokie, 432 U.S. 43(1977); Brandenburg v. Ohio, 395 U.S. 444 (1969); Terminiello v. City of Chicago, 337 U.S. 1 (1949); Gitlow v. People of State of New York, 268 U.S. 652 (1925); Snyder v. Phelps, 131 S. Ct. 1207 (2011).

[37] David L. Hudson Jr., *Hate Speech and Campus Speech Codes*, FIRST AMENDMENT CENTER (Sept. 13, 2002), http://www.firstamendmentcenter.org/hate-speech-campus-speech-codes.

[38] Chaplinsky v. State of New Hampshire, 315 U.S. 568, 572 (1942).

[39] UWM Post, Inc. v. Bd. of Regents of Univ. of Wisconsin Sys., 774 F. Supp. 1163, 1174 (E.D. Wis. 1991).

A literal interpretation of the First Amendment suggests any law abridging speech is unconstitutional; however, the Supreme Court has taken a more nuanced approach, recognizing legitimate competing interests. As Justice Holmes articulated, "the most stringent protection of free speech would not protect a man in falsely shouting fire in a theater, and causing a panic...."[40]

This statement, endorsed by every subsequent US Supreme Court decision, reflects an understanding that similar to other constitutionally guaranteed protections, there is no absolutism with respect to free speech. Powerful interests must be balanced against other powerful interests; the question is whether the balancing reflects a rights minimization or rights maximization paradigm. Free speech jurisdiction has traveled a long road in American jurisprudence, arguably in concert with society, which superficially—at least—is more tolerant of dissent than in the past.

The caveat is pertinent because one must never forget the rigid, Puritan roots of the American culture; a casual perusal of public discussion regarding same sex marriage, children of same sex parents, and abortion highlights a constant strain of ideological rigidity, largely premised on a literalist interpretation of religious scripture.

Some argue that the marketplace of ideas should take precedence over efforts to limit free speech protections; however, reality is more complicated. Analysis whether speech is to be protected must determine whether the proposed restriction is content-based or content-neutral. The former refers to restrictions that apply to particular viewpoints; in such cases, the proposed restriction carries a heavy presumption that it violates the First Amendment. In such a paradigm, the Court applies a strict scrutiny standard in evaluating the restriction's lawfulness; to survive strict scrutiny, the restriction must be *narrowly tailored* to achieve *an important governmental interest*. That means that it cannot be, among other things, over-inclusive, under-inclusive, or vague. This standard effectively places a heavy burden on the government in defending the restriction.

However, if the restriction is content-neutral, whereby the concern is not with the speech itself but rather pertains to the details surrounding the speech, then the government is allowed to set certain parameters involving time, place, and manner. Content-neutral restrictions on speech are reviewed under intermediate scrutiny rather than strict scrutiny because the speech is restricted solely in the manner in which the information is communicated rather than its content.

In *United States v. O'Brien*,[41] the Supreme Court established a four-part test to determine whether a content-neutral restriction on speech is constitutional: (1) Is the restriction within the constitutional power of government?, (2) Does the restriction further an important or substantial governmental interest?, (3) Is the governmental interest unrelated to the suppression of free expression?, and (4) Is the restriction narrowly tailored (i.e., no

[40] Schenck v. United States, 249 U.S. 47, 52 (1919).
[41] United States v. O'Brien, 391 U.S. 367 (1968).

greater than necessary)? Subsequently, a fifth factor was added in *City of Ladue v. Gilleo*[42] inquiring whether the restriction leaves open ample opportunities of communication.

The American public has been confronted with a number of significant free speech issues in the past few years; three shall be discussed below: a Koran-burning pastor, Christian extremists demonstrating at funerals of US military personnel, and an assistant attorney general (Michigan) who specifically targeted a University of Michigan student who was student body president and a homosexual. In examining these the point of departure is whether the test articulated by the Supreme Court in *Brandenburg* sufficiently protects the speaker, his or her audience, the larger public, and the intended target of the speech.

Pastor Terry Jones, of Florida, leads a small but vocal congregation. On March 20, 2011, he burned a Koran; his actions resulted in anti-American violence in Afghanistan, killing at least 12 people. Jones was urged not to do this by virtually every national leader including President Obama, Secretary of State Clinton, and perhaps most important, General Petraeus, the commander of US forces in Afghanistan. Petraeus argued that Pastor Jones's conduct would endanger US military personnel in Afghanistan. While Jones burned the Korans, his actions present a significant First Amendment dilemma: is speech protected even though harm is both encouraged and/or *may* result both domestically and internationally?

In that vein, although Jones did not advocate violence he was arrested for attempting to protest outside a mosque in Dearborn, Michigan. After a brief trial, a jury upheld the city's injunction, claiming that Jones's protest would disturb the peace; ultimately, Jones was held on $1 bail and then released.[43] Although Jones's conduct is considered by many to be reprehensible, numerous constitutional law experts claim the court's action was a gross miscarriage of justice and a violation of Jones's First Amendment rights.[44]

The same concerns are relevant regarding a pastor who, along with his tiny but vocal community, shouts degrading comments at family and friends of fallen soldiers gathered to bury their loved one killed while serving the United States. The basis for the pastor's conduct: the soldier died because God hates the United States for its tolerance of homosexuality, particularly in America's military. The Supreme Court recently addressed this issue in *Snyder v. Phelps*,[45] where members of the Westboro Baptist Church protested the funeral of a US marine killed in Iraq. The protesters carried signs, as they have done at nearly 600 funerals throughout the country over the past 20 years, displaying placards

---

[42] City of Ladue v. Gilleo, 512 U.S. 43 (1994).

[43] *Pastor Who Planned Mosque Protest out of Jail*, CBS NEWS (Apr. 22, 2011), http://www.cbsnews.com/stories/2011/04/22/national/main20056660.shtml.

[44] *See generally* Narij Warikoo, *Terry Jones, Second Pastor, Briefly Jailed after Tense Day*, DETROIT FREE PRESS, Apr. 23, 2011, http://www.freep.com/article/20110423/NEWS02/104230425/Terry-Jones-second-pastor-briefly-jailed-after-tense-day.

[45] Snyder v. Phelps, 131 S. Ct. 1207 (2011).

such as "America is doomed," "You're going to hell," "God hates you," "Fags doom nations," and "Thank God for dead soldiers."[46]

Dissenting justice Samuel Alito likened the protests of the Westboro Baptist Church members to fighting words and of a personal character, and thus not protected speech. However, the majority disagreed, stating that the protester's speech was not personal but public, and that local laws, which can shield funeral attendees from protesters, are adequate in the context of protection from emotional distress.

Andrew Shirvell, a former assistant attorney general for Michigan, was sued for stalking Chris Armstrong, the first openly gay University of Michigan student body president. Armstrong claims that Shirvell showed up everywhere he went, including school and home. In addition, Shirvell started a blog campaign against Armstrong and his "radical homosexual agenda." Shirvell claims that the stalking charges are moot because he has never actually spoke to Armstrong, and that he was exercising his First Amendment rights.[47] Should Shirvell be allowed to exercise his free speech rights in this manner? How does the doctrine of hate speech apply? Mike Cox, the state's attorney general and Shirvell's boss, initially defended Shirvell's actions claiming the First Amendment protected them. However, shortly after Armstrong filed harassment charges, Cox changed his stance and fired Shirvell.[48] A jury later agreed with Armstrong and awarded Armstrong $4.5 million in damages[49]

The First Amendment has traveled an extraordinary journey, from clear limits imposed on free speech to an understanding that protecting free speech is important to a vital and vibrant democracy. The road taken has been full of pitfalls and pratfalls reflective both of the extraordinary importance of this protection and the dangers that free speech, potentially, poses. The rocky road directly reflects this tension; to suggest that the tension has been resolved and that limitations will not be posed in the future would be to mis-read American history.

After all, American history is replete with rollbacks of rights in times of crisis, whether real or imagined. This tendency, in the speech context, is compounded by the ever-changing nature of speech and the media. Rearticulated: given the power of social media, and the speed with which information can be transmitted, it is not unforeseeable

---

[46] *Id.* at 1213.

[47] David Jesse, *Shirvell Fires Back, Claims He's Victim of Gay Agenda*, DETROIT FREE PRESS, May 10, 2011, *available at* http://www.freep.com/article/20110510/NEWS05/110510041/Shirvell-fires-back-claims-he-s-victim-gay-agenda?odyssey=mod|mostcom.

[48] Brian Montopoli, *Andrew Shirvell Fired After Harassment Charges*, CBSNEWS (Nov. 8, 2010), http://www.cbsnews.com/8301-503544_162-20022143-503544.html.

[49] Kevin Dolak, *Attorney Andrew Shirvell Ordered to Pay 4.5 Million for Attacks on Gay Student*, ABC NEWS, Aug. 17, 2012, http://abcnews.go.com/US/attorney-andrew-shirvell-ordered-pay-45-million-attacks/story?id=17028621#.UDeXv9ZlSS0.; For the transcript of Andrew Shirvell's interview with Anderson Cooper (CNN). http://transcripts.cnn.com/TRANSCRIPTS/1009/28/acd.02.html

that both government and the courts will consider imposing additonal limits on free speech when public safety is perceived to be endangered.

Although the Supreme Court's holding in *Snyder*[50] suggests an expansive articulation of free speech, possibility of a "rollback"—particularly in the context of national security and public order—cannot be easily dismissed. Though American society has significantly matured over the past 200 years, the public's reaction when under threat is surprisingly consistent: accepting a rights minimization paradigm imposed by the government and upheld by the Court.

The question, in a nutshell, is whether national security and public order justify minimizing free speech. In some ways, American history has demonstrated a ready willingness to answer in the affirmative. The costs are significant with respect to both First Amendment principles and on a human, individual basis. However, disregarding legitimate threats to national security is *also* dangerous. The dilemma, then, is determining the seriousness of the threat to public order and ascertaining whether limiting free speech will mitigate that threat and at what cost to individual liberty.

The risk in finger pointing is extraordinary; there is always a danger in identifying the "other" ' as posing a threat to society. That tension is palpable; numerous questionnaire respondents correctly identified *that* risk as potentially troubling; as discussed in the pages that follow, this tension is palpable. The tolerating intolerance paradigm espoused by Professor Minow is directly on point regarding the limits of free speech: whether religious and secular extremists pose a sufficient enough threat to society that their freedom-of-speech protections need be redefined. There is, clearly, danger in raising this question for it suggests identification of a specific group as worthy of special attention in the context of establishing a rights minimization paradigm. The risk in this proposal is significant; similarly, the possible risk to public safety and individuals alike in failing to recognize the possible harm posed by religious and secular extremists is also fraught with danger.

Because of the dangers inherent to this discussion the definition of extremism offered above is deliberately limited. The recommendation that extremism be defined in a minimalist manner seeks to balance the requirement to protect society while protecting the rights of those who challenge society but do not threaten public order by inciting to violence, directly or indirectly, or cause harm to vulnerable members of society. Vibrant democracies benefit from those who think "outside the box" though discomfort is concomitant to their actions. Extremists who pose a danger may perceive themselves as thinking outside the box whereas, in reality, the harm they may cause warrants limiting their rights.

With this, we turn our attention to ascertaining the harm extremists pose to society; the assumption is that extremists do, indeed, pose a threat. That, however, does not mean that rights minimization is an absolute; rather it requires determining the extent to which intolerance is to be tolerated and at what price.

---

[50] *Phelps*, 131 S.Ct. 1207.

THE DANGERS EXTREMISM POSES TO SOCIETY

THIS CHAPTER'S TITLE highlights the inherent tension in this project: although extremism can pose a danger to society, it is important that mature society tolerate dissent, and perhaps encourage, if not facilitate, powerful opposition voices. The question, then, is one of balance: imposing undue and unjustified limits on voices outside the consensus is the antithesis of a vibrant democracy. These voices may well engender discomfort, anger, and resentment among the mainstream population; however, that does not mean that these voices must necessarily be stifled. However, it is similarly undeniable that extremism, under certain conditions, poses clear danger to society; the burden is narrowly defining specific danger. Loosely articulating danger is harmful for it facilitates unjustified silencing of legitimate dissent; however, failure to define—and act against—clear danger unnecessarily endangers society and individuals alike.[1]

The most obvious harm extremism poses is physical injury to members of society; in that vein, it is the primary responsibility of the nation-state to ensure the physical safety of the populace, from internal and external threats alike. To dismiss the possibility that extremists have the capability, and under certain conditions willingness, to cause harm is to undermine the social compact that Rousseau brilliantly outlined in *The Social Contract*.[2] After all, in

---

[1] *See* David Sirota, *Are Evangelicals A National Security Threat?*, SALON (Nov. 29, 2011, 1:50 PM), http://www. salon.com/2011/11/29/are_evangelicals_a_national_security_threat/.

[2] *See generally* JEAN-JACQUES ROUSSEAU, THE SOCIAL CONTRACT (1923), *available at* http://www.archive. org/stream/therepublicofplaoorousuoft#page/n3/mode/2up.

exchange for entering into a social compact with the state, the individual expects protection and safety. That is, by willfully entering into an association with other individuals under the umbrella provided by the state, the person rightfully demands protection and safety. In addition, the individual in agreeing to the social compact expects laws that reflect the majority will. Nevertheless, the individual has the right to oppose laws the majority has viewed favorably.

That is, after all, the essence of democracy: although the individual may oppose particular laws he or she is guaranteed protection from the majority when expressing a particular viewpoint. The social compact, in establishing an association, articulates a paradigm whereby the individual sacrifices liberty for protection; that, however, does not mean the individual agrees to be subjected to violence and harm. After all, the motivation in forming an association and joining society is to be free from harm and danger. In examining the harm posed by extremism the question is not only existential harm to society but also physical harm to individual members of society who are, potentially, at risk.

The willingness of the individual to voluntarily join society is based on understanding that some freedom and liberty is voluntarily relinquished in exchange for protection and safety. In other words, the individual has made a "deal" with society whereby protection is proffered in exchange for minimization of personal rights.

However, if society neither satisfactorily nor sufficiently protects the individual either from external or internal threats, then the social contract has been violated. Under such circumstances, society fails to meet its obligation to the individual.[3] While the failure violates the contract, it, more importantly, enhances the vulnerability of individuals by exposing them to harm from which they are unprotected. In the context of examining extremism one of the most important—and troubling—realities is that the nation-state tolerates conduct that, as history has consistently demonstrated, harms individuals, whether randomly or specifically. The social contract model articulated by Rousseau sought to create a model whereby harm to individuals is minimized; yet, the pages of history are replete with examples where the contract has been violated by the nation-state turning a blind eye to extremism.

The specific examples discussed in this book reflect the tension between individual rights and national security rights; the social contract is at the confluence between these competing rights for it establishes state responsibility to the individual. When the nation-state chooses not to confront extremism or extremists, the social contract has been violated.

The social contract is predicated on an understanding that neither national security nor individual rights are absolute, and that respect for both is essential to a thriving civil, democratic society. After all, the voluntary joining of society necessarily implies rights minimization in exchange for protection. One of the great dilemmas from the perspective

---

[3] *See* THOMAS HOBBS, LEVIATHAN (Hackett 1994) (1651).

of the individual is what alternatives exist if the contract is violated; prima facie, three options seem viable: submissiveness, peaceful civil disobedience,[4] and violent protest.

As discussed in Chapter One, the US civil rights movement is of particular importance: societal and institutionalized racism against African Americans arguably left civil rights leaders no alternative but to organize, demonstrate, and protest. The extremism confronted on a daily basis, based on deep-seated racism enabling systemic, callous, and institutionalized disregard of their constitutionally guaranteed rights, was a primary motivation in Dr. Martin Luther King, Jr.'s efforts to seek justice and redress for African Americans.

Although King was a profound believer in nonviolence he was incarcerated on a number of occasions by local law enforcement[5] and convicted for his actions.[6] King's convictions were for nonviolent crimes including preventing the operation of a business without "just or legal cause," trespassing, loitering, and obstructing the sidewalk.[7] These stemmed from organizing and participating in sit-ins, boycotts, marches, and standing in a public place.[8] Although King largely, but not exclusively, sought change legally, the Black Panthers' conduct was overtly violent, illegal, and openly disdainful of government, white society, and King. Broadly speaking, albeit with caveats and cautionary flags raised, we can say King's civil rights movement was inclusionary[9] whereas the Panthers excluded whites and moderate blacks alike.

The King–Black Panthers discussion is important not only with respect to the civil rights movement but also in the broader context of how to respond to extremism. Rearticulated: should extremism be fought with extremism, or are moderate measures more effective and ultimately more successful? If those whose rights are violated reach the conclusion that working within the system and tolerance of intolerance is no longer effective, then violent measures may be adopted. If society and/or law enforcement overreact to extremism—real or perceived—then not only is government legitimacy in question but the ranks of the extremists may, inadvertently from the perspective of government, increase.

How society reacts to the moderate/extreme paradigm is of the utmost importance; however, as the civil rights movement demonstrated even moderate groups, though

---

[4] *See generally* PETER SINGER, DEMOCRACY AND DISOBEDIENCE (1st ed. 1973).

[5] *See* Mitchell Brown, *Timeline of Events in Martin Luther King, Jr.'s Life*, LSU, *available at* http://www.lib.lsu.edu/hum/mlk/srs216.html (last visited Jan. 10, 2012) (listing dates and locations where King was arrested by local law enforcement).

[6] *See Dr. Martin Luther King, Jr. Chronography*, UNIV. OF HAW., *available at* http://www.hawaii.edu/mauispeech/html/mlk.html (last visited June 11, 2012) (listing dates, arrests, and convictions of King).

[7] The King Center, *The Life and Legacy of Dr, King*, GWIRED, http://gwired.gwu.edu/sac/index.gw/Site_ID/7/Page_ID/13579/ (last visited Aug. 24, 2012).

[8] *Id.*

[9] Pictures from civil rights marches consistently show significant white participation; that is in direct contradiction to the Panthers.

engaged in illegal activity as defined by the criminal code, may be subjected to extremist responses by society and law enforcement alike. Government's extreme response to real or perceived extremism is, generally, justified as necessary to protect society in accordance with the social contract violated when government denies otherwise guaranteed rights. In addressing rights guaranteed either by a national constitution or specific laws it is necessary to inquire whose rights are at stake and what protections can be demanded.

I. Failure to Act

The decision to protect harmful religious practices rather than the individual endangers vulnerable members of society. It, frankly, reflects an unjustified defense of extremism by government reflecting misguided priorities largely predicated on a disturbing failure to understand harm posed by extremism. That decision, however, represents a failure of the larger responsibility owed by the nation-state; the duty owed paradigm requires protecting individuals from extremists and extremism. In that sense, the danger emanating from government's failure to minimize the potential threat of extremism is no less potent than the harm caused by extremists.

Protecting religious extremism has the clear potential to result in harm to vulnerable individuals; it is the modern-day articulation of appeasement. It is disturbing because it reflects an unwillingness to learn from history; true extremism, as compared to perceived extremism, is emboldened in the face of government weakness. Although Warren Jeffs was ultimately convicted, the harm he caused both underage girls and young males, specifically, and members of the Fundamentalist Church of Jesus Christ of Latter-day Saints (FLDS) society, generally, is extraordinary. That damage could have been significantly mitigated had law enforcement officials acted decisively years, if not decades, before. Not doing so reflects a troubling failure to understand the clear and present danger posed by extremism, in this case religious extremism. Essential to this discussion is recognizing that government policy resulted in a failure to protect those to whom a duty is owed.

Asking to whom is a duty owed is integral to a discussion regarding the decision to try Geert Wilders, the head of the Dutch Party of Freedom. The decision to prosecute Wilders was imposed on the public prosecutor by the Amsterdam Court of Appeals.[10] Comparing Wilders to Jeffs is, on the face of it, akin to comparing apples and oranges. Nevertheless, a closer examination of decisions taken by prosecutors and judges alike suggests interesting, if not disturbing, parallels. Warren Jeffs is, as a thoughtful observer commented, a serial pedophile,[11] responsible for untold forced marriages of underage

---

[10] *See* Andrew G. Bostom, *Geert Wilders and the Rise of Islamic Correctness*, AMERICAN THINKER (Oct. 18, 2010), http://www.americanthinker.com/2010/10/geert_wilders_and_the_rise_of.html.

[11] Private email in my records.

girls; when the Utah Fifth District Court convicted him of "accomplice to rape"[12] the relevant question was what took you so long?

The question should, obviously, have been directed at the state attorney general and public prosecutors who for an extended period of time granted immunity to an extremist whose harm-inducing interpretation of religious scripture was widely known and much discussed. Although various theories were suggested justifying the failure to aggressively prosecute Jeffs, the reality is that state action, actually inaction, directly facilitated the heinous crimes committed. Jeffs's subsequent conviction and life sentence in 2011 for sexually assaulting two teenage girls in Texas[13] does not justify the State of Utah's tolerance of his conduct. The studied non-action by Utah law enforcement officials reflects both unjustified toleration of intolerance and an institutionalized failure to protect vulnerable members of society facing known and documented threats.

This stands in direct contrast to Wilders whose prosecution was ordered by the District Court of Amsterdam after the public prosecutor determined that prosecution was not warranted. In overruling the prosecutor the court held that both Wilders's movie *Fitna*[14] and a series of public statements and writings violated section 137 of the Dutch criminal code[15] and therefore ordered his prosecution.

Although the Amsterdam District Court acquitted Wilders, after a mistrial had initially been declared,[16] the importance of the case is less in the judicial process and more in its legal, political, and social connotations. In a nutshell, the Wilders trial requires addressing a number of issues including the limits of free speech, concern in the Netherlands (and elsewhere in Europe) regarding Islam,[17] and increasing tension between traditional European society and the integration and acculturation of immigrants.[18]

---

[12] Lateshia Beachum, *Sect Leader Jeffs Convicted of Rape by Accomplice*, NOW.ORG (Sept. 26, 2007), http://www.now.org/issues/violence/092607jeffs.html.

[13] In Texas, Jeffs was convicted of sexually assaulting two girls he claimed were his spiritual wives. Jeffs was sentenced to life in prison for aggravated sexual assault of a 12-year-old and 20 years for sexual assault of a 15-year-old. He must serve at least 35 years of the life sentence and half of the 20-year sentence. *See generally* SAM BROWER, PROPHET'S PREY: MY SEVEN-YEAR INVESTIGATION INTO WARREN JEFFS AND THE FUNDAMENTALIST CHURCH OF LATTER-DAY SAINTS (2011); CNN Wire Staff, *Polygamist Leader Warren Jeffs Sentenced to Life in Prison*, CNN JUSTICE (Aug. 9, 2011), http://articles.cnn.com/2011-08-09/justice/texas.polygamist.jeffs_1_warren-jeffs-sexual-assault-brent-jeffs?_s=PM:CRIME; Paul Bentley, *Shaved and Shamed: Haunting Prison Photos Show Paedohile "Prophet" Warren Jeffs as He Begins Life Sentence for Raping Girls*, DAILY MAIL (Aug. 10, 2011, 3:49 PM), http://www.dailymail.co.uk/news/article-2024530/Warren-Jeffs-trial-Prison-photos-paedophile-shaved-ashamed.html.

[14] *See* Geert Wilders, *Fitna*, YOUTUBE (Feb. 5. 2001), http://www.youtube.com/watch?v=kIKCgRlwQUA.

[15] *Netherlands: Hate Crimes*, LEGISLATIONLINE, http://www.legislationline.org/topics/country/12/topic/4 (last visited June 21, 2012).

[16] *See Geert Wilders Cleared of Hate Charges by Dutch Court*,BBCNEWS, http://www.bbc.co.uk/news/world-europe-13883331 (last updated June 23, 2011, 6:34AM).

[17] *See* Bill Muehlenberg, *Free Speech on Trial: Geertz Wilders*, NEWS WEEKLY, Feb. 6, 2010, http://www.news-weekly.com.au/article.php?id=4173; Steven Erlanger, *Amid Rise of Multiculturalism, Dutch Confront Their Questions of Identity*, N.Y. TIMES, Aug 13, 2011, http://www.nytimes.com/2011/08/14/world/europe/14dutch.html?pagewanted=all.

[18] *See* Racheal Donadio, *Fears about Immigrants Deepen Divisions in Europe*, N.Y. TIMES, Apr. 12, 2011, http://www.nytimes.com/2011/04/13/world/europe/13europe.html.

In ordering Wilders's prosecution, the Amsterdam Court of Appeal *believed* his conduct was offensive to Moslems;[19] this is in direct contrast to the decades-long decision by Utah state officials not to prosecute Jeffs for conduct that *unequivocally* harmed vulnerable members of society.[20] The two reflect distinct approaches to protecting individuals and society. Although Wilders's public statements and film were, undoubtedly, controversial and offensive to Moslems, they were not intended to harm or threaten individuals. Their purpose was to raise, in a provocative and edgy manner, social issues highly relevant to contemporary Dutch society.

Conversely, Jeffs's actions although cloaked in religious scripture unequivocally caused harm; after all, statutory rape is a crime, and invoking religion does not, and must not, grant it either legitimacy or immunity. Extending protections to extremism, whether religious or non-religious, violates the social contract if harm is caused. Similarly, unwarranted and over-broad restrictions on free speech, devoid of rigorous analysis of possible harm to the larger society, is antithetical to Western jurisprudence. The decision to prosecute Wilders is troubling on numerous levels, particularly because it seeks to silence non-harmful provocation while those who incite to harm based on interpretation of religious scripture are, largely, granted immunity.[21] The Wilders–Jeffs comparison is stark: provocation is deemed to be silence-able whereas a serial pedophile is, until recently, granted immunity by state officials protecting the criminal at the expense of innumerable victims. The danger that extremism poses to society occurs on multiple levels; to view it otherwise is to deliberately minimize its powerful impact.

II. Tolerating Intolerance

To cut to the chase: those members of white society who chose to ignore the horrors of lynching in the Deep South adopted the same attitude that secular Jews in Israel did in the face of unremitting incitement by extremist rabbis prior to Prime Minister Rabin's assassination. The attitude is best described as tolerating intolerance. The failure of the mainstream Israeli public, as well as the stunning failure of law enforcement and Justice Ministry officials to fully appreciate the power of religious extremist incitement prior to the Rabin assassination, is a collective tragedy. More disturbing, or at least no less disturbing, is the continued failure to recognize the danger extremist rabbis pose to civil democratic society.

---

[19] *See* David Jolly, *Dutch Court Acquits Anti-Islam Politician*, N.Y. Times, June 23, 2011, http://www.nytimes.com/2011/06/24/world/europe/24dutch.html.

[20] *See generally* Danielle Tumminio, *Warren Jeffs' Appalling Abuse of Religion*, Huffington Post (Aug. 6, 2011, 10:34 AM), http://www.huffingtonpost.com/danielle-tumminio/warren-jeffs-trial-religious-abuse_b_919607.html; http://www.latimes.com/news/la-na-sect12may12,0,5778341.story.

[21] *See generally* Paul Canning, *The Netherlands: Islamic Extremists Call for Lesbian's Death*, LGBTQNation (Dec. 14, 2011) http://www.lgbtqnation.com/2011/12/islamic-extremists-call-for-lesbians-death/; Soeren Kern, *German Cartoon Riots: Clubs, Bottles, and Stones*, Gatestone Inst. (May 8, 2012, 5:00 AM), http://www.gatestoneinstitute.org/3052/german-cartoon-riots.

Recent examples of this danger are found in remarks made by right-wing extremists toward Defense Minister Ehud Barak when West Bank settlements were put on a 10-month freeze: "If you think of destroying the settlements, you are mistaken, and I will kill you...I will harm you or your children, be careful... If not now, then when you are no longer a minister and have no security around you."[22] An additional example is a warning given by the former Head of the Israeli Security Agency, Yuval Diskin, to Prime Minister Benjamin Netanyahu and Defense Minister Ehud Barak: "The Rabin assassination can repeat itself. There are extremist Jews within the Green Line as well, not only in the territories. It's an optical illusion that they're all in the territories... There are dozens willing to use firearms against their Jewish brothers."[23]

On the face of it, refusal of religious male soldiers to attend official military ceremonies where women either participate or sing seems quaint and insignificant.[24] Nothing could be further from the truth. The refusal is a direct challenge by extremist rabbis to civil, secular Israeli society; the Israel Defense Forces (IDF), after all, is the true melting pot where Israelis—Jews, Druze, Bedouin, Circassian, religious, secular, male, female— contribute to society in the name of collective national defense. Political maneuvering in the state's infancy resulted in religious-based deferments[25] from service in the IDF; today, the question is whether the state will bow to the demands of extremist rabbis.

Although public criticism is voiced regarding deferments granted to 18-year-old male Yeshiva students (Haredim), the Israeli public has largely accepted them in the context of political reality and machinations.[26] In addition, the deferments were largely legalized when the Israeli Knesset enacted the "Tal Bill"[27]; while the legislation created a bifurcated responsibility paradigm amongst Israelis, public opposition was mild and inconsistent. However, the incitement by extremist rabbis directed at male soldiers urging them to disrespect their female colleagues[28] raises significant challenges to both the IDF specifically

---

[22] *See* Amos Harel,*Barak Gets Death Threat over West Bank Settlement Freeze*, HAARETZ (Jan. 5, 2010, 8:23 PM), http://www.haaretz.com/news/barak-gets-death-threat-over-west-bank-settlement-freeze-1.260859.

[23] *See* Chaim Levison, *Yuval Diskin: West Bank Evacuation Could Lead to Another Political Assassination*, HAARETZ (Apr. 28, 2012, 7:08 PM), http://www.haaretz.com/news/diplomacy-defense/yuval-diskin-west-bank-evacuations-could-lead-to-another-political-assassination-1.426979.

[24] *See* Barak Ravid, *Israeli Secular, Religious Ministers Hold Heated Debate over Women's Rights*, HAARETZ (Nov. 27, 2011, 5:12 PM), http://www.haaretz.com/news/national/israeli-secular-religious-ministers-hold-heated-debate-over-women-s-rights-1.398061.; Rabbi Leibowitz, *It Ain't over 'til the IDF Soldier Sings*, HAARETZ (Nov. 27, 2011, 2:25 PM), http://www.haaretz.com/jewish-world/it-ain-t-over-til-the-idf-soldier-sings-1.398037.

[25] DONNA ROSENTHAL, THE ISRAELIS: ORDINARY PEOPLE IN AN EXTRAORDINARY LAND 176 (2003).

[26] A yeshiva or yeshivah () (Hebrew: הבישי, "sitting (n.)"; pl. yeshivot or yeshivas) is a Jewish institution for Torah study and the study of Talmud. Yeshivot are usually Orthodox Jewish institutions, and generally cater to boys or men http://yeshiva.askdefine.com/. (last visited Aug. 1, 2013).

[27] *See* Gideon Alon, *Knesset Committee Expected to Pass Haredi Draft Bill*, HAARETZ (July 15, 2012, 12:00 AM), http://www.haaretz.com/news/knesset-committee-expected-to-pass-haredi-draft-bill-1.39643 (explaining that Tal bill grants deferments to yeshiva students).

[28] *See* Israel Hayom, *IDF Bans Talks by Advocates of Women's Exclusion*, ISRAELHAYOM, Jan. 2, 2012, *available at* http://www.israelhayom.com/site/newsletter_article.php?id=2475 (discussing recent discriminatory acts

and society in general. The issue goes beyond whether male soldiers choose to participate or not in a military ceremony where women sing;[29] the larger question is whether secular society acquiesces to religious extremist demands that violate the existential core of the IDF.[30]

A military unit is distinct from civilian society; its codes and rules are different as exemplified by distinct disciplinary and punishment rules. To that end, for a military to be divided between religious and secular soldiers, with the former determining under what conditions they can (and cannot) participate in specific events, poses significant danger to civil democratic society. In the same vein, the continued incitement by extremist rabbis against members of the Israeli political left[31] and Israeli Arabs[32] presents a threat both to specific individuals and members of a particular group. Harkening back to the pre-Rabin assassination hate-filled incitement, the silence of mainstream Israeli society emboldens extremism. Underestimating the threat posed by extremism raises profound questions regarding human nature; whether it reflects a determined unwillingness to understand the danger posed, or apathy, is uncertain.[33]

That question is relevant to the child abuse tragedy at Penn State University.[34] Jerry Sandusky's fellow coaches and employers disregarded horrors he committed because protecting the Penn State brand was more important than coming to the rescue of innocent and vulnerable underage boys. The Penn State affair reflects the combustable

---

against women in the Israeli military); *"Women Sit in Cockpits, They Can Sit Anywhere,"* JERUSALEM POST, Dec. 29, 2011, http://www.jpost.com/NationalNews/Article.aspx?id=251441 (discussing rising discrimination against Jewish women).

[29] Some Orthodox Jews believe that a man is forbidden to hear a woman sing. This prohibition is known as Kol Isha and is derived from Song of Solomon 2:14: "Let me hear your voice, for your voice is sweet ("arev") and your face is beautiful." The Talmud classifies this as *ervah* (literally "nakedness"). *See* Shmuel Rosner, *The Voice of a Woman*, N.Y. TIMES, Nov. 18, 2011, http://latitude.blogs.nytimes.com/2011/11/18/the-voice-of-a-woman/; Amos Harel, *IDF: Soldiers Cannot Skip Ceremonies with Women Singing*, HAARETZ (Sep. 14, 2011, 3:14 AM), http://www.haaretz.com/print-edition/news/idf-soldiers-cannot-skip-ceremonies-with-w omen-singing-1.384288.

[30] *See* Amos Harel, *IDF Freezes Implementation of Report Calling for Gender Equality*, HAARETZ (Nov. 30, 2011, 2:07 AM), http://www.haaretz.com/print-edition/news/idf-freezes-implementation-of-report-calling-for-gender-equality-1.398544.

[31] *See* Oz Rosenberg, *"Price Tag" Suspect Emailed Death Threats from House Arrest, Police Says*, HAARETZ (Nov. 27, 2011, 8:45 PM), http://www.haaretz.com/news/diplomacy-defense/price-tag-suspect-emailed-de ath-threats-from-house-arrest-police-says-1.398087.

[32] *See* Dan Williams, *Israel Targets Top Rabbis for Anti-Arab Incitement Backing "King's Doctrine,"* REUTERS (July 3, 2011), http://blogs.reuters.com/faithworld/2011/07/03/israel-targets-top-rabbis-for-anti-arab-incitement-backing-kings-doctrine/.

[33] The danger posed to individuals and society alike by a failure to actually minimize extremist behavior. *See generally* Parliamentary Assembly, *Doc. 9890: Threat Posed to Democracy by Extremist Parties and Movements in Europe*, COUNCIL OF EUR. (July 25, 2003), *available at* http://assembly.coe.int/documents/workingdocs/doc03/edoc9890.htm; James Zumwalt, *Extremes Stream a Common Theme*, UPI.COM (May 31, 2012, 6:30 AM), http://www.upi.com/Top_News/Analysis/Outside-View/2012/05/31/Outside-View-Extremes-stream-a-common-theme/UPI-91841338460200/?spt=hs&or=an.

[34] *See* Ken Belson, *Sandusky Trial Opens with Accuser's Testimony*, N.Y. TIMES, June 11, 2012, http://www.nytimes.com/2012/06/12/sports/ncaafootball/jerry-sandusky-child-sexual-abuse-trial-begins.html.

danger of a closed society[35] and harm caused by ignoring risk to the vulnerable.[36] The alleged failure of university officials, who are state employees, to respond forcefully to an eyewitness report[37] is deeply troubling. It reflects a deliberate minimization of a clear threat, manifesting disturbing prioritization. Not to mix apples and oranges but it reflects mainstream German society ignoring murders, largely of immigrants, committed over the past decade.[38] It took German authorities almost 10 years to piece together evidence revealing a neo-Nazi group linked to a string of murders, bank robberies, and bomb attacks.[39]

The ignoring of clear danger signs reflects violation of the social contract; there is little doubt that extremism benefits from this willful blindness, which, depending on the circumstance is either a criminal act or an extraordinary moral failure. In either paradigm—criminal or moral—the results are similar: harm is caused to the vulnerable because mainstream society and government officials failed to sufficiently protect those most in need of that very protection. There is something about extremist behavior that fosters reticence on the part of the larger society; that very weakness emboldens extremists committed to a worldview intolerant of compromise that brooks no dissent. That reality defines an internal society that poses extraordinary dangers to those deemed apostates or insufficiently devout; those deemed not true believers are at risk. As history demonstrates, vulnerable members of an internal society are subject to unrelenting abuse with little hope of outside mitigation of their distress. In other words, the price of tolerating intolerance is neither abstract nor ephemeral; it is very real with tragic consequences.

Society's turning of a blind eye to extremism is a pattern that tragically repeats itself. It is insignificant whether the deliberate ignoring of the threat posed by extremists is a crime or only a moral failure. In both cases, the victims of extremism are unprotected; whether Penn State officials, in positions of authority entrusted to ensure child abuse desist and Sandusky's prosecution, committed a crime (i.e., child endangerment) or failed morally (brand/institution protection rather than child protection) will be determined by prosecutors and courts. An investigative report written by former FBI director Louis Freeh found Penn State officials guilty not of simple negligence but rather willfulness in

---

[35] *See* Jason Sickles, *Report: Penn State Officials May Have Tried to Conceal Jerry Sandusky Child Abuse Allegations*, YAHOO NEWS (June 11, 2012, 3:47 PM), http://news.yahoo.com/blogs/lookout/report-penn-state-officials-may-tried-conceal-jerry-154753288.html.

[36] *See* Mark Gado, *The Kitty Genovese Murder*, TRUTV (2012), http://www.trutv.com/library/crime/serial_killers/predators/kitty_genovese/1.html.

[37] Sickles, *supra* note 35.

[38] *See Neo-NaziMurders, Film Confession Shock Germany*, REUTERS (Nov. 13, 2011, 1:23 PM), http://www.reuters.com/article/2011/11/13/us-germany-crime-neonazis-idUSTRE7AC0TQ20111113; Nicholas Kulish, *Neo-Nazis Suspected in Long Wave of Crimes, Including Murders, in Germany*, N.Y. TIMES, Nov. 13, 2011, http://www.nytimes.com/2011/11/14/world/europe/neo-nazis-suspected-in-wave-of-crimes-in-germany.html?pagewanted=all.

[39] *Id.*

covering up Sandusky's abuses.[40] Currently, Penn State officials responsible for the cover-up are awaiting trial.[41] What is clear, reminiscent of the Catholic Church's historical response to horrific and unceasing reports of child abuse by priests, is policy intended to protect the institution rather than the victim. In both cases, Penn State and the Church, the damage to the institution would be extraordinary; in both cases, institution leaders made egregious errors reflecting willful blindness at its most unconscionable extreme.[42]

Although neither Penn State nor the Catholic Church is the focus of this book, each is instructive in examining dangers extremism poses to society. The failure to act in the face of a clear wrong largely defines society's response to extremist behavior. Perhaps, by analogy, it is akin to the schoolyard bully whose actions fellow students and authorities alike know; yet, response time has historically been painfully delayed. Whether that hesitation, recently the subject of extensive media attention,[43] will change is an open question. The historical pattern reflects a policy best described as fear of confronting.

What Professor Minow phrased as tolerating intolerance is intellectually and philosophically akin to Winston Churchill's prophetic words in the 1930s.[44] After all, Churchill, more than any other public figure, clearly recognized the threat posed by Hitler. That recognition, in direct contrast to Neville Chamberlin's appeasement policy, is as appropriate today as it was 80 years ago. Chamberlin's failure to recognize, much less appreciate, Hitler's true intentions are akin to those who prefer to understate direct and indirect threats alike. Minow's tolerating intolerance paradigm and Churchill's early and prescient warnings highlight the dangers extremism poses when mainstream society flinches in the face of clear danger.

There is, obviously, risk in overstating the danger; after all, history is replete with harm incurred by otherwise innocent people wrongly suspected of posing a threat to society. That is the harm of finger pointing and painting broad strokes regarding possible threats to society. However, extremists arguably benefit from overreaction because perceived excess by the state can serve to galvanize supporters feeling like outliers and enhance recruitment of new membership. In that sense, government excess can directly facilitate unintended growth of extremist organizations. There is, then, a danger in both insufficiently

---

[40] Rana L. Cash, *Penn State Report: Freeh Says Paterno, Administrators Engaged in Sandusky Cover-Up*, AOL SPORTINGNEWS, (July 12, 2012), http://aol.sportingnews.com/ncaa-football/story/2012-07-12/penn-state-report-joe-paterno-role-sandusky-scandal-louis-freeh-investigation.

[41] *Jan. Trial for Ex-PSU Officials Curley, Schultz*, N.Y. TIMES, Aug. 17, 2012, http://www.nytimes.com/aponline/2012/08/17/us/ap-us-penn-state-abuse-administrators.html.

[42] *See Roman Catholic Church Sex Abuse Cases*, N.Y. TIMES, Mar. 12, 2012, http://topics.nytimes.com/top/reference/timestopics/organizations/r/roman_catholic_church_sex_abuse_cases/index.html; *see also* Erik Kain, *How Penn State and the Catholic Church Covered Up Sexual Abuse and What We Can Do to Stop It*, FORBES (Nov. 7, 2011, 2:19 PM), http://www.forbes.com/sites/erikkain/2011/11/07/how-penn-state-and-the-catholic-church-covered-up-sexual-abuse-and-what-we-can-do-to-stop-it/.

[43] *See* Kirk Semple, *Army Charges 8 in Wake of Death of a Fellow G.I.*, N.Y. TIMES, Dec. 21, 2011, http://www.nytimes.com/2011/12/22/us/8-charged-in-death-of-fellow-soldier-us-army-says.html?pagewanted=all.

[44] WINSTON CHURCHILL, THE GATHERING STORM (1948).

reacting to and preventing extremism and in overreacting to perceived threats posed by extremists. After all, the essence of a vibrant and robust democracy is free speech; the tension is in articulating, developing, and implementing a balance regime that protects society while respecting guaranteed rights.

Clearly, multiple themes and threads are woven into this discussion; whether current examples conjure visions of Chamberlin returning to London promising "peace in our time"[45] is a matter of debate. However, the warning signs that Churchill so eloquently expressed were overwhelmingly ignored both by his fellow Englishman and much of the Western world. Whether Churchill's warnings, if articulated by a different politician, would have been disregarded as cavalierly is a moot question; the reality is that Western society and leadership alike believed that Hitler could be appeased were Sudetenland made part of Germany.[46] Although historical analogies are inherently dangerous the quick discarding of lessons offered by history comes with a cost.

That cost is forgetting extremists are characterized by clear vision, mission dedication, enormous energy, and unrelenting will. Those four traits—vision, dedication, energy, and will—are essential to understanding extremists. Equally important, these traits do not depict society at large, except in times of crisis and national emergency. Furthermore, mainstream society largely emphasizes inclusivity; this is in contrast to the exclusivity of extremist groups that focus on a particular issue. The difference between inclusivity and exclusivity is essential to understanding extremists; by emphasizing the centrality of their group, at the expense of the state, they deny the legitimacy of state laws and institutions. In creating an internal governance system divorced from the nation-state, extremists pose a direct challenge to the social contract. That is not to say they necessarily challenge the very survival of the nation-state, but potential harm to individual members of the nation-state is a very real possibility. That, in and of itself, endangers society.

The tolerance/intolerance debate is critical to understanding extremism in the context of the social contract. When extremism that poses harm is tolerated, the contract is violated; when society, on rare occasions, rebukes or rejects extremism, the social contract is honored. From the abstract to the concrete: whereas law enforcement attacked King and the civil rights movement at the behest of state agents, FLDS child brides were abandoned by state officials. In both cases, whether state actors actively or passively violate the social contract, harm to the individual is all but ensured.

However, on innumerable occasions decision-makers have failed to decisively act in the face of internal harm to an individual. As an Israeli journalist ruefully commented[47] the failure of the Israeli media, including this journalist, to soberly recognize the clear danger posed by extremist right-wing rabbis inciting against Rabin was based on a secular assumption that religious-based incitement is not a sufficient motivator for action.

---

[45] DAVID FABER, MUNICH: 1938 APPEASEMENT CRISIS 5–7 (2008).

[46] *See generally* PETER NEVILLE, HITLER AND APPEASEMENT (2007).

[47] Notes in author's records.

In other words, to paraphrase the journalist, no one *really* takes religious extremism seriously.

The media's failure to sufficiently appreciate the power of religious extremist speech was a malady that permeated throughout Israeli society prior to Rabin's assassination. It was only after Yigal Amir assassinated Rabin—acting in the spirit of unrestrained and unmitigated religious extremist incitement—that mainstream society asked itself "where were we?" The question, posed in anguish and deep remorse by many, was the wrong one; the correct query is "why did we consistently fail to underestimate the power of religious extremist speech?" In many ways, the answer is arrogance: a secular arrogance that religious leaders must not be taken seriously by their congregants, who should understand that religious speech is just that, religious speech, and is therefore inapplicable to modern society.

This arrogance born of inability to understand the power of religious extremist speech is not restricted to a powerful disconnect between religious extremists and secular members of society, for it extends to secular extremist speech. That, too, is minimized by mainstream society largely convinced that extremist speech represents mere venting by a disaffected few and does not pose a threat to society or individuals. As McCarthyism made clear, ignorance is not bliss, and the price to be paid for willfully disregarding extremist speech is indeed high. The sheer numbers of careers ruined, lives destroyed, and irreversible harm caused to innumerable innocent victims highlights the dangers of speech dismissed by society as the ranting of a lone individual.[48]

III. Extremist Speech

Without doubt, Senator McCarthy benefited from the Red Scare that pervaded American culture in the aftermath of World War II; just as important, the acquiescence of American leadership and society in the face of McCarthy's rants was outrageous. The former, in particular President Eisenhower, chose to ignore the extraordinary harm McCarthy's speech caused, whereas the latter were either scared into silence or deliberately chose to ignore the danger posed by McCarthy. Perhaps, some identified with McCarthy, believing American society was, indeed, threatened by Communists holding positions of influence and power in the State Department, Hollywood, or leading intellectual circles. Eisenhower and others, who turned a deaf ear to McCarthy and a blind eye to the harm caused, illustrate the harm that results when extremists are not confronted.

In the same manner that mainstream Israeli society ignored the incitement Rabin was subjected to, mainstream American society similarly responded in the 1950s. Deafening silence is the most apt description of that response. Whereas right-wing rabbis directed

---

[48] *See generally* ELLEN SCHRECKER, THE AGE OF MCCARTHYISM: A BRIEF HISTORY WITH DOCUMENTS (Bedford 2nd ed. 2001) (1994).

their venom at the prime minister, McCarthy targeted particular categories of American society, particularly the elites easily identified by their liberal values and broad-minded thinking. That, largely, was tolerated by mainstream society; what, ultimately, caused McCarthy's downfall were unabated and virulent attacks on the US Army. Then, and only then, did President Eisenhower respond; however, the true hero's in confronting McCarthy were CBS correspondent Edward R. Murrow and the Secretary of the Army, Joseph N. Welch.[49]

In examining the power of extremism and the tragic consequences of acquiescence by mainstream society, the importance of McCarthyism as a teaching moment must not be minimized. Message framing, verbal or symbolic, requires intimate knowledge of the audience and its core needs and beliefs. The ability of extremists, religious or secular, to concisely frame an idea, devoid of nuance, is essential to shaping public opinion. The message is critical to the dissemination of extremism: the more concise and direct, the more powerful and compelling. The concise message is essential to extremist movements: the simpler the message, the more powerful the punch. Nuance is perceived as weakness whereas themes that are focused have greater ability to move people to action, particularly when a target group has been identified.

Extremist speech creates a black-white paradigm of us-them with the other clearly identified and castigated. Important to the extremist is identifying the other, someone not like me; the other can be a member of the same internal group, a member of a particular external community, or the larger society as a whole. An effective message clearly defines individuals—internal and external communities alike—as legitimate targets, based on their race, ethnicity, religion, degree of devoutness, and sexual preference. Extremists have assumed the position—existentially and practically—of society's defenders as they define society.

In addition to protecting society, extremists are wedded to the absolute requirement to protect their own way of life, regardless of possible harm caused to others. It is that absolutism the that extremists, to be effective, must capture and bottle. In doing so, the message must articulate the threat posed to larger society or to the particular group by an identified target, and propose concrete measures protecting threatened values, mores, and ways. Extremists articulate a paradigm whereby they are the last bastions of protecting at risk values; if not for their efforts and resolve, the larger society or the specific group will be endangered. However, unlike mainstream groups—including nongovernmental organizations (NGOs) that focus on particular issues, whether the environment, human rights, or child safety—extremists articulate a paradigm whereby compromise and dialogue with existing institutions is rejected.

---

[49] *See* AdmiralMoo, *Army-McCarthy Hearings*, YOUTUBE (Mar. 9, 2008), http://www.youtube.com/watch?v=lAur_Io77NA; *see also* W.H. Lawrence, *Welch Assails M'Carthy's "Cruelty" And "Recklessness" in Attack on Aide; Senator, on Stand, Tells of Red Hunt*, N.Y. TIMES, June 9, 1954, http://www.nytimes.com/learning/general/onthisday/big/0609.html.

The requirement to protect –whether a group or society—is an essential aspect of the extremists' worldview; in the protection paradigm the extremist has clearly identified both what needs to be protected and what poses the threat. In other words, clearly identifying the legitimate target justifies the legitimacy of their actions. What facilitates the extremists' ability to act against the target defined as legitimate is mainstream society's traditional lethargic response to extremism.

However, the response to extremist speech must not be excessive, for freedom of speech is a guaranteed right; the tension is in balancing between the two competing interests. That is, although the message articulated by extremists may be objectionable to a majority of the population that does not, inherently, mean the speech must be banned and the speaker defined as an inciter. Conversely, freedom of speech must not be viewed so broadly that the speaker be granted immunity regardless of the potential harm the speech may cause. Freedom of speech, after all, is not an unlimited right. The requisite line drawing requires great sensitivity: not recognizing the potential harm posed by extremist speech is clear, and the harm to democratic values when harmful speech goes unabated is equally troubling.

IV. Extreme Expressions of Faith

Although religious extremism presents a significant threat to contemporary society, this does not mean that all religions or all people of religious faith present a threat. It is not religion, but religious extremism as understood, articulated, and practiced by extremists that warrants careful attention.

If viewed on a spectrum, belief is the most private and intimate of the three aspects of religiosity and, therefore, the least subject to the imposition of limitations. Conversely, speech and conduct—if outside the intimacy of the home—are the most public manifestations of religion. However, speech and conduct in the home is not immune from the imposition of limitations; crimes committed in the home in the name of religion[50] are punishable and justice must be meted out to the perpetrators. Clear distinctions are drawn between private and public religion; nevertheless private religion is not immune from law enforcement, even if the motivation for the crime is religion.

In accordance with Supreme Court's holding in *Reynolds v. United States*[51] that federal law prohibiting polygamy did not violate the Free Exercise Clause of the US Constitution regarding a Mormon who claimed polygamy a fundamental tenet of his faith,[52] religious belief must be protected but religiously inspired conduct need not necessarily be protected. Similarly in *Employment Division, Department of Human Resources of Oregon*

---

[50] Honor killings are a prime example of religious-based crimes committed within the home.

[51] Reynolds v. U.S., 98 U.S. 145 (1878).

[52] *Id.* at 166.

v. Smith,[53] the Supreme Court ruled that even were peyote used as part of a religious ceremony, if the Oregon Supreme Court prohibited religious use of peyote, it was proper to deny unemployment benefits to those fired for using the drug.[54]

Whether religious extremism is a function of the manipulation of religion or an extremist understanding of sacred scripture is an important question. It is, however, not the critical one. Hundreds of millions of individuals worldwide practice their faith while neither imposing themselves on the rights of their neighbors nor endangering them. Recommending that limits be imposed on how religion is practiced directly affects the rights of religious moderates. The critical question, then, is how does society protect itself against religious extremism without unnecessarily trammeling on the rights of those whose religious beliefs and practices are in full accordance of the law? That is, how should the rights of those who engage in moderate expressions of faith be protected while similar protections are not extended to those who engage in religious extremism?

In April 2008, I had dinner with the District Mayor of Slotervaart, a "ward" of Amsterdam,[55] Mr. Ahmed Marcouch.[56] The dinner was held shortly after Sheikh Fawaz Jneid, a radical imam of the As-Soenna mosque in The Hague, issued a fatwa[57] against Marcouch, who suggested on a national TV show that Islam must "come to terms with homosexuality."[58] In addition, Marcouch said that full assimilation into the Netherlands was possible only if young Islamic men sought gainful employment and learned Dutch.[59]

Marcouch said on the television program *Pauw & Witteman* during a debate with Fawaz Jneid that the Imam had signed a statement referring to Marcouch as a "hypocrite" and "disguised unbeliever." According to Marcouch, the statement has the status of a fatwa (Islamic curse), as a result of which his life may be in danger.[60] On the day we met, the Volkskrant published Marcouch's open letter to Jneid, challenging him both to rescind the fatwa and to openly debate the issues.[61] Marcouch indicated he had received numerous private expressions of support but none publicly. Shortly thereafter at an academic conference,[62] the fatwa was discussed at my initiative. Reaction was limited, as

---

[53] Emp't Div. v. Smith, 485 U.S. 660 (1988).

[54] *Id.* at 672.

[55] Amsterdam is divided into thirteen sub-districts.

[56] The dinner was one of innumerable meetings organized on my behalf during a week-long visit to the Netherlands (April 2008). Similar meetings were held in December 2007.

[57] A fatwa is "a legal opinion or decree handed down by an Islamic religious leader." WEBSTER'S DICTIONARY 456 (11th ed. 2003).

[58] Penwtv, *Pauw & Witteman—2 April 2008*, YOUTUBE (Apr. 3, 2008), http://www.youtube.com/watch?v=xkr8RGtX89g (Pauw & Witteman Show, VARA television broadcast, Apr. 2, 2008).

[59] *Id.*

[60] *Fatwa against PvdA Politician Marcouch*, NIS NEWS BULL, Apr. 26, 2008, http://www.nisnews.nl/public/260408_2.htm.

[61] Forum, *Imam Fawaz vs. Broeder Marcouch*, DE VOLKSKRANT (Amsterdam, Neth.), Apr. 25, 2008, at 11, *available at* http://extra.volkskrant.nl/opinie/artikel/show/id/410/Imam_vs._Ahmed_Marcouch.

[62] Exit Strategies for Terrorists, April 2008, at The Hague (organized by the Center for Terrorism and Counterterrorism by the University of Leidens and the National Counterterrorism Coordinator).

many participants were unaware (at least publicly) of its existence; one individual sought to limit its importance by arguing "you must understand its context."[63] My obvious—but unstated—response would (should) have been: "if Mr. Marcouch were to be killed by a follower of Mr. Fawaz Jneid, would his three children have understood its 'context?'" This is not meant to trivialize the discussion—quite the opposite.

Proposing limiting rights regarding religious conduct requires concretizing the discussion. With respect to Fawaz Jneid, his words could have had the same effect that the pronouncements of right-wing rabbis in Israel had on Yigal Amir when he assassinated Prime Minister Rabin. Although Jneid subsequently retracted the fatwa[64] and moderate Islamic leaders denounced it, there are a number of irrefutable, inescapable conclusions germane to this discussion.

The criticism of the fatwa was not immediate; to an outside observer dependent on translation of culture and language, the response of moderates, decision-makers, and thought leaders seems best described as "wait and see." The question, then, is how extremism is to be limited; ignoring its dangers comes with great peril. With that, we turn our attention to multiculturalism.

---

[63] I found this comment troubling, so much so that I immediately phoned an American colleague who suggested such a response echoes statements more closely associated with Europe in the late 1930s.

[64] *See* Claudia van Zanten, *Marcouch: Code Should Ban Fatwa Record*, ELSEVIER (Apr. 25, 2008), http://www.elsevier.nl/web/10191369/Nieuws/Nederland/Marcouch-Wetboek-moet-verbod-fatwa-opnemen.htm.

3

MULTICULTURALISM

THE LIBERAL DEMOCRATIC nation-state is founded on a contract between the individual and the state; the former willingly joins the latter primarily for protection and safety. In so doing, he voluntarily waives certain freedoms and rights he would otherwise enjoy were he to remain truly independent; he does not, however, waive protections. Quite the opposite. For that reason, the nation-state's failure to directly confront extremism and its resulting harms reflects a rearticulation of Rousseau's social contract.[1] In seeking to preserve one set of rights (freedom of religion/freedom of speech), the state is relinquishing its responsibility to protect other, equally important rights. That is the essence of multiculturalism: acceptance and accommodation of practices and conduct that violate laws of the host country.

How one defines multiculturalism is less important than what it represents: an embrace, or at least understanding by society of different communities, ethnicities, and religions living in the nation-state. Without doubt, a laudatory goal; nevertheless, we must ask whether an embrace of *all* aspects of *all* cultures comes at a cost. Society must not tolerate extremist beliefs that impact protected rights of others, whether secular or those held by persons of moderate faith.

---

[1] JEAN-JACQUES ROUSSEAU, THE SOCIAL CONTRACT (1762).

I. The Effects of Multiculturalism

Some, such as Will Kymlicka,[2] embrace multiculturalism, arguing it reflects acknowledgment and acceptance of minority rights by government recognition and celebration of diverse and distinct groups living in the modern day nation-state. According to this theory, multiculturalism ensures the protection of a minority's human rights by enabling groups, to varying degrees, to conduct their lives in accordance with their particular norms and mores. Protecting minority groups' human rights is an important principle of civil democratic society, manifested by domestic legislation and international conventions.[3] The resulting embrace of distinct groups reflects "disaggregation,"[4] in which state power declines relative to group power.

Although enabling group power is not inherently a negative, and may even be a positive, the state cannot absolve itself from responsibility to prevent harm to group members. To suggest otherwise is to relinquish state responsibility; nonstate actors free of responsibility and accountability requirements fill the resulting void.[5] The embrace of multiculturalism is, perhaps, understandable in the context of expanding rights to minority groups; however, all is not well with multiculturalism.

My thesis reflects concern that in seeking to respect, advance, and embrace the rights of minority groups the state, unwittingly, endangers two distinct categories: individual members of the group identified as having violated group morals and the national population at risk from overprotection extended to minority groups. To best understand these threats, multiculturalism must be viewed through the lens of immigrant communities who came to Western Europe largely in search of employment opportunites not otherwise available in their native lands.

Examining immigrant communities and multiculturalism requires answering what is the nature of the relationship between the immigrant community and the host country? In essence, if members of the immigrant community live in a parallel society, segregated from mainstream culture, rather than functioning as vibrant, contributing members of the host country, red flags regarding multiculturalism's beneficence must be raised. Brian Barry has suggested that whereas assimilation requires ratification by the receiving

---

[2] WILLIAM KYMLICKA, MULTICULTURAL ODYSSEYS: NAVIGATING THE NEW INTERNATIONAL POLITICS OF DIVERSITY (2009).

[3] See International Covenant on Civil and Political Rights (members of minority groups shall not be denied the right to profess and practice their religion) and European Convention on the Protection of Human Rights and Fundamental Freedoms (individuals have the right to freedom of religion including the right to manifest religion in practice and observance).

[4] I borrow the term from Neil Craik and Joseph DiMento, *avaliable at* http://papers.ssrn.com/sol3/papers.cfm?abstract_id=128557 (last visited Nov. 13, 2009; selected for inclusion in TOP TEN GLOBAL JUSTICE LAW REVIEW ARTICLES (Amos N. Guiora, ed., 2009).

[5] The issue of nonstate governance was addressed at a University of Utah Law School symposium, Non-state Governance, Feb. 2009; Symposium, Non-state Governance, 2010 UTAH L. REV.

group, in acculturation the individual comes to acquire cultural practices belonging to a tradition of another group.[6] Parallel societies, or what Tariq Modood calls "creating an alternative society"[7] pose a significant danger to liberal society because, as Modood explains, they foster or shelter radicalism. Disturbingly, radicalism manifests itself in the immigrant community in two primary ways: sexual and political violence. The inherent isolationism of parallel societies makes the state largely unable—perhaps unwilling is a more accurate term—to engage those that it *otherwise* would. In doing so, the state facilitates nonstate governance unencumbered by government oversight or intervention.[8]

Political philosophers argue that the essence of liberal society is tolerance of diverse communities predicated on state encouragement of individual expressions of speech and conduct. However, according to Martha Minow,[9] the amount of intolerance that can be tolerated is a pressing question demanding our fullest attention. Minow's suggestion is particularly poignant in the context of immigrant communities whose illiberalism—predicated on the mores of their former cultures—runs counter to the liberal societies that nevertheless tolerate them even though harm occurs to internal apostate members.[10] State tolerance of group intolerance raises questions regarding the cost of tolerance and liberalism. This dilemma suggests an intellectual paradox, if not practical conundrum: the liberal state has fostered illiberalism that, as Melanie Phillips suggests, goes unabated.

Although multicultural manifestations including distinct language, attire, music, and food are celebrated,[11] other manifestations are, frankly, less deserving of laudatory embrace or even tolerance. The tension is both complex and stark: if multiculturalism is not embraced, the liberal state may be accused of illiberalism. For the liberal democratic state, predicated on "the ingathering of the exiles," the majestic words on the Statue of Liberty ring as loudly today as when Emma Lazarus wrote them:

> *Give me your tired, your poor,*
> *your huddled masses yearning to breathe free,*
> *The wretched refuse of your teeming shore.*

---

[6] Brian Barry, Culture and Equality: An Egalitarian Critique of Multiculturalism 73 (2001).

[7] Tariq Modood, Multiculturalism (2007).

[8] For additional information, see Frank J. Buijs, Froukje Demant & Atef Handy. *strijders van eigen bodem. radicale en democratische moslims in nederland* (2006); 40 percent of Dutch Moroccans think Islamic and Euopean lifestyles do not reconcile, citing K. Phalet, C van Lotringen & H. Entzinger, Islam in de Multiculturele Samenleving. Opvattingen van jongeren in Rotterdam 207 (2000), who studied youths in Rotterdam.

[9] Martha Minow, *Tolerance in an Age of Terror*, 16 U.S.C. Inter. L.J. 453 (2007).

[10] Modood, *supra* note 7; this theme, articulated by Modood, was discussed at the University of Utah Law Review Symposium; *see supra* note 5 and *see* Interview by Jennifer Dunham with Syylvia Maier, SNYU professor, scholar, and activist, in Perspectives on Global Issues (Spring 2008), *available at* http://www.perspectivesonglobalissues.com/0302/SilviaMaier.htm.

[11] In the American context, ethnic fairs/weeks are a representative example.

Send these, the homeless, tempest-tost to me,
I lift my lamp beside the golden door!"[12]

However, the crux of the contemporary existential dilemma facing the liberal European state is this: disturbing evidence suggests that some in immigrant communities, despite welcoming host country largesse and embrace, subsequently reject that embrace, in particular values of tolerance and inclusiveness.[13] This is clearly seen in a recent report conducted by the German Interior Ministry, which found that nearly one in four non-German Muslims reject integration, question Western values, and tend to accept violence.[14] In France, a study by the French Domestic Intelligence Services revealed that many French city suburbs are becoming ethnic ghettos. These suburbs are plagued with unemployment, crime, and violence, and a high proportion of immigrant families—some still practicing polygamy—hold anti-Western and anti-Semitic opinions. Particularly, the intelligence services noted "many families of immigrant origin were rejecting French values and even the French language, following instead more traditional ways of life associated with their ethnic origin—including an increasing religious radicalisation among young Muslims, and a backlash against young Muslim women who wore Western clothing."[15]

In other words, the radicalization[16] that defines particular immigrant communities stands at variance with the liberal values and culture of the host country. Although Europe has witnessed extraordinary—and unimaginable—acts of inhumanity throughout history, the European nation-state is, at its core, liberal and tolerant. However, that liberalism is being challenged, literally, on a daily basis in the current milieu; the question is how and whether the state protects itself against the voices of extremism and intolerance. Re-articulated: what are the limits of tolerance, in the face of threats or harm to both internal members and the population at large?.[17]

---

[12] See Emma Lazarus, "The New Colossus," *avaliable at* http://www.libertystatepark.com/emma.htm (last visited Aug. 6, 2013).

[13] *See generally* Andrew Reding, *Can Europe Keep Its Western Values with Unassimilated Immigrants?*, PACIFIC NEWS SERVICE (May 22, 2002), http://www.worldpolicy.org/sites/default/files/uploaded/image/SAEN-2002-Can%20Europe%20keep%20values%20despite%20its%20immigrants.pdf; Emily Abbey, *Ventriloquism: The Central Role of an Immigrant's Own Group Members in Negotiating Ambiguity in Identity*, CULTURE & PSYCHOLOGY 409–15 (Dec. 2002); Leon de Winter, *Tolerating a Time Bomb*, N.Y. TIMES, July 16, 2005, http://www.nytimes.com/2005/07/16/opinion/16winter.html?_r=2&pagewanted=all.

[14] *Many German Muslims "Refuse to Integrate,"* LOCAL (Mar. 1, 2012), http://www.thelocal.de/society/20120301-41079.html; *see* Toni Johnson, *Europe: Integrating Islam*, COUNCIL ON FOREIGN RELATIONS (July, 25, 2011), http://www.cfr.org/religion/europe-integrating-islam/p8252.

[15] Caroline Wyatt, *France "Forming Ethnic Ghettoes,"* BBCNEWS, http://news.bbc.co.uk/2/hi/europe/3871447.stm (last updated July 6, 2004, 4:49PM).

[16] For an important study examining radicalization see JEAN TILLIE, PROCESS OF RADICALISATION, INSTITUTE FOR MIGRATION AND ETHNIC STUDIES (2006).

[17] *See* Patrick Weil, *Why the French Laicite Is Liberal*, 30 CARDOZO L. REV. 2699 (2009); Paul Cliteur, *State and Religion against the Backdrop of Religious Radicalism*, 10 INT'L J. CONST. L. 127 (2012); *see generally* Adam Silverman, *Drift into Extremism: Immigrant Communities*, A COMMITTEE OF CORRESPONDENCE

As Bruce Bawer suggested:

in recent years, something has happened to complicate the left's fanciful picture even further: Western European voters' widespread reaction against social democracy.

The shift has two principal, and related, causes. The more significant one is that over the past three decades, social-democratic Europe's political, cultural, academic and media elites have presided over, and vigorously defended, a vast wave of immigration from the Muslim world—the largest such influx in human history. According to Foreign Affairs, Muslims in Western Europe numbered between 15 million and 20 million in 2005. One source estimates that Britain's Muslim population rose from about 82,000 in 1961 to 553,000 in 1981 to two million in 2000—a demographic change roughly representative of Western Europe as a whole during that period. According to the London Times, the number of Muslims in the U.K. climbed by half a million between 2004 and 2008 alone—a rate of growth 10 times that of the rest of the country's population.

Yet instead of encouraging these immigrants to integrate and become part of their new societies, Western Europe's governments have allowed them to form self-segregating parallel societies. Many of the residents of these patriarchal enclaves subsist on government benefits, speak the language of their adopted country poorly if at all, reject pluralistic democracy, and support—at least in spirit—terrorism against the West. A 2006 *Sunday Telegraph* poll, for example, showed that 40 percent of British Muslims wanted shariah in Britain, 14 percent approved of attacks on Danish embassies in retribution for the famous Mohammed cartoons, 13 percent supported violence against those who insulted Islam, and 20 percent sympathized with the July 2005 London bombers. Too often, such attitudes find their way into practice. Ubiquitous youth gangs, contemptuous of infidels, have made European cities increasingly dangerous for non-Muslims—especially women, Jews, and gays. In 2001, 65 percent of rapes in Norway were committed by what the country's police call "non-Western" men—a category consisting overwhelmingly of Muslims, who make up just 2 percent of that country's population. In 2005, members of immigrant groups, the majority of them Muslims, committed 82 percent of crimes in Copenhagen.[18]

(Jan. 6, 2010), http://turcopolier.typepad.com/sic_semper_tyrannis/2010/01/drift-into-extremism-imm igrant-communities-and-terrorism-adam-silverman-ph-d.html; Stephen Borthwick, *Immigrant Violence in Sweden Reaches New High*, EXAMINER, June 10, 2010, http://www.examiner.com/article/immigrant-violence-sweden-reaches-new-high; *State of Emergency Declared in France*, FOXNEWS (Nov. 8, 2005), http://www.foxnews.com/story/0,2933,174868,00.html.

[18] *See* Bruce Bawer, *Heirs to a Fortuyn?*, WSJ, Apr. 29, 2009, http://online.wsj.com/article_email/ SB124043553074744693-lMyQjAxMDI5NDEwMDQxMzA1Wj.html.

Religious extremists question the state's legitimacy; for them, state law is not inherently superior to religious law. As Margit Warburg explains,

> In some religious circles the emphasis in human rights on the individual above all is a thorn in the flesh. For example, an outstanding Danish right-wing Lutheran theologian, Søren Krarup argues against the concept of human rights precisely because it places humans and not God in the centre (Krarup 2000). A parallel to this is the Muslim argument that in an Islamic state any acceptance of such a human-centred concept of universal human rights would be a denial of the religious supremacy of Allah and an acceptance of secularism. In both cases, it concerns the relationship between religion and state. The extreme interpretation of the Lutheran doctrine of two kingdoms which calls for a sharp division between religion and politics, or the extreme Islamic call for the adoption of shari'a in family law are both challenged by human rights as universal rights that can only be exercised in a secular state.[19]

II. The State's Role and Responsibility

The question is how should the nation-state respond to the challenge of protecting *both* vulnerable members of the internal community and the larger civilian population? Recent polls suggest many Europeans feel their state has failed in its duty; this concern is predicated on the belief the nation-state is devoting resources, time, and protection to those perceived as "attacking" their country—immigrants.[20] This sentiment has been manifested in recent European elections with the rise in popularity of anti-immigrant groups.[21] This rise has pushed mainstream parties to interject anti-immigrant themes into their campaigns and messages.[22] As Melanie Phillips suggests, the unwillingness of state actors to recognize (or acknowledge) that the nation-state is under attack is particularly disconcerting.

---

[19] Margit Warburg, *Dynamics of Religious Boundaries: A European Perspective,* Europeanization, Welfare and Democracy—International Conference, Centre for Modern European Studies, Apr. 16, 2009.

[20] Soeren Kern, *European Concerns over Muslim Immigration Go Mainstream*, GATESTONE INST. (Aug. 15, 2011), http://www.gatestoneinstitute.org/2349/european-concerns-muslim-immigration.

[21] *See generally* Rachel Donadio, *Hard Times Lift Greece's Anti-immigrant Fringe*, N.Y. TIMES, Apr. 12, 2012, http://www.nytimes.com/2012/04/13/world/europe/far-right-golden-dawn-sees-opening-in-greeces-woes.html?_r=2; *Golden Dawn: Leader of Far-Right Party Lashes Out at Greece's "Traitors,"* GUARDIAN, May 6, 2012, http://www.guardian.co.uk/world/2012/may/06/golden-dawn-far-right-greece. Jon Henley, *Marine Le Pen's 17.9% Is Not a Breakthrough for the Far Right*, GUARDIAN, Apr. 25, 2012, http://www.guardian.co.uk/world/french-election-blog-2012/2012/apr/25/marine-le-pen-french-elections-2012; Andrew Willis, *Gains for Wilders' Anti-immigration Party in Dutch Elections*, EU OBSERVER (Apr. 3, 2010), http://euobserver.com/political/29605.

[22] *Sarkosy: "We Have Too Many Foreigners in France,"* FRANCE 24 (July 3, 2012), http://www.france24.com/en/20120306-france-sarkozy-immigrants-presidential-election.

International legal norms regarding intervention in failed states offer an instructive analogy. Scholars examining contemporary trends in international law suggest states justify intervention in failed states to protect both vulnerable population groups in the failed state and their own national self-interest. Although there is not a general consensus regarding the definition of a failed state, common characteristics are agreed upon by many scholars.[23] These characteristics, according to the US think tank Fund for Peace, include a central government that is so weak or ineffective that it has little practical control over much of its territory, non-provision of public services, widespread corruption and criminality, refugees and involuntary movement of populations, and sharp economic decline.[24] The failed state concept has justified both American military presence in Afghanistan[25] and targeting of al-Qaeda and Taliban targets in a number of countries including Pakistan, Yemen, and Afghanistan.[26] Identifying a state as failed is grounds for intervention; by analogy, failure to protect individuals within the immigrant community reflects failure to fulfill the duty-owed obligation.

With respect to the question to whom does the state owe a duty, Churchill's response was unequivocal: protect the general public and thwart danger. That duty, according to Churchill, was essential and primary. Churchill was unique in that he both saw the future and acted on what he saw; unlike many who prophesize, Churchill's genius was not in saying I told you so but in minimizing damage done by others that he had correctly

---

[23] Hugo Grotius, a jurist who laid the foundations of international law in *De Jure Belli ac Pacis* (1625 [On the Law of War and Peace]) wrote, "where a tyrant 'should inflict upon his subjects such a treatment as no one is warranted in inflicting' other states may exercise a right of humanitarian intervention." Thus, it is widely accepted that military intervention is justified where massive violations of human rights occur.

Although Ferdinand Teson acknowledges international law in general bans the use of force, he contends that "cases that warrant humanitarian intervention disclose…serious violations of international law: genocide, crimes against humanity, and so on." In some cases, Teson writes regardless of what action we take we tolerate the "violation of some fundamental rule of international law"; therefore "either we intervene and put an end to the massacres, or we abstain from intervening, in which case we tolerate the violation by other states of the general prohibition of gross human rights abuses." Ferdinando R. Teson, *The Liberal Case for Humanitarian Intervention, in* HUMANITARIAN INTERVENTION: ETHICAL, LEGAL, AND POLITICAL DILEMMAS 110 (J.L. Holzgrefe & Robert O. Keohane eds., 2003).

Christopher Greenwood rightly argues that "it is no longer tenable to assert that whenever a government massacres its own people or a state collapses into anarchy international law forbids military intervention altogether." Christopher Greenwood, quoted in OLIVER RAMSBOTHAM AND TOM WOODHOUSE, HUMANITARIAN INTERVENTION IN CONTEMPORARY CONFLICT: A RECONCEPTUALIZATION 143 (1996).

[24] *The Failed States Index: Frequently Asked Questions: What Does "State Failure" Mean?*, FUND FOR PEACE, http://www.fundforpeace.org/global/?q=fsi-faq#5 (last visited Aug. 6, 2013).

[25] Failed in the Afghanistan paradigm is defined as a failure to prevent the presence of al-Qaeda pre-9/11 and the resurgence of the Taliban; both are considered to simultaneously threaten the domestic Afghan population and present a threat to American national interests.

[26] This is, perhaps, more in accordance with a partial failed state as, according to conventional wisdom, Pakistan has all but relinquished control of western Pakistan (Buchistan) to al-Qaeda and the Taliban. Whether the US policy is in accordance with Pakistani agreement (tacit or complicit) is beside the point; what is of critical importance is US violation of Pakistani sovereignty.

foreseen. In doing so he was a lone and brave voice against appeasement and an advocate for use of necessary force in resisting evil. His infamous phrase "never have so many owed so much to so few" applies to Churchill with a small twist: "never have so many owed so much to one individual."

Contrast Churchill with Tony Blair, the darling of European liberals.[27] Blair's response to 9/11 is reflective, frankly, of blind acceptance of multiculturalism devoid of significant and rigorous analysis of its dangers: "[w]e celebrate the diversity in our country, we get strength from the cultures and races that go to make up Britain today."[28] Apparently, the British public viewed Blair's words favorably: "a Mori poll for the BBC in August 2005, following the London July bombings,[29] showed that, although 32% of the population thought that multiculturalism 'threatens the British way of life', 62% believed that 'multiculturalism makes Britain a better place to live.' "[30] Some might suggest the poll numbers reflect an unwillingness to accept certain realities;[31] others would respond modern society is predicated on different communities living under "one roof." According to a YouGov poll conducted shortly after the July 2005 bombings, 18 percent of Muslims living in the United Kingom stated they felt little loyalty toward Britain; 32 percent answered they believe Western society is decadent and immoral and that Muslims should seek to bring it to an end; 56 percent, whether or not they sympathized with the bombers, at least understood why some people might want to behave this way; 6 percent insisted that the bombings were fully justified. In absolute numbers, that amounts to approximately 100,000 people whom, if not willing to actually conduct a terrorist attack, support those who do.[32]

---

[27] Until his decision to send British forces to Iraq, for which he was subsequently castigated both in the United Kingdom and Europe.

[28] MARGARET BREARLEY, THE ANGLICAN CHURCH, JEWS AND BRITISH MULTICULTURALISM, http://sicsa.huji.ac.il/ppbrearley.pdf (last visited Nov. 13, 2009). See generally Conform to Our Society, Says PM, BBCNEWS, http://news.bbc.co.uk/2/hi/uk_news/politics/6219626.stm (last updated Dec. 8, 2006). It is important to add that surveys regarding multiculturalism are inherently controversial because of different definitions regarding the term.

[29] Fifty-two people were killed in the attacks with over 770 injured. 7 July Bombings, BBCNEWS, http://news.bbc.co.uk/2/shared/spl/hi/uk/05/london_blasts/investigation/html/introduction.stm (last visited Jan. 7, 2013).

[30] BREARLEY, supra note 28; for an additional perspective on this issue see Norman Berdichevsky, Mutliculturalism in the U.K.: Faith Based and Ethnic Schools, ENGLISH REV. (Feb. 2008), http://www.newenglishreview.org/custpage.cfm/frm/9971/sec_id/9971.

[31] When researching Freedom from Religion I traveled to London. In response to my question regarding "political correctness," more than one interlocutor explained the British suffer from colonial guilt; although meant sardonically, I would suggest there is more than a grain of salt of truth in that self-assessment.

[32] See generally MUHAMMAD TAHIR-UL-QADRI, JOHN ESPOSITO & JOEL HAYWARD, FATWA ON TERRORISM AND SUICIDE BOMBINGS (2011); Michael Radu, London 7/7 and Its Impact, FOREIGN POLICY RESEARCH INST. (July 2005), http://www.fpri.org/ww/0605.200507.radu.londonbombings.html; see also Anthony King, One in Four Muslims Sympathises with the Motives of Terrorists, TELEGRAPH, July 23, 2005, http://www.telegraph.co.uk/news/uknews/1494648/One-in-four-Muslims-sympathises-with-motives-of-terrorists.html.

In the middle of this discussion is the delta—human rights. Numerous conventions[33] and treaties[34] create obligations for states to protect human rights and facilitate monitoring by NGOs.[35] Post–World War II, human rights have become a critical component of international geopolitics.[36] The essence of human rights is to protect the individual[37] from egregious governmental action violating otherwise protected or valued rights. Discussing human rights requires asking whose human rights are involved and how are competing concepts of human rights balanced. In the balancing dilemma, the human rights community places great emphasis on legitimate individual rights rather than on equally legitimate national security considerations of the state,[38] inherently tipping the scale in favor of the former. A legitimate and defensible position, this approach has been upheld in both courts of law[39] and the court of international opinion.[40] Nonetheless, one must question whether it adequately and equally protects both society and an otherwise unprotected class.[41]

To protect both the larger society and vulnerable individuals the state must impose limits on human rights. Simply stated, human rights are not an absolute. Multiculturalism ostensibly celebrates human rights, but it has the unintended opposite effect: it directly contributes to violations of human rights, for the reasons discussed above. Human rights demands fair treatment and justice and that basic needs, including food, shelter, and education, are respected.[42] Multiculturalism, when examined theoretically is intended to ensure the protection of religious, cultural, and moral rights in accordance with human rights as traditionally understood. However, multiculturalism in practice is

---

[33] Charter of Fundamental Rights of the European Union; European Council's Framework Treaty for the Protection of National Minorities, *available at* http://www.un.org/en/documents/udhr/ (last visited Jan. 7, 2013).

[34] Leading international human rights treaties can be found at http://www2.ohchr.org/english/law/ (last visited Jan. 7, 2013).

[35] See Amnesty International Reports, etc *available at* www.amnesty.org.

[36] See the Jackson-Vanik amendment in Title IV of the 1974 Trade Act, which denies most favored nation status to countries with non-market economies that restrict emigration. See http://georgewbush-whitehouse. archives.gov/news/releases/2001/11/20011113-16.html (last visited Jan. 7, 2013).

[37] *See* David Koller, *The Moral Imperative: Toward a Human Rights–Based Law of War*, 46 HARV. INT'L L.J. 231 (2005).

[38] *Id.*

[39] *See generally Sahin v. Turkey*, Application no. 44774/98, Council of Europe: European Court of Human Rights, 10 November 2005, *available at* http://www.unhcr.org/refworld/docid/48abd56ed.html (last visited Jan. 17, 2013); Immigration and Refugee Board of Canada, *Turkey: Situation of Women Who Wear Headscarves*, May 20, 2008, TUR102820.E, *available at* http://www.unhcr.org/refworld/docid/4885a91a8.html (last visited Jan. 17, 2013).

[40] *See generally, Germany: Headscarf Bans Violate Rights*, HUMAN RIGHTS WATCH (Feb. 26, 2009), http://www.hrw.org/news/2009/02/26/germany-headscarf-bans-violate-rights.

[41] *See* University of Utah conference, http://www.law.utah.edu/news/show-news.asp?NewsID=206 (last visited Nov. 13, 2009).

[42] Jens-Martin Eriksen & Frederik Stjernfelt, *The Democratic Contradictions of Multiculturalism*, E-INTERNATIONAL RELATIONS (Mar. 22, 2012), http://www.e-ir.info/2012/03/22/the-democratic-contradictions-of-multiculturalism/.

not individualistic but rather communistic. Jens-Martin Eriksen and Frederik Stjernfelt termed this version as "hard" multiculturalism;[43] the actual practice of multiculturalism, then, is contrary to that of human rights and freedom for it facilitates significant denial of individual human rights. Multiculturalism allows a community to enforce its own mores and traditions, whatever it holds sacred.[44] In its most extreme form "the community may even mobilize its own police force and legal system in order to demand, to some extent or another, the conformity of individuals."[45] This is, tragically, particularly evident in domestic affairs.

A compelling example occurred in Canada when a father, wife, and son were accused and convicted of killing three of their family members in the name of honor.[46] Tarek Fatah, founder of the Muslim Canadian Congress, when speaking on the case lamented, "These girls went to the school, the cops, child services and everyone wanted to protect multiculturalism—not the lives of these young women."[47]

Similarly, in advocating the supremacy of religious law rather than civil law, religious extremism inherently limits human rights. According to Eriksen and Stjernfelt:

> A concrete example...can be seen in the famous case of the Danish cartoons of Muhammad. An analysis of the central drawing of Muhammad with a bomb in his turban points out that it is normal, in everyday international caricature, to portray the originator of a doctrine as a symbol of that doctrine. Thus, the famous Muhammad caricature addresses the doctrine of Islam rather than targeting Muslims as worshippers of the doctrine. In the same vein, equipping politicians or thinkers with bombs, grenades or other weapons to convey their violent intent is just as common a device in caricature drawing. Despite the normalcy of such drawings, many of the arguments against them (in Muslim countries as in the West) rest on a multiculturalist assumption that certain groups are entitled not to be offended, to have religious belief protected, to attack people taken to offend them, etc. The Cartoon Crisis thus offers a conspicuous example of the clash between basic, universal human rights claimed for all individuals, such as free speech, and the group rights claims of hard multiculturalism.[48]

Whereas civil law and liberal society celebrate individual rights, extremism emphasizes absoluteness and justifies, even authorizes, violence in the name of a particular belief.

---

[43] *Id.*

[44] *Id.*

[45] *Id.*

[46] *See Jury Hears Wiretap of Accused in Canal Deaths*, CBC News, Nov. 10, 2011, http://www.cbc.ca/news/canada/montreal/story/2011/11/10/shafia-trial-nov10.html.

[47] Stephanie Fidley, *Were Shafia Murders "Honour Killings" or Domestic Violence?*, STAR, Jan. 30, 2012, http://www.thestar.com/news/gta/article/1123403--were-shafia-murders-honour-killings-or-domestic-violence.

[48] Eriksen & Stjernfelt, *supra* note 42.

Extremists, after all, are convinced of their truth; absolution requires adherence to a conviction that *the truth* is known but only to members of *that group* and compromise is not possible. This conviction applies whether the group is secular or religious.

The notion of human rights as a zero-sum game represents a fundamental misunderstanding of the tenuous relationship among different internal communities and between those communities and the nation-state. A more realpolitik approach would be to ask the following: human rights—at what cost and to whom?. This question is particularly relevant to the multiculturalism discussion. In an age fraught with extraordinary danger, the instinctive reaction that all rights must be respected equally is a philosophical fallacy and practical misconception.

The premise of this chapter is that society cannot allow itself the luxury of denying that multiculturalism causes harm. The state's duty is to minimize harm caused to citizens; duty is not owed to concepts. In the face of dangers posed by multiculturalism, the state has a number of appropriate responses, according to political scientists and political philosophers. Rafael Cohen-Almagor and Marco Zambotti have suggested, for example:

> The business of government is to protect and foster the interests of the public, and allowing entry to this group does not coincide with these aims. Democracy ought to defend itself against threats, even if sometimes the measures include steps which exclude members of intolerant groups altogether from a democratic state. Thus, we have a strong case for exclusion where fascists are concerned, since their ideas are incompatible with a commitment to human dignity and respect for others, and since they are likely to resort to violence to achieve their political aims. Similarly, what countermeasures should the government of a liberal democracy put in place if a considerable number of radical Islamist zealots were to immigrate in mass to England with the aim of pursuing a political agenda based on the literal application of the Qur-an? We refer here to the verses regarding the relations between Muslim believers and infidels, that—if read in their literal meaning—would escalate the level of inter-faith violence within the country. In this case, again, the principles and values characterizing the community of immigrants are not compatible with the preservation of a liberal democratic society. Just as in the case of fascists, England's democratic society would be entitled to defend itself and the bases on which peaceful coexistence in a liberal democracy rest. Access into the country, therefore, could be legitimately denied on the grounds that instigation to violence and inter-faith hatred are not compatible with the rules of a liberal democracy.[49]

---

[49] Raphael Cohen-Almagor & Marco Zambotti, *Liberalism, Tolerance and Multiculturalism: The Bounds of Liberal Intervention in Affairs of Minority Cultures*, in ETHICAL LIBERALISM IN CONTEMPORARY SOCIETIES 79–88 (Krzysztof Wojciechowski & Jan C. Joerden eds., 2009).

Domestic legislation, judicial holdings and political paradigms influence how society can most effectively protect belief in the face of multiculturalism that tolerates intolerance, therefore placing individuals and society at risk. Insular groups benefit from liberal society's tolerance of multiculturalism; the irony, of course, is that this tolerance results in tolerating intolerance. To protect society, the following measures can serve as a blueprint:

> **Limit the civil and political rights of those who limit the rights of others (e.g., the group suppressing/repressing the individual rights of group members);**
>
> **Rearticulate rights otherwise granted by constitution or statute;**
>
> **Use language as a condition for citizenship;**
>
> **Impose limits on independent (e.g., beyond the purview of state control) educational systems;**
>
> **Impose limits on attire (e.g., the veil/burkha);**
>
> **Rearticulate judicial regimes so that family issues are adjudicated not in religious courts, but in the preexisting national court structure;**
>
> **Enforce the criminal law;**
>
> **Investigate and prosecute crimes committed in the name of religious extremism and facilitated by multiculturalism;**
>
> **Impose restrictions on religious extremist speech;**
>
> **Rearticulate criminal codes to broaden the definition of crimes predicated on religious extremism/multiculturalism;**
>
> **Combat the immunity from which religious extremism and multiculturalism currently benefit;**
>
> **Minimize nonstate governance;**
>
> **Engage immigrant communities;**
>
> **Resolve to protect the unprotected.**

Although each recommendation warrants a detailed and thorough analysis, discussion will be limited to protecting the unprotected for that is the practical manifestation of the tolerating intolerance paradigm. Two principles are at the core of this recommendation: granting immunity to religious practices and religion endangers members of closed groups and extremist communities must not be allowed to step into the shoes of the sovereign, regardless of the weakening of sovereignty in the context of international law and geopolitics. National constitutions protect the practice and conduct of religion,[50] but must not protect crimes committed in the name of religious belief.

---

[50] See the constitutions of the United States, Turkey, France, Australia, Germany, etc. for examples of constitutional protection of religious conduct/choice.

III. Responding to the Dangers: Recommendations

The harm produced at the intersection of multiculturalism and religious and secular extremism must be recognized even if contemporary democratic civil society embraces the former while failing to recognize its inherent intolerance. Although understandable from an intellectual and instinctual perspective, embracing multiculturalism must be rejected when it causes harm to otherwise unprotected individuals.

By embracing multiculturalism and insufficiently responding to the threat extremism poses, the state has facilitated, whether deliberately or not, the emergence of the nonstate actor whose *known* criminal actions are largely unchallenged. Professor Amnon Rubenstein has concisely articulated the paradigm:

> The Islamist crisis administered a serious blow to this concept and led to a renewed awareness of the need to defend the freedom and equality of individuals as well as to the right of the majority preserve its culture and identity. The multicultural approach in its absolutist interpretation—the claim that all cultures are equal and have an equal legal status—has been weakened, but the multicultural approach in its liberal–tolerant interpretation—consideration given to religious traditions and cultures of various communities—remains intact. In cases in which the multicultural approach clashes head-on with human rights, it must vacate its place and withdraw. Otherwise, this collision can be readdressed by balancing the two interests. Demarcation of borders between the two types of collisions and balancing those interests is within the field of expertise of judges and jurists.[51]

If immigrant communities successfully assimilate, society benefits; self-enclosed communities endanger society and individual group members alike. Assimilation and inclusion into mainstream society enhances educational, economic, and political opportunities; parallel society engenders isolation, radicalization, poverty, anger, and, in many cases, religious extremism. Although this paints a stark picture of clear diametric opposites, it represents a reality in much of Europe today. Although the original population may welcome[52] multiculturalism, there are increasing reports and significant anecdotal evidence that the immigrant community is increasingly turning inward and to religion, specifically religious extremism.[53]

---

[51] Amnon Rubenstein, *The Decline, but Not Demise, of Multiculturalism*, IDC, Oct. 30, 2006, *available at* http://papers.ssrn.com/sol3/papers.cfm?abstract_id=941370.

[52] For an example of original society rejecting immigrants, see Owen Matthews, *The Kremlin Vigilantes*, NEWSWEEK, Feb. 13, 2009, http://www.newsweek.com/id/184777. Measures against immigrants can be seen in many countries where there are language requirements and cultural teachings such as in the Netherlands. Rubenstein, *supra* note 51.

[53] *Muslims in Europe: Economic Worries Top Concerns about Religious and Cultural Identity*, PEW GLOBAL ATTITUDES PROJECT (July 6, 2006), http://pewglobal.org/reports/pdf/254.pdf. Only 7 percent of

Thomas Friedman described the world as flat in the age of globalization; perhaps, however, the reality is that of a flat world with walls.[54] The walls are largely, albeit not exclusively, self-imposed by immigrant communities who choose to separate themselves and shun the mainstream society of host countries. This reality raises important philosophical questions; however, in the interim practical concerns regarding the physical well-being of internal group members demand attention. A flat world with walls is extraordinarily dangerous for those living within the walls. The proverbial proof in the pudding is female genital mutilation (FGM) and honor killing.[55]

Ayaan Hirsi Ali[56] and Fauziya Kassindja[57] describe FGM graphically and unflinchingly. Law enforcement officials in the United States, Europe, and the Middle East are aware of the harm caused to females in the name of religious extremism yet fail to protect the victims. The practice of female circumcision varies from country to country and in its degree of intrusiveness. Even in its least invasive form the description is often hard to stomach; the World Health Organization classifies the practice in four degrees. The following is a witness's description of one of the more intrusive forms:

> It is the twelfth of June, a day that promises to be as hot and as demanding as any yet experienced. I am to witness the circumcisions of the two little girls. Zaineb calls for me at sunup; it seems we are late. We run to a *hosh* (courtyard) in the interior

---

British Muslims think of themselves as British first (81 percent say "Muslim" rather than "Briton"); *Muslim Americans: No Signs of Growth in Alienation or Support Extremism*, Pew Research (Aug. 30, 2011), http://www.people-press.org/2011/08/30/section-6-terrorism-concerns-about-extremism-foreign-policy/. (21 percent of Muslim-Americans say there is a fair-to-great amount of support for Islamic extremism in their community); *Muslim Americans: Middle Class and Mostly Mainstream*, Pew Research (May 22, 2007), http://pewresearch.org/assets/pdf/muslim-americans.pdf#page=60; Denis MacEoin, *Sharia Law or "One Law for All?"* Civitas (June 2009), http://www.civitas.org.uk/pdf/ShariaLawOrOneLawForAll.pdf.

26 percent of younger Muslims in America believe suicide bombings are justified; 35 percent of young Muslims in Britain believe suicide bombings are justified (24 percent overall); 42 percent of young Muslims in France believe suicide bombings are justified (35 percent overall); 22 percent of young Muslims in Germany believe suicide bombings are justified (13 percent overall); 29 percent of young Muslims in Spain believe suicide bombings are justified (25 percent overall)). http://www.cbsnews.com/stories/2006/08/14/opinion/main1893879.shtml&date=2011-04-06. (62 percent of British Muslims do not believe in the protection of free speech. Only 3 percent adopt a "consistently pro-freedom of speech line.").

[54] Thomas L. Friedman, The World Is Flat: A Brief History of the Twenty-first Century (2005).

[55] FGM is considered by its practitioners to be an essential part of raising a girl properly—girls are regarded as having been cleansed by the removal of "male" body parts. It ensures premarital virginity and inhibits extramarital sex, because it reduces women's libido. Women fear the pain of reopening the vagina, and are afraid of being discovered if it is opened illicitly. See Female Genital Mutilation, World Health Organization (Feb. 2012), http://www.who.int/mediacentre/factsheets/fs241/en/index.html. The tradition underlying honor killing defines a woman's chastity as her family's property. "It comes from our ancient tribal days, from the Hammurabi and Assyrian tribes of 1200 B.C."—Norma Khouri, a Christian Arab and author of Honor Lost: Love and Death in Modern-Day Jordan (2003).

[56] Ayanan Hirsi Ali, Infidel (2007).

[57] Fauzia Kassindja & Layli Miller Bashir, Do They Hear You When You Cry (1999).

of the village. When we arrive, we find that Miriam, the local midwife, has already circumcised one sister and is getting ready to operate on the second. A crowd of women, many of them grandmothers (*habobat*), has gathered outside the room, not a man in sight. A dozen hands push me forward. "You've got to see this up close," says Zaineb, "it's important." I dare not confess my reluctance. The girl is lying on an *angareeb* (native bed), her body supported by several adult kinswomen. Two of these hold her legs apart. Then she is administered with a local injection. In the silence of the next few minutes Miriam takes a pair of what look to me like children's paper scissors and quickly cuts away the girl's clitoris and labia minora. She tells me this is the *lahma djewa* (the inside flesh). I am surprised that there is so little blood. Then she takes a surgical needle from her midwife's kit, threads it with suture, and sews together the labia majora, leaving a small opening at the vulva. After liberal application of antiseptic, it is all over.[58]

According to the World Health Organization there are currently 100 to 140 million girls and women worldwide who have been subjected to FGM.[59] In Africa alone there is an estimated 3 million girls at risk of undergoing FGM.[60] Although most of the girls and women who have undergone FGM or who are at risk of undergoing FGM live in underdeveloped countries, recent statistics indicate the practice also occurs in Western countries. A study conducted in 2007 estimated that over 24,000 girls in England and Wales are at risk of undergoing FGM each year.[61]

Honor killings are beyond description; they are also, tragically, not uncommon in cultures that treat women as property whose actions directly impact a family's reputation.[62] According to the principle justifying honor killings, if a woman brings dishonor to her family her family members must kill her.[63] In the overwhelming majority of honor killings, those responsible go unpunished. It is estimated by women's groups that over

---

[58] Janice Body, *Womb as Oasis: The Symbolic Context of Pharaonic Circumcision in Rural Northern Sudan*, 9(4) Am. Ethnologist 683 (1982).

[59] *Female Genital Mutilation and Other Harmful Practices*, WHO, http://www.who.int/reproductivehealth/topics/fgm/prevalence/en/index.html (last visited Jan. 8, 2013).

[60] *Id.*

[61] *See A Statistical Study to Estimate the Prevalence of Female Genital Mutilation in England and Wales*, FORWARD (2007), http://www.forwarduk.org.uk/download/96.

[62] For a discussion regarding honor killings, see *Case Study: "Honour" Killings and Blood Fueds*, GENDERCIDE, http://www.gendercide.org/case_honour.html (last visited Jan. 8, 2013); Phyllis Chesler, *Are Honor Killings Simply Domestic Violence?*, MIDDLE EAST Q. 61–69 (Spring 2009), *avaiable at* http://www.meforum.org/2067/are-honor-killings-simply-domestic-violence; Hillary Mayell, *Thousands of Women Killed for Family "Honor,"* NAT. GEOGRAPHIC, Feb. 12, 2002, http://news.nationalgeographic.com/news/2002/02/0212_020212_honorkilling.html.

[63] For a discussion regarding the controlling of women in certain cultures, see Susan Moller Okin, *Feminism and Multiculturalism: Some Tensions*, 108(4) ETHICS 661–84 (July 1998); Susan Moller Okin, *Is Multiculturalism Bad For Women*, in IS MULTICULTURALISM BAD FOR WOMEN?, (Joshua Cohen & Matthew Howard eds., 1999).

20,000 women are killed each year in the Middle East and Asia in the name of honor.[64] In addition, in 2011 there were almost 3,000 victims of honor-based violence in the United Kingdom. Precise statistics on how many women die in honor killings in European countries and other parts of the world are hard to come by. This is largely due to the fact that most honor crimes are a political hot potato and rarely reported. Politicians, community leaders, and feminist groups fear singling out one group of perpetrators, particularly immigrant groups, and are reluctant to call honor killings for what they really are.[65] Rather they use terms such as "domestic violence" to describe the crimes. In the Middle East and Asia honor killings are rarely prosecuted, and when they are, the sentences are often light.[66]

When I sat as a judge in an honor killing case, involving two brothers killing their sister at the behest of their mother, I was struck by the overwhelming lack of remorse those involved expressed and their absolute conviction as to the rightness of the killing. The mother instructed her sons to kill her daughter in a manner that was beyond gruesome. As was explained to me, removing the stain to family honor caused by the daughter's alleged behavior required the killing be conducted in a particularly brutal manner. The two brothers spent over eight hours torturing their sister, ultimately dismembering her by tying her legs to two different beds pulled in separate directions. The description is important not for purposes of sensationalism or to dishonor her memory but to emphasize, graphically, the sheer horror of honor killings. This horror is magnified by a disconcerting failure by state agents to consistently prosecute those responsible for honor killings, inciters and perpetrators alike.

But if the state defers to cultural mores accepting—even demanding—such behavior, it abdicates its duty to the individual. The very fact that honor killings go unpunished in many cultures highlights the harm multiculturalism causes. In questioning whether society owes a duty to the culture or to the individual harmed by that culture, the answer must resoundingly be the latter; celebration of the former must be tempered by reality of the harm caused.

In the United States, for example, the "cultural defense" has been argued and, in some cases, accepted as a mitigating factor or defense to violent crimes. For example, in *People v. Wu*,[67] the Court of Appeals of California held that "upon retrial [for murder of her

---

[64] Robert Fisk, *The Crimewave That Shames the World*, INDEPENDENT, Sept. 7, 2010, http://www.independent. co.uk/voices/commentators/fisk/robert-fisk-the-crimewave-that-shames-the-world-2072201.html.

[65] *See* Phyllis Chesler, *A Civilized Dialogue about Islam and Honor Killing: When Feminist Heroes Disagree, available at* http://muslimsagainstsharia.blogspot.com/2009/03/civilized-dialogue-about-islam-and.html (last visited Apr. 6, 2013); *Jordanian Journalist Rana Husseini on "Murder in the Name of Honor: The True Story of One Woman's Heroic Fight against an Unbelievable Crime,"* DEMOCRACY NOW (Oct. 21, 2009), http://www.demo cracynow.org/2009/10/21/jordanian_journalist_rana_husseini_on_murder.

[66] Yotam Feldner, *"Honor" Murders—Why the Perps Get Off Easy*, MIDDLE EAST Q. 41–50, (Dec. 2000), *available at* http://www.meforum.org/50/honor-murders-why-the-perps-get-off-easy.

[67] People v. Wu, 286 Cal. Rptr. 868, 887 (Ct. App. 1991).

child, ANG] defendant is entitled to have the jury instructed that it may consider evidence of defendant's cultural background in determining the existence or nonexistence of the relevant mental states."[68] I am neither the first—nor the last—to ask this question: "at what point must the criminal law be willing to undermine culture?"[69] In the ideal, society would respect culture and cultural heritage, mores, and norms; but just as important, society must protect those who are harmed by cultural heritage, mores, and norms. That is not to suggest that culture necessarily harms, but rather to advocate, indeed emphasize, that *when* culture harms it must be viewed as just that—a harm to an otherwise unprotected population group that society owes a clear duty to. The fundamental weakness of the embrace of multiculturalism and its ensuing celebration is its inability to address when and how society protects those harmed, directly and indirectly, by that very multiculturalism. After all, the defendant in *Wu* argued her "cultural background"[70] was a major reason she murdered her child.

No less problematic, the world is also dangerous for those outside the walls described above. After all, members of immigrant communities have committed post-9/11 terrorist attacks in Europe. Madrid, London, Glasgow, and Amsterdam all represent domestic terrorism committed in the name of Islamic extremism; those committing acts of terrorism in Europe are immigrants and their children. That is not to say that all immigrants are terrorists; it is, however, to highlight that immigrants commit terrorist attacks in contemporary Europe. This is distinguishable from the 1970s when radical groups comprised of native Europeans committed terrorist attacks in West Germany and Italy. The contemporary trend whereby immigrants commit terrorism in Europe suggests that rather than becoming fully engaged members of the home country, some immigrants are retreating to their community, vulnerable to religious extremist faith leaders encouraging and facilitating acts of terrorism.

As a government policy, therefore, unmitigated multiculturalism enables harm to both specific individuals within closed groups and random targets within the general population. It is harmful to those within specific immigrant communities deemed to have violated their mores; it is also harmful to the random victims of terrorism within the larger population. Both categories are victims—unintentionally by government, intentionally by the actors—of multiculturalism. By embracing the concept that nongovernmental groups can engage in self-governance without government monitoring, much less accountability, the state is neglecting its primary responsibility. In the context of embracing different cultures and—in essence—facilitating their operation beyond the state's reach, the nation-state is actually minimizing its own sovereignty, thereby rearticulating the definition of the state.

---

[68] *Id.*

[69] John Kaplan, Robert Weisberg & Guyora Binder, Criminal Law 378 (6th ed. 2008).

[70] *Wu*, 286 Cal. Rptr. 868.

IV. Societal Responses

A government's fundamental responsibility is to protect the community at large; determining what protections must be extended to particular communities within the larger community is a critical question in the limits-of-freedom discussion. Those protections are not absolute; indeed, no rights can be absolute.[71] Rousseau's social contract depends on an understanding that the rights of an individual are not absolute. In essence, the individual trades rights (such as freedom) for protection (as part of the larger community); in so doing, the individual both implicitly and explicitly recognizes that individual rights are not absolute. As John Locke explained:

> The toleration of those that differ from others in matters of religion is so agreeable to the Gospel of Jesus Christ, and to the genuine reason of mankind, that it seems monstrous for men to be so blind as not to perceive the necessity and advantage of it in so clear a light.... But, however, that some may not colour their spirit of persecution and unchristian cruelty with a pretence of care of the public weal and observation of the laws; and that others, under pretence of religion, may not seek impunity for their libertinism and licentiousness; in a word, that none may impose either upon himself or others, by the pretences of loyalty and obedience to the prince, or of tenderness and sincerity in the worship of God; I esteem it above all things necessary to distinguish exactly the business of civil government from that of religion and to settle the just bounds that lie between the one and the other. If this be not done, there can be no end put to the controversies that will be always arising between those that have, or at least pretend to have, on the one side, a concernment for the interest of men's souls, and, on the other side, a care of the commonwealth. The commonwealth seems to me to be a society of men constituted only for the procuring, preserving, and advancing their own civil interests.[72]

The obvious challenge to individual and state is in defining the limits the latter may impose on the former. The equation, however, is not binary because there is an additional—critical—variable that must be factored in: members of society potentially injured by the individual actor's actions. That is, while the individual seeks protection by joining society and therefore voluntarily agreeing to limitations on her otherwise absolute rights,

---

[71] Thomas Hobbes 1651 book *Leviathan* describes the structure of society and legitimate governments and is one of the best-known examples of social contract theory—the idea that in exchange for social order/rule of law people give up some rights. John Stuart Mill's *On Liberty*, first published in 1859, can be viewed as a reaction to social contract theory. Mill believed that "the only purpose for which power can be rightfully exercised over any member of a civilized community, against his will, is to prevent harm to others."

[72] John Locke, *A Letter Concerning Toleration, available at* http://www.constitution.org/jl/tolerati.htm (last visited Jan. 8, 2013).

other members of society must be similarly protected from that individual. The state has an obligation to protect members of society; doing so may well require imposing limits on specific religious-based conduct. These limits do not gainsay either the centrality or vitality of religion; rather, they clearly demonstrate that rights—even if predicated on religious belief—are not absolute. At a basic level, this appears to be an obvious truism, but the more complicated issue is determining which rights should be limited and how in the face of potential conflict with divinely ordained conduct.

Government, in protecting society, must both define threats and assess the dangers they pose. In so doing, it is essential to weigh the costs of action and inaction alike in response to those threats. Obviously, this is not a scientific exercise because threats cannot be empirically determined, but the potential harm they pose must be carefully analyzed even in the absence of numerical certainty. To cut to the chase: as I have suggested, multiculturalism as presently practiced by government and religious extremists alike directly poses a clear and present danger to two distinct population groups: specific targets and the broader population. Although the intended consequence of multiculturalism is not to cause harm, the failure to aggressively rectify the harm it causes is—if not intended— certainly inexcusable and reflects a fundamental governmental failure with respect to an absolute obligation to protecting innocent citizens. It is also not the essence of the nation-state, but may perhaps reflect the reality of the contemporary nation-state.

Human rights of the individual are more important than governmental policies playing to particular groups and communities. What Churchill called appeasement with respect to Chamberlain has, I suggest, once again reared its extraordinarily dangerous head. That appeasement was in response to an external threat; today's threat is largely internal. McCarthyism, a manifestation of the great harm of domestic finger-pointing showed us the potential harm in suggesting internal threats and dangers, but its remaining scars and fears are the extreme. Society cannot turn a blind eye to harm caused by an excessive embracing of a policy—however well intended—that causes harm. There is a middle ground: after all the essence of human rights is to balance competing rights of individuals and groups living under one roof in the nation-state that is responsible for the public good and welfare.

4

RELIGIOUS EXTREMISM

Causes and Examples of Harm

I. State Law versus Religious Law

In liberal Western democracies, religion—although important—is not superior to state law. Religion must not be granted unlimited powers or special rights; this needs to be the case both theoretically and practically for practitioners of faith and theologians alike. An individual accused of violating state law must find little recourse in claiming before a court of law that the illegal conduct was premised on adherence to religious law. Despite this premise, the core of the modern nation-state, the concept of the supremacy of state law, is met with resistance in numerous quarters.

The resistance is particularly acute when lives of at risk individuals are in danger as the tension between religious law and state law moves from the abstract and philosophical to the concrete and real. Although the state is obligated to respect faith it must never tolerate extreme manifestation of faith that endangers vulnerable members of closed religious communities. As case law discussed in this chapter highlights, the risk posed to children in the context of religious extremism illustrates the tension between state law and religious law. That tension cuts to the question as to whom does the state owe a duty, and whether religious doctrine, regardless of the harm it potentially causes, receives precedence over state law intended to protect vulnerable members of society. As discussed in this chapter, the harm caused to children in the name of religious extremism is, tragically, a reality that must be directly confronted by law enforcement and larger society alike. To suggest that religious law has precedence and, therefore, injury to children is justified is a clear violation of the social contract that must be extended, unequivocally, to children. Otherwise, children at risk because of their parents' belief will be abandoned by the state and left helpless in the face of harm caused by religious extremism.

As child endangerment legislation and case law make clear the duty owed is to the at risk child, not the relevant harmful belief system. However, the state fails to consistently meet this obligation; turning a blind eye typifies actions of some officials who, doubtlessly, understand the harm that awaits children. Although laws are clear, implementation requires state officials understand that limits need be imposed on religious extremism; otherwise, harm is inevitable.

Civil laws have been imposed on citizens in order to protect individual rights and society alike. Change in these laws is inevitable; that is how society progresses, reflecting modernity and changes in society and culture. Protecting the democratic process is the obligation of government. Checks and balances and separation of powers ensure changes reflect protection of civil and political rights; otherwise, rights—created by man for man—will be trampled on, threatening the very essence of civil democratic states.

Conversely, religious law is governed by God and according to extremists may not be altered by man, who is obligated to live in accordance with God's laws. That is, it is not for man to question God, whose infallibility is unquestioned. As the conversation with my airplane seatmate[1] made clear people of extremist faith are convinced both of the supremacy of their faith and the infallibility of their God. Questioning God's laws is, therefore, akin to heresy for the obligation of man is to respect and accept, unquestioningly, God's laws. In many ways, that is the essence of religious extremism: the requirement to live in absolute accordance with God's laws, which must not be questioned by man whose obligation is to respect those laws but does not have the right to alter them. Religious law dictates how people of faith live their lives. Civil democratic regimes are endangered when religious extremists—violently or through dangerous intimidation— seek to impose religious law on civil society.

Unlike democratic values, which are inherently broad and liberal, religious extremists aspire to impose a narrow, dogmatic interpretation of religious scripture both on civil society and their coreligionists. To that end, there is significant danger to civil society when absoluteness dictates the conduct of religious extremists. Tolerance of religion is a core value of democracies; however, that tolerance must not be unlimited or otherwise harm may befall innocent members of society.

Does this suggestion correctly identify the primary source of potential danger facing civil society? It may be suggested that religion is a convenient scapegoat and that other significant dangers are lurking around the proverbial corner. In discussing the question of religious-based violence, the inevitable comparison to non-religious violence is raised. Is religion another form of "absolutism" undistinguishable from mass movements that have wreaked well-documented havoc throughout history?

---

[1] See Introduction.

The Rev. Dr. John Lentz wisely observed:

In general religion is not, by definition, another form of absolutism. However, any religious perspective that seeks to control behavior of believers, limits the access to other points of view, and demands strict adherence to a particular world-view, code of ethics, or manner of living moves along the trajectory toward absolute control and is hardly distinguishable from other forms of political or social absolutism.[2]

II. Harm Caused by Religious Extremism

There is no intention to engage in "religion bashing"; it is important to recall that millions have been killed for purely non-religious reasons. Obvious examples include Nazism, Italian Fascism, Pol Pot (Cambodia), and the Cultural Revolution (China); all four regimes were marked by absolute loyalty, in particular to a national leader. In fulfilling real or perceived loyalty requirements, citizens of those regimes committed mass murder on an unparalleled scale.

DEATHS CAUSED BY NON-RELIGIOUS REGIMES

	Nazism	Italian Fascism	Pol Pot	Cul. Rev. (China)
Estimated Deaths	17 million[3]	1–2 million[4]	1.7–2.5 million[5]	7.73 million[6]

---

[2] E-mail correspondence with the author (e-mail in author's records).

[3] According to Donald Niewyk (DONALD L. NIEWARK & FRANCIS R. NICOSIA, THE COLUMBIA GUIDE TO THE HOLOCAUST 45–52 (2000), Nazism caused the murder, using the broadest definition, of roughly 17 million people. Estimates of the death toll of non-Jewish victims vary by millions, partly because the boundary between death by persecution and death by starvation and other means in a context of total war is unclear. Overall, approximately 5.7 million (78 percent) of the 7.3 million Jews in occupied Europe perished (GILBERT MARTIN, ATLAS OF THE HOLOCAUST 242–44 (1988). In addition, 5 to 11 million (1.4 percent to 3.0 percent) of the 360 million non-Jews in German-dominated Europe. MELVIN SMALL & J. DAVID SINGER, RESORT TO ARMS: INTERNATIONAL AND CIVIL WARS 1816–1980 (1982); MICHAEL BERENBAUM, A MOSAIC OF VICTIMS: NON-JEWS PERSECUTED AND MURDERED BY THE NAZIS (1990).

[4] Mussolini's Fascist dictatorship was responsible for over a million deaths. These deaths resulted from political violence during the regime's rise to power; however, most deaths occurred abroad. For example: Ethiopians estimate that between 300,000 and 600,000 Ethopians perished during the Italian invasion and subsequent annexation.

[5] Pol Pot was a Cambodian Maoist revolutionary who came into power in the 1970s. During his reign, he imposed agrarian socialism forcing urban dwellers to relocate to the countryside to work in collective farms and forced labor projects. The combined effects of forced labor, malnutrition, poor medical care, and executions resulted in the deaths of approximately 21 percent of the Cambodian population. ("The Cambodian Genocide Program," *Genocide Studies Program.* Yale University (1994–2008) In all, an estimated 1.7 to 2.5 million people (out of a population of slightly over 8 million) died as a result of the policies of his three-year premiership. Patrick Heuveline, *The Demographic Analysis of Mortality in Cambodia, in* FORCED MIGRATION AND MORTALITY (Holly E. Reed & Charles B. Keely eds., 2001); MAREK SLIWINSKI, LE GÉNOCIDE KHMER ROUGE: UNE ANALYSE DÉMOGRAPHIQUE (1995); Judith Banister & Paige Johnson, *After the Nightmare: The Population of Cambodia, in* GENOCIDE AND DEMOCRACY IN CAMBODIA: THE KHMER ROUGE, THE UNITED NATIONS AND THE INTERNATIONAL COMMUNITY (Ben Kiernan ed., 1993).

Is the absolutism that characterized certain non-religious regimes similar to murder committed in the "name of God"? The doctrine of certitude[7] proposes that religious actors are (1) certain of a deity, and (2) certain that they are acting in the name of that deity. The certitude, then, is a two-step process that requires the believer to fully internalize both belief in a higher power and belief in action on behalf of a higher power. Otherwise, the religious belief is not absolute. Furthermore, religious belief is predicated on the notion that its deity (or deities) is supreme. The concept of supremacy has led individuals of faith throughout history to commit horrific acts of violence against two categories of "nonbelievers"—those who are nominally members of the same faith, but whose fervency is doubted by the actor, and those of other faiths.

The Fundamentalist Church of Jesus Christ of Latter-day Saints (FLDS) has recently been the focus of intense government and media scrutiny regarding the practice of plural marriage involving underage girls. Girls as young as fourteen, when their prophet proclaims that God has commanded them to marry men (in some cases three times their age), are forced to have sexual relations with their husbands. These girls, and their parents, submit to the command believing their prophet's words are, in fact, the words of God.

Similarly—and just as tragically—boys in the FLDS community, some as young as thirteen, are placed in compromising and dangerous situations. Although difficult to determine the exact number, it is estimated that as many as 1,000 boys have been expelled from the community for breaking its strict standards since Warren Jeffs became the prophet.[8] Breaking these standards involves doing things as simple as wearing short-sleeved shirts, listening to CDs, watching movies and TV, staying out past curfew, and having a girlfriend.[9] According to experts, these "Lost Boys"[10] are banished from their community

---

[6] The Cultural Revolution took place in the People's Republic of China from 1966 through 1976; Mao's stated goal was to enforce socialism and to impose Maoist orthodoxy within the Party. The widespread phenomenon of mass killings in the Cultural Revolution consisted of five types: (1) mass terror or mass dictatorship encouraged by the government—victims were humiliated and then killed by mobs or forced to commit suicide on streets or other public places; (2) direct killing of unarmed civilians by armed forces; (3) pogroms against traditional "class enemies" by government-led perpetrators including local security officers and militias; (4) killings as part of political witch-hunts (a huge number of suspects of alleged conspiratorial groups were tortured to death during investigations); and (5) summary execution of captives. The most frequent forms of massacres were the first four; the degree of brutality in the mass killings during the Cultural Revolution was very high. Estimates by various scholars range from 500,000 to 8 million victims. According to Rummel's 1991 analysis, the figure should be around 7.73 million (R. J. RUMMEL, CHINA'S BLOODY CENTURY: GENOCIDE AND MASS MURDER SINCE 1900 (1991).

[7] Phrase used in private conversation with author (details in author's records).

[8] Julian Borger, *The Lost Boys, Thrown Out of US Sect so That Older Men Can Marry More Wives*, GUARDIAN, June 14, 2005, http://www.guardian.co.uk/world/2005/jun/14/usa.julianborger.

[9] David Kelly, *Polygamy's "Lost Boys" Expelled from Only Life They Knew*, BOSTON GLOBE, June 19, 2005, http://www.boston.com/news/nation/articles/2005/06/19/polygamys_lost_boys_expelled_from_only_life_they_knew/.

[10] The term "Lost Boys" refers to teenage boys who have been asked to leave, or have voluntarily left the FLDS community. According to The Diversity Foundation, the Lost Boys are also referred to as the "Children of Diversity." The Diversity Foundation, *Strenthening and Aligning Global Communities, available at* http://www.smilesfordiversity.org/cod.php (last visited Jan. 8, 2013).

primarily in order to minimize competition for older men seeking to marry child brides. Simply put, male and female children alike are victims of child abuse and neglect in the name of FLDS religious doctrine.[11]

Although others have addressed "terror in the name of God,"[12] attacking internal and external targets alike, child endangerment in the religion paradigm is, I suggest, fundamentally different. Simply put, it is the deliberate injury to *one's own* child predicated on religious faith, in particular religious extremism. Though God tested Abraham[13] with respect to the sacrifice of his son, Isaac,[14] the sacrifice (thankfully, never brought to fruition) was the result of a direct interaction between God and Abraham. The modern-day religious extremism–predicated endangerment of children is not between the divine and man; rather, it is between man and man when one of the two *purports to act in the name of God.*

This is fundamentally and philosophically different from the original sacrifice. Unlike Abraham, who ultimately did *not* sacrifice Isaac—for God ordered him to not do so— religious extremists *do* endanger their children.[15] From a theological perspective, polygamy as practiced by FLDS is an essential tenet of how FLDS members articulate and practice their faith. Members believe that plural marriage is a requirement for exaltation and entry into the highest "degree" of the Celestial Kingdom (the highest of the three Mormon heavens).[16] The FLDS Church perceives itself as the "true" Mormon Church, asserting its members practice what the prophet Joseph Smith *truly* believed. The practice of child brides in plural marriages is essential in ensuring obedience and subservience; the practice involves sexual contact between adult males and underage girls. Sexual contact with a minor is illegal and should result in criminal liability. FLDS members violate the law when they have sexual relations with underage girls—the child brides. FLDS parents *do* endanger their children,[17] which raises profoundly important legal, moral, and theological questions pertaining to the essence of two relationships: parent–child and individual–faith/faith leader. The question before us is who protects the otherwise

---

[11] 4 The Juvenile Court Act of 1996, UTAH CODE ANN. § 78A-6-105(1)(a) (2006) defines abuse as "(i) nonaccidental harm of a child, (ii) threatened harm of a child, (iii) sexual exploitation, or (iv) sexual abuse." .

[12] JESSICA STERN, TERROR IN THE NAME OF GOD (2004).

[13] *Why Did God Tell Abraham to Sacrifice Isaac?*, http://www.rationalchristianity.net/abe_isaac.html (last visited Jan. 31, 2010).

[14] *See generally Abraham's Sacrifice of Isaac*, http://www.apocalipsis.org/Abraham.htm (last visited Jan 8, 2013).

[15] *See generally* Gen. 22:5 & 8; Why Did God Tell Abraham to Sacrifice Isaac?, http://www.rationalchristianity. net/abe_isaac.html (last visited Jan. 8, 2013)

[16] JOHN KRAKAUER, UNDER THE BANNER OF HEAVEN: A STORY OF VIOLENT FAITH 6 (2003).

[17] This is, undoubtedly, a relative point for people of faith. Those who engage in practices related to their children's health, safety, and welfare would argue that their actions are in accordance with their faith whereas the state attaches criminal liability to those same practices. *See generally* Adam Lamparello, *Taking God Out of the Hospital: Requiring Parents to Seek Medical Care for Their Children Regardless of Religious Belief*, 6 TEX. FORUM CIVIL LIBERTIES & CIVIL RIGHTS 47 (2001); Jennifer L. Hartsell, *Mother May I ... Live? Parental Refusal of Life-Sustaining Medical Treatment for Children Based on Religious Objections*, 66 TENN. L. REV. 499 (1999); Amos Guiora, *Protecting the Unprotected: Religious Extremism and Child Endangerment*, 12 J. L. & FAMILY STUDIES 393 (2010).

unprotected;[18] the question, complicated as it is, is exponentially more complex when framed in a religious paradigm.

"Who owes what duty to whom" is the subtext of this chapter; the intellectual, philosophical, and constitutional premise must be that the state owes a duty and obligation to children *regardless* of their parents' faith. That is neither to delegitimize faith nor to cast aspersions on people of faith; it is however, to articulate the position that the state has the proactive, positive responsibility to protect children. This is particularly true when the threat to the child is faith-based. Although this is neither the first, nor tragically the last, time this issue will require resolution, it is one that urgently requires candid examination and analysis.

III. History of the Church of Jesus Christ of Latter-day Saints

According to the Church of Jesus Christ of Latter-day Saints (Mormon Church), its founder, Joseph Smith, had revelations and visions that he was ordained as a prophet of God. Smith's followers believed that he had a relationship with God and was His spokesman and prophet on earth. Unquestioning obedience to the latter-day prophet was instrumental to Church members who believed the only way to heaven was to follow Smith's commandments. That faith was tested in the 1830s as Smith gradually began introducing polygamy, claiming that it was a divinely inspired practice. Brigham Young led the Mormons across the continent, ultimately settling in Utah in order to "escape the intense persecution members faced for their unique religious beliefs."

As members of the Church began to live in Utah, "polygamy became a part of their culture and religion." While Utah quickly developed into a unique frontier theocracy under Young's guidance, Church leaders understood the benefit of becoming a state. However, the US government strongly opposed polygamy and refused to grant statehood unless the practice was rescinded. Outside pressure to forbid polygamy increased as the Church grew in Utah. In 1856, the newly created Republican Party declared that "[i]t is the duty of Congress to prohibit in the territories those twin relics of barbarism, polygamy and slavery."[19] True to its promise, the federal government sent law enforcement officials to Utah to end polygamy, confiscating land and possessions of those who practiced plural marriage.

---

[18] The Juvenile Court Act of 1996, UTAH CODE ANN. § 78A-6-317(4) (2008), specifies: In every abuse, neglect, or dependency proceeding…the court shall order that the child be represented by a guardian ad litem, in accordance with Section 78A-6-902. The guardian ad litem shall represent the best interest of the child, in accordance with the requirements of that section, at the shelter hearing and at all subsequent court and administrative proceedings, including any proceeding for termination of parental rights in accordance with Part 5, Termination of Parental Rights Act.

[19] 1 NATIONAL PARTY PLATFORMS 1840–1956, at 27 (Donald B. Johnson & Kirk H. Porter eds., 1973). *Cf.* HENRY CHARLES LEA, BIBLE VIEW OF POLYGAMY BY MIZPAH 1 (n.d.) (asserting the American liberty to possess "as many slaves as Abraham, and as many wives as Solomon.").

IV. History of Polygamy

The Republican Party first compared polygamy to slavery in 1856;[20] in 1862, Congress passed the Morrill Act for the Suppression of Polygamy (the "Morrill Act"). Section One of the Morrill Act states:

> Every person having a husband or wife living, who shall marry any other person, whether married or single, in a Territory of the United States, or other place over which the United States have exclusive jurisdiction, shall...be adjudged guilty of bigamy, and, upon conviction thereof, shall be punished by a fine not exceeding five hundred dollars, and by imprisonment for a term not exceeding five years.[21]

However, the Morrill Act proved to be ineffective in outlawing the practice of polygamy, primarily because those involved were key witnesses who, generally, had no interest in cooperating with the prosecution. Additionally, "no grand jury in Utah would indict Church leaders for violating the [Morrill] Act, so the Act was never used or challenged in court."[22]

In 1878, the question of polygamy reached the Supreme Court for the first time in *Reynolds v. United States*. George Reynolds, a member of the Church of Jesus Christ of Latter-day Saints, was charged with bigamy under the Morrill Act after he married Amelia Jane Schofield while still married to his first wife. Reynolds was originally convicted in the District Court for the 3rd District of the Territory of Utah. Before the Supreme Court, Reynolds argued that his conviction should be overturned for a number of reasons: the statute exceeded Congress's legislative power; his challenges to jurors in the original case were improperly overruled; testimony from his second wife should not have been permitted; and most significant, he had a constitutional right to engage in polygamy as it was part of his religious duty.[23]

Justice Waite distinguished between government control of beliefs and government control of actions. He concluded that "[l]aws are made for the government of actions, and while they cannot interfere with mere religious belief and opinions, they may with practices."[24] An example of this is, if one believes that human sacrifice is an integral part of worship, the government can validly restrict the religious practice. Justice Waite concluded that to permit illegal practices in the name of religion would be "[t]o make the professed doctrines of religious belief superior to the law of the land, and in effect to

---

[20] 24 *Republican Philadelphia: GOP Convention of 1856 in Philadelphia*, July 4, 1995, http://www.ushistory.org/gop/convention_1856.htm.

[21] Morrill Act, ch. 126, § 1, 12 Stat. 501 (1862).

[22] Shayna M. Sigman, *Everything Lawyers Know about Polygamy Is Wrong*, 16 CORNELL J.L. PUB. POL'Y 101, 119 (2006).

[23] Reynolds v. United States, 98 U.S. 145, 155 (1878).

[24] *Id.* at 166.

permit every citizen to become a law unto himself."[25] Nevertheless, problems in prosecuting under the Morrill Act persisted; therefore, in 1882 Congress passed the Edmunds Act, making it significantly easier to prosecute polygamy as prosecutors did not need to prove actual marriage but only cohabitation, which the act prohibited.[26] Additionally, the act allowed prosecutors to strike jurors who practiced polygamy, as well as those who did not practice polygamy, but believed it acceptable.[27] Nearly 1,300 polygamists were prosecuted under various anti-polygamy statutes after the Edmunds Act.[28]

On October 6, 1890, the Church's then prophet, Wilford Woodruff, issued an official declaration stating that the Church would obey the laws of the federal government and cease the practice of polygamy. Woodruff explained to Church members that he had received a revelation from God and had been shown a vision in which the Church would be destroyed if the practice of polygamy were to continue. Most Church members followed the new commandment from Woodruff; others believed he was a fallen prophet who had succumbed to pressure from the United States. Shortly after the official renunciation of polygamy, Utah became a state in 1896. As a condition to statehood, Utah included in its constitution a provision that "polygamous or plural marriages are forever prohibited."[29]

V. Fundamentalism—The Break Off

Those who refused to give up polygamy, believing it an eternal principle, were the predecessors of the Fundamentalist Church of Jesus Christ of Latter-day Saints (FLDS). FLDS members claim that in 1886, four years before the Church's renunciation of polygamy, the then prophet and president of the Church, John Taylor, received a very different revelation. According to FLDS historians, in Taylor's revelation the Lord declared that polygamy was an everlasting covenant, and that God would never revoke it. Lorin C. Woolley, who later became a FLDS leader, testified that he was outside Taylor's room during this vision when he saw a light appearing from beneath the door. Woolley claims to have heard three distinct voices coming from the room, which Taylor later told him was the Lord and the deceased prophet Joseph Smith delivering the revelation of eternal polygamy. FLDS members claim that the following morning Taylor placed five men under covenant to practice polygamy as long as they lived, and gave them power to ordain others to do the same. For some time those practicing polygamy stayed in Salt Lake City, alongside the Mormons who renounced plural marriage. However, as polygamy became less acceptable in mainstream Utah, many polygamists went into hiding.

---

[25] *Id.* at 167.

[26] Edmunds Act, ch. 47, § 3, 22 Stat. 30 (1882).

[27] *Id.* at § 5.

[28] Sigman, *supra* note 22, at 128.

[29] 39 UTAH CONST. art. III, § 1.

Eventually Short Creek, Arizona (now known as Colorado City), became a stronghold for polygamists. FLDS members felt comfortable in this remote area surrounded by desert, over a hundred miles away from law enforcement, and believed they could safely practice polygamy unbothered by the outside world.

VI. Government Intervention and FLDS Isolation

The FLDS's belief that law enforcement would tolerate their polygamist practices was mistaken; government officials have conducted a number of raids on FLDS compounds, dramatically affecting the outside world's opinion of the Church. One of the most traumatic is known as the "Short Creek Raid." In the summer of 1953, over a hundred Arizona police officers and National Guardsmen descended on the FLDS compound in Short Creek. The reason given for the raid by Arizona governor John Pyle was to stop a pending insurrection by the polygamists. Pyle accused FLDS members of being involved in the "foulest conspiracy you could possibly imagine" designed to produce white slaves. The governor even invited reporters to witness the raid with him. However, the attempt to demonize those practicing polygamy failed. Church members had been tipped off to the impending raid. As law enforcement entered the compound, they found the community's adults congregated in a schoolhouse singing hymns, while their children played outside. Instead of reporting on the evils of polygamy, the media focused on the overreaction of government officials. Regardless of the media reaction, the government removed over 400 children from their families at Short Creek.[30] It took more than two years for 150 of those children to be reunited with their families. The Short Creek Raid became a rallying cry for FLDS members—a manifestation of the secular world's desire to destroy God's chosen people.

Shortly after his father's (the previous prophet) death, Jeffs married all but 2 of Rulon's 20 wives, increasing the number of his wives to approximately 70, according to some ex-members. Jeffs claimed that this was necessary to ensure the preservation of his sacred bloodline; it is important to recall that Jeffs decreed that God sanctioned his actions. As the only person who possessed the authority to perform marriages, and assign wives, Jeffs often used this power to discipline members by reassigning their wives, children, and homes to another man. This was made clear in 2004 when Jeffs exiled 20 male members from the community and assigned their wives to men Jeffs determined were more worthy.

Similar to his predecessors, Jeffs teaches that it is only through plural marriage that a man may enter heaven. To that extent, Jeffs has taught that any worthy male member should have at least three wives, and the more wives a man has, the closer he is to heaven. In 2004, the FLDS, especially Jeffs as the then-current prophet, began facing trouble from the outside world once again. In 2004, several of Jeffs's nephews alleged that Jeffs

---

[30] *See Texas Takes Legal Custody of 401 Sect Children*, CNN (Apr. 7, 2008), http://web.archive.org/web/20080411050954/http://www.cnn.com/2008/CRIME/04/07/texas.ranch/.

and his brothers sodomized them in the late 1980s, leading the nephews to file a lawsuit.[31] In 2005, Jeffs was charged with sexual assault on a minor and with conspiracy to commit sexual misconduct with a minor for arranging a marriage between a 14-year-old girl and her 19-year-old first cousin.[32]

In late 2005, Jeffs was placed on the FBI's most wanted list;[33] he was charged in Utah with rape as an accomplice and in Arizona with two counts of sexual conduct with a minor, one count of conspiracy to commit sexual conduct with a minor, and unlawful flight to avoid prosecution.[34] While a fugitive, Jeffs nevertheless continued to perform marriages between underage girls and older men.[35] In August 2006, Jeffs was captured in Nevada during a traffic stop[36] and, in September 2007, he was convicted in Utah on the accomplice-to-rape charge.[37] He was given a sentence of 10-years-to-life.[38] However, on July 27, 2010, the Utah Supreme Court, citing deficient jury instructions, reversed Jeff's convictions and ordered a new trial.[39]

The FLDS Church faced additional difficulties at a second compound, the Yearning for Zion Ranch, near Eldorado, Texas. On April 16, 2008, Texas state authorities entered the community after they had received calls[40] from an individual claiming to be an abused child from the ranch. Child Protective Services determined that the children living in the compound required protection from forced underage marriages. As a result,[41] 416 children were removed from the FLDS compound while over a hundred adult women chose to leave the ranch in order to accompany their children. The state determined that as of that time, of 53 girls aged 14 to 17, 31 had children or were pregnant. On May 22, 2008, after a state court ruled that there was insufficient evidence to justify holding the

[31] David Kelly & Gary Cohn, *Insider Accounts Put Sect Leader on the Run*, SEATTLE TIMES, May 16, 2006, http://seattletimes.nwsource.com/html/nationworld/2002996905_secttwo16.html.

[32] Christine Hauser, *Man Near Top of Most-Wanted List Is Captured*, Aug. 29, 2006, http://www.nytimes.com/2006/08/29/us/30jeffscnd.html?_r=1&ref=us&oref=slogin.

[33] *Have You Seen This Man? FBI Announces New Top Tenner, available at* http://www.fbi.gov/news/stories/2006/may/jeffs050606.

[34] *Id.*

[35] Brooke Adams & Pamela Manson, *Polygamist Sect Leader Warren Jeffs Arrested in Las Vegas*, S.L. TRIB., Sept. 30, 2007, http://www.sltrib.com/polygamy/ci_4254653.

[36] *Id.*

[37] John Dougherty & Kirk Johnson, *Sect Leader Is Convicted as an Accomplice to Rape*, N.Y. TIMES, Sept. 26, 2007, http://www.nytimes.com/2007/09/26/us/26jeffs.html?_r=1.

[38] *See* Ben Winslow, *Jeffs Is Now an Inmate at Utah State Prison*, DESERET NEWS, Nov. 22, 2007, http://www.deseretnews.com/article/695229917/Jeffs-is-now-an-inmate-at-Utah-State-Prison.html.

[39] *See* Dan Frosch, *Polygamist Convictions Overturned*, N.Y. TIMES, July 27, 2010, http://www.nytimes.com/2010/07/28/us/28jeffs.html.

[40] Subsequently, these calls were discovered to be "hoax" phone calls impersonating an abused child. Ryan Owens, *Polygamist Sect Marks First Anniversary of Texas Ranch Raid*, ABC News (Apr. 3, 2009), http://www.abcnews.go.com/TheLaw/Story?id=7252149&page=3.

[41] Susan Duclos, *Polygamist Group, FLDS Children to be Placed in Foster Homes This Week*, DIGITAL J. (Apr. 20, 2008), http://www.digitaljournal.com/article/253535.

children in custody, they were returned to their families within 10 days.[42] One year after the raid only one child remained in state custody, though 12 of the men from the group were indicted on a variety of sex charges, including assault and bigamy.[43] On August 9, 2011, Jeffs was convicted on two counts of sexual assault of a child and sentenced to life in prison.[44] During the sentencing phase his nephew testified to having been raped since he was five and Jeffs's niece testified as to having been raped since she was seven.[45]

VII. Forced Marriage of Daughters

Adolescent girls are the best-known victims of polygamy in the FLDS community as they are forced to marry significantly older, married men. These girls lack a meaningful choice in deciding whether to get married; they have been taught the world outside their community is evil. Furthermore, avoiding the marriage by leaving is extraordinarily difficult as FLDS communities are physically isolated, making escape nearly impossible. By example: Jane Kingston was forced by her father, Daniel Kingston, to marry her uncle 16 years her senior, and therefore became his 15th wife.[46] When Jane tried to escape the marriage, her father captured her and beat her until she was unconscious.[47] When she woke up from the beating, Jane walked seven miles to a gas station and called 9-1-1.[48] Although Jane's uncle, David Ortell Kingston, was charged and convicted of incest and unlawful sexual conduct with a minor, he was not charged with bigamy.[49]

Although there is no doubt that many underage girls such as Jane are forced into marriage with much older men, prosecuting the crime is difficult because of significant evidentiary barriers. First, the key witnesses usually have no interest in aiding the prosecution as children are taught that authorities are not to be trusted, and if they cooperate by testifying, they could be placed in foster care.[50] Girls have been taught that the outside world is evil; there is no one safe for them to turn to when they do not want to enter into a marriage. Furthermore, because of the remote physical location of these communities, the victim must go to extreme lengths to escape the abuse, as Jane did by walking seven miles to seek help after being beaten unconscious. In addition, typically only the first marriage

---

[42] Ismael Estrada, *Returning the Children, with Conditions*, AC360 (May 30, 2008), http://ac360.blogs.cnn.com/2008/05/30/returning-the-children-with-conditions/.

[43] Owens, *supra* note 40.

[44] *See* Lindsay Whitehurst, *Warren Jeffs Gets Life in Prison for Sex with Underage Girls*, SALT LAKE TRIB., Aug, 10, 2011, http://www.sltrib.com/sltrib/news/52354441-78/jeffs-sexual-child-jurors.html.csp.

[45] *See Nephew, Niece Allege Polygamist Sect Leader Warren Jeffs Abused Them*, CNN (Aug. 6, 2011), http://articles.cnn.com/2011-08-06/justice/texas.polygamist.jeffs_1_warren-jeffs-alta-academy-polygamist-sect-leader?_s=PM:CRIME.

[46] Leti Volpp, *Blaming Culture for Bad Behavior*, 12 YALE J.L. & HUMAN. 89, 100 (2000).

[47] *Id.*

[48] Sigman, *supra* note 22, at 179.

[49] *Id.*

[50] *Id. at 180*

of a polygamist is recorded with the state; thus, the state has no paper trail of the other marriages. Finally, as the FLDS community is located on both sides of the Utah–Arizona border, prosecutors have difficulty proving in which state the abuse occurred and, thus, are hard pressed to determine the appropriate jurisdiction for prosecution purposes.[51]

VIII. The Lost Boys

Another group of children/individuals that have suffered from FLDS extremism are a group of male children known as the "Lost Boys." Over 1,000 male children between the ages of 13 and 23 have left the FLDS community, typically by being banished and becoming a "Lost Boy,"[52] as polygamy unavoidably leads to a shortage of girls and a surplus of boys. Critics of the FLDS maintain that these Lost Boys are kicked out of the community so that older, established men have less competition for the young wives.[53] The community tells the boys that they are being banished for not meeting rigorous FLDS religious standards.[54] Once expelled, the boys are not allowed contact with their former community. The Church forbids parents from visiting their banished sons, and violating the rule can result in eviction from their Church-owned homes.[55] This means that the boys have no emotional and financial support from their former communities, and they suddenly find themselves in the outside world, which they have been taught is "evil." Furthermore, "most have no money, no real education and nowhere to live."[56]

Not surprisingly, many of the boys turn to drugs and alcohol. Although there are state laws preventing child abandonment and neglect, Utah and Arizona authorities have yet to systematically enforce them. Additionally, authorities have not sought child support from FLDS members who abandon their sons.[57] Similar to the prosecution of sexual abuse, prosecution against parents for child abandonment has evidentiary challenges primarily because the Lost Boys are largely unwilling to testify against their parents. According to the Utah Attorney General, Mark Shurtleff, "the kids don't want their parents prosecuted; they want us to get the number one bad guy—Warren Jeffs. He is chiefly responsible for kicking out these boys."[58] However, in 2006 a group of six Lost Boys filed a landmark suit against Warren Jeffs and the FLDS for "unlawful activity, fraud, and

---

[51] Emily J. Duncan, *The Positive Effects of Legalizing Polygamy: "Love Is a Many Splendored Thing,"* 15 Duke J. Gender L. & Pol'y 315, 324 (2008).

[52] Borger, *supra* note 8; New Frontiers for Families, *The House Just off Bluff: Pilot Proposal,* http://www.newfrontiersforfamilies.org/bluffhouse.asp (last visited Jan. 8, 2013).

[53] Borger, *supra* note 8.

[54] *Id.*

[55] *Id.*

[56] Dan Simon & Amanda Townsend, *Warren Jeffs "Lost Boys" Find Themselves in Strange World,* CNN (Sept. 7, 2007), http://www.cnn.com/2007/US/09/07/lost.boys/index.html.

[57] Sigman, *supra* note 22, at 184.

[58] Kelly, *supra* note 9.

breach of fiduciary duty, and civil conspiracy."[59] The suit alleged that the boys were kicked out of the community so that it would be easier for the older men to marry the younger girls, because without the boys there would be less competition.[60] The suit was settled out of court; the Lost Boys received $250,000 for housing, education, and other assistance to help other Lost Boys forced to leave the FLDS community.[61]

In 2006, Utah governor Jon Huntsman signed House Bill 30, also known as the "Lost Boys Law," which allows minors to petition to district court judges on their own behalf for emancipation.[62] The Lost Boys, and other homeless youth trying to survive face numerous hurdles because of the fact that they are minors. Everyday concerns, such as signing leases and receiving healthcare, are difficult for this population as legally they are minors and cannot represent themselves.[63] Although the effects remain to be seen, the bill undoubtedly represents an effort to facilitate the Lost Boys' integration into society.

IX. Who Defines the Best Interest of the Child?

The essence of the parent–child relationship is the "duty to care" obligation that the parent owes to the child. That duty, obligation, and responsibility has been one of the core essences of the human condition since time immemorial:

> "But if any provide not for his own, and specially for those of his own house, he hath denied the faith, and is worse than an infidel."
>
> "And, ye fathers, provoke not your children to wrath: but bring them up in the nurture and admonition of the Lord."
>
> "But whoso shall offend one of these little ones [a child] which believe in me, it were better for him that a millstone were hanged about his neck, and that he were drowned in the depth of the sea." [64]

---

[59] Sigman, *supra* note 22, at 182 (citing Complaint, Ream v. Jeffs, No. 040918237 (Utah Dist. Ct. Aug. 27, 2004)).

[60] *Id.*

[61] Simon & Townsend, *supra* note 56.

[62] H.R. 30, 2006 Gen. Sess. (Utah 2006), *available at* http://www.le.state.ut.us/%7E2006/bills/hbillenr/ hb0030.htm.

[63] For further discussion, see Brieanne M. Billie, Note, *The "Lost Boys" of Polygamy: Is Emancipation the Answer?*, 12 J. GENDER RACE & JUST. 127, 138 (2008), and T. Christopher Wharton, Statute Note, *Deserted in Deseret: How Utah's Emancipation Statute Is Saving Polygamist Runaways and Queer Homeless Youths*, 10 J.L. & FAM. STUD. 213, 220 (2007).

[64] "Take heed that ye despise not one of these little ones..." *Matthew* 18:10 (King James); "And whosoever shall offend one of *these* little ones that believe in me, it is better for him that a millstone were hanged about his neck, and he were cast into the sea." *Mark* 9:42 (King James); "Lo, children *are* an heritage of the Lord: *and* the fruit of the womb *is his* reward." *Psalm* 127:3 (King James); "It were better for him that a millstone were hanged about his neck, and he cast into the sea, than that he should offend one of these little ones." *Luke* 17:2 (King James); "And the King shall answer and say unto them, Verily I say unto you, Inasmuch as ye have done *it* unto one of the least of these my brethren, ye have done *it* unto me." *Matthew* 25:40 (King James).

The May 15, 2009 decision of Brown County (Minnesota) District Judge John Rodenberg that 13-year-old Daniel Hauser was "medically neglected"[65] by his parents, Colleen and Anthony Hauser (who refused to provide him with appropriate medical treatment), and was in need of child protection services, is an important illustration of this issue.[66] The parents, who religiously believe in natural healing, cited their beliefs as the principle reason for refusing treatment.[67] Daniel, whose cancer has a 85–90 percent chance of being successfully treated, was determined to have a "rudimentary understanding at best" of his condition and simply went along with his parents' beliefs.[68] Rodenberg, in describing the state's interest, stated "the state's interest in protecting the child overrides the constitutional right to freedom of religious expression and a parent's right to direct a child's upbringing."[69]

In *In re Clark*, a three-year-old child suffered third degree burns over 40 percent of his body. As the child's blood condition deteriorated the parents, who belong to the Jehovah Witness Church, were asked to consent to blood transfusions if such became necessary to save his life. The parents refused. The doctor then petitioned a local court for permission to administer blood transfusions if such became medically necessary. The court granted the petition, citing Ohio's Juvenile Code, which provided for emergency medical and surgical care for children, as well as the court's right under common law to act on behalf of the interests of the child. The child's condition gradually improved, and it appeared that a blood transfusion would not be necessary. The parents then attempted to vacate the outstanding court authorization—contending that Kenneth's situation was not an emergency. Judge Alexander rejected the argument and addressed the duty of the state: "The child is a citizen of the State. While he 'belongs' to his parents he belongs also to his State...When a religious doctrine espoused by the parents threatens to defeat or curtail such a right of their child, the State's duty to step in and preserve the child's right is immediately operative."[70] Although the judge stressed that parents have an absolute right

---

[65] Minnesota Criminal Code, MINN. STAT. ANN. § 609.378 (2010) specifies that a person is guilty of neglect or endangerment when: (a)(1) A parent, legal guardian, or caretaker who willfully deprives a child of necessary food, clothing, shelter, health care, or supervision appropriate to the child's age, when the parent, guardian, or caretaker is reasonably able to make the necessary provisions and the deprivation harms or is likely to substantially harm the child's physical, mental, or emotional health is guilty of neglect of a child and may be sentenced to imprisonment for not more than one year or to payment of a fine of not more than $3,000, or both. If the deprivation results in substantial harm to the child's physical, mental, or emotional health, the person may be sentenced to imprisonment for not more than five years or to payment of a fine of not more than $10,000, or both. If a parent, guardian, or caretaker responsible for the child's care in good faith selects and depends upon spiritual means or prayer for treatment or care of disease or remedial care of the child, this treatment or care is "health care," for purposes of this clause.

[66] Amy Forliti, *Minnesota Judge Rules Teen Must See Cancer Doctor*, NEWVINE (May 15, 2009), http://www.newsvine.com/_news/2009/05/15/2819712-minn-judge-rules-teen-must-seecancer-doctor.

[67] *Id.*

[68] *Id.*

[69] *Id.*

[70] *In re* Clark, 185 N.E.2d 128, 132 (Ohio Com. Pl. 1962).

to believe that blood transfusions are forbidden by Holy Scripture and to act in accordance with that belief, "this right of theirs ends where somebody else's right begins."[71]

However, in *Newmark v. Williams*, the court limited this right when state action had a low chance of actually benefiting the child. In that case the court grappled with the proposed treatment of a three-year-old suffering from Burkitt's Lymphoma when his Christian Scientist parents wanted to refuse medical intervention. The parents argued that removing the child from their home violated their First Amendment right to freedom of religion and that the Delaware abuse and neglect statutes exempted those who treat their children's illnesses "solely by spiritual means." The court ruled in favor of the parents because the state sought to administer, against the parents' wishes, an "extremely risky, toxic, and dangerously life threatening medical treatment offering less than a 40% chance for success."[72]

There is clear tension: although scripture articulates parental responsibility and obligation regarding children, some religious extremists are endangering their children. That endangerment violates both the criminal law and religious scripture.

There are at least two categories of private interests at stake in parental rights termination proceedings: the fundamental liberty interest of the parents in the care and custody of their children,[73] and the parents' and children's shared interest in preventing an "erroneous termination" of their natural relationship.[74] "Consequently, courts could consider both the parents' and the children's rights when determining the state's burden of proof at the best interests stage."[75] The lack of aggressiveness in enforcing child protection laws—often predicated on deference to religious belief—has the tragic effect of leaving children unprotected and vulnerable.

X. Recommendations: Civil Society or Religious Society?

Membership and participation in civil democratic society explicitly demands that citizens respect the rule of law as supreme. According to Rousseau, as citizens of a society we are signatories to the social contract; in essence, we give up *absolute* rights for the safety and comfort that government can provide. We agree to be subject to laws imposed by a civil society, including restrictions on religious practice and speech, regardless of the fact that religious rights are generally granted immunity.

That is not to minimize the importance, relevance, or centrality of religion in the lives of untold millions. We simply must recognize that the core of civil society is the primacy

---

[71] *Id.*

[72] Newmark v. Williams, 588 A.2d 1108 (Del. 1991).

[73] *Id.* at 753.

[74] *Id.* at 760.

[75] Brian C. Hill, *The State's Burden of Proof at the Best Interests Stage of a Termination of Parental Rights*, 2004 U. CHI. LEGAL F. 557, 567 (2004).

of civil law rather than religious law. Some people of faith—particularly those for whom religion is the essence of their temporal existence—may find this perspective objectionable. However, civil society cannot endure if religious law is supreme to state law.

Civil society owes an obligation to protect its otherwise unprotected—particularly children who are its most vulnerable members. Religious belief and conduct cannot be used as justification for placing children at risk; government, law enforcement, and the general public cannot allow religion to hide behind a cloak of "religious immunity." The focus of a religious extremist is singleminded dedication and devotion to serving his or her God. Based on innumerable conversations with terrorists and members of the intelligence community alike, I have written elsewhere of the extraordinary hardships imposed on wanted terrorists. I have come to the conclusion that those hardships, when understood in the context of terrorists serving their God, are both *explainable* to the terrorist and *tolerable* by the terrorist. Although difficult, these hardships are not nearly as foreboding as the alternative, according to their worldview. For them it is better to incur physical discomfort than to incur the wrath of God. Where does that leave the secular state? Precisely because of the absolutism of the religious extremist, the state has no choice but to respond accordingly.

Perhaps the fundamental weakness of my argument is that I am suggesting that the state restrict the rights of citizens even at the cost of curtailing otherwise guaranteed rights. Perhaps society in order to protect the unprotected may have no choice but to consistently and aggressively monitor and prosecute religious extremists who endanger their children. The specific danger posed by religious extremists not only justifies but also demands that law enforcement and prosecutors rearticulate their approach to child endangerment in a religious paradigm.

The traditional argument that prosecution is difficult as witnesses are hesitant to come forward can be addressed by an aggressive intelligence gathering policy similar to concerted law enforcement efforts regarding the manufacturing and supplying of illegal drugs.[76] The danger posed by religious extremists to their internal community requires the immediate adoption of this aggressive policy. Although there is an undeniable and understandable difficulty in persuading child brides and lost boys to testify against their parents and community—akin to children who are victims of sexual abuse committed by a parent or family member[77]—the state's obligation to protect the otherwise unprotected requires that intelligence gathering be aggressive.

---

[76] "In an effort to achieve a 'drug free society', the United States Government approaches its national drug problem through criminal sanctions for the possession, manufacture, sale, transport, and distribution of illegal drugs in the United States; the establishment of a complex law enforcement apparatus at both the federal and state levels with the purpose of reducing drug availability, increasing drug prices, and reducing drug use in America; and the development of drug use prevention and treatment programs that seek to stop drug use and heal drug users." Margarita Mercado Echegaray, Note, *Drug Prohibition in America: Federal Drug Policy and its Consequences*, 75 REV. JUR. U.P.R. 1215, 1273 (2006).

[77] According to the Supreme Court, child abuse is "one of the most difficult crimes to detect and prosecute, in large part because there are often no witnesses except the victim." Pennsylvania v. Ritchie, 480 U.S. 39, 60

Although religious extremism presents a significant threat to contemporary society, this does not mean that all religions or all people of religious faith present a threat. Far from it. It does, however, suggest that religious extremism needs to be analyzed, discussed, and understood. It is not religion, but religion as articulated and practiced by extremists that draws our greatest concern and attention. The distinction is critical for otherwise "guilt by association" and "round up the usual suspects" are inevitable byproducts. That said, the role of religion cannot be denied. Precisely because of that reality, the debate as to whether limits should be imposed on the practice of religion is legitimate.

If viewed on a spectrum or sliding scale, belief is the most private and intimate of the three aspects of religiosity and, therefore, the least subject to the imposition of limitations. Conversely, speech and conduct—if outside the intimacy of the home—are the most public manifestations of religion. However, with respect to speech and conduct, the home, as previously discussed, is not immune from the imposition of limitations. Crimes committed within the home in the name of religion[78] are punishable, and justice must be meted out to the perpetrators. Although clear distinctions are drawn between private and public religion, the home—the essence of private religion—is not immune from law enforcement, even if the motivation for the crime is religion.

In proposing that limits be imposed, it is essential to clearly and candidly address what I propose limiting. It is neither faith itself nor beliefs of particular faiths; with the exception of regimes that practice "thought police" or re-education camps, belief cannot be limited. Rather, it is how extremism is articulated and practiced that must be limited. Limits must not be blindly imposed devoid of standards, criteria, and review. Such an approach would reflect government action best described as arbitrary and capricious, resulting in denial of due process before the law. The requirement to impose limits subject to constitutional protections must not deter policymakers from limiting the rights of those who endanger society even if the basis for that endangerment is religion.

The Supreme Court's holding in *Reynolds v. United States*[79] that federal law prohibiting polygamy did not violate the Free Exercise Clause rights of a Mormon who claimed polygamy a fundamental tenet of his faith[80] is of enormous importance in this discussion. The same is true with respect to the Supreme Court's holding in *Smith*[81] that even if peyote were used as part of a religious ceremony, if the Oregon Supreme Court prohibited

---

(1987). Most often, the abuse is not reported because it takes place in the family setting and children do not understand what is happening or fear retribution if they report it, and because adult family members similarly fail to report the abuse. Raymond C. O'Brien, *Clergy, Sex and the American Way*, 31 Pepp. L. Rev. 363, 377 (2004).

[78] Honor killings are a prime example of religious-based crimes committed within the home.

[79] 98 U.S. 145 (1878).

[80] *Id.* at 166

[81] 485 U.S. 660 (1988).

the use of peyote even if for religious purposes, it was proper to deny unemployment benefits to those fired for using the drug.[82]

These cases are, in many ways, the constitutional basis for recommending that limits be imposed on how religion is practiced and the parameters of tolerable religious conduct. To that end, I propose religious belief be protected but that religiously inspired conduct, when harmful, not be protected. A proposal to proactively limit otherwise guaranteed protections must, necessarily, extend to speech that incites to violence. However, as this chapter makes clear, protected speech directly contributes to harmful conduct. Obviously, not all protected speech directly contributes to harm; to argue that would be engaging in unconscionable exaggeration devoid of any basis in reality. Nevertheless, as history has repeatedly shown, failure to limit speech that incites poses risks that society need not tolerate. The instinctual response that free speech is a "holy grail" (maybe *the* holy grail) of civil democratic society is justified and understandable. However, given the clear danger posed by extremist speech, exploring limits reflects government responsibility to the larger society. That is the essence of protecting the vulnerable and unprotected who are "at risk" from extremism.

---

[82] *Id.* at 672.

5

THE POWER OF THE INTERNET AND SOCIAL MEDIA IN

FACILITATING EXTREMIST MOVEMENTS AND IDEAS

THE INTERNET AND social media have dramatically affected our lives. We are, obviously, living in a communications-technology age predicated on accessibility, interconnectivity, and instant and unlimited information being easily available. Whether one Twitters, Facebooks, or emails, contemporary society is predicated on being connected. Questions—perhaps concern—are raised regarding the social, cultural, and personal price of "alone together."[1] The adage "if you are not connected, you do not exist" is an honest reflection of the times; watch any child nimbly engage an i-Phone and the evidence is best described as "I rest my case". Facebook's extraordinary initial public offering (IPO)[2] is but an obvious illustration of the influence of the social media and Internet. Perhaps more than any other development it highlights the remarkable ability of the Internet to connect people worldwide who have never met or engaged in actual, verbal conversation. Without doubt, the Internet has made an extraordinarily positive impact on society and individuals alike.

However, those benefits must be tempered when analyzing the relationship between modern communication-technology and extremism. In particular, the emphasis is on the profound difference between "traditional" media (newspapers, radio, TV) that has been

---

[1] SHERRY TURKLE, ALONE TOGETHER: WHY WE EXPECT MORE FROM TECHNOLOGY AND LESS FROM EACH OTHER (2012); *see also* Sherry Turkle, *Connected, but Alone?*, Web2forDev (June 8, 2012, 2:44 PM), http://www.web2fordev.net/component/content/article/1-latest-news/160-sherry-turkle-connected-but-alone.

[2] Marc Davis, *How Facebook's IPO Will Make People Rich*, INVESTOPEDIA.COM., Feb. 28, 2012, http://www.investopedia.com/financial-edge/0212/how-facebooks-ipo-will-make-people-rich.aspx

largely supplanted by "nontraditional" media (blogs, social media). As one responder to the questionnaire thoughtfully commented:

> I suspect that the media not only facilitates extremism but may indeed cause and foster it. After all, in order to catch the media's attention, one needs to do something extreme. In order for people to get their message across in a short "sound bite" or "single picture frame", they need to do or say something extreme. Normal is boring; extremism is interesting and newsworthy. There have even been studies demonstrating that media people actually verbally and explicitly encourage extreme behavior for the cameras, which immediately ends once the camera lights are turned off. It is a win-win situation for all involved. The media gets their headline, the "actors" get their story covered and the viewers get their excitement.
>
> I believe the Internet and social media will play a greater and greater role in extremism. Religious extremists have had a captive audience among those who share their faith. Religion provides others with a mechanism for communication. In my position, I see a lot of individuals who are anti-government. They search the Internet for others who share their ideas and are willing to believe the ideas that others have spread. Some people would argue that the founder of Wikileaks is an extremist in his ideas on sharing government secrets. He has found an audience of those who share his beliefs through the Internet. Internet hacker groups such as LulzSec have found an audience of individuals who believe that it is okay to disrupt the Internet as well as steal identifying information. Just as the Internet can be powerful in spreading popular ideas, such as occurred in places such as Egypt and Tunisia, the Internet can spread extremism. The birther movement has life because of the Internet.[3]

Contemporary language reflects how the Internet has penetrated our lives. "Google it," "Facebook friends," and "tweeting" are an inherent part of our dialogue having replaced relics such as "please Xerox this" and the Kodak camera. This is, perhaps, a natural progression of human development in the same manner that previous generations referenced terms relevant to their human experience. The next Steven Jobs, Steve Wozniak, and Mark Zuckerberg are, doubtlessly, developing technology that will replace instruments created by Apple and social networking facilitated by Facebook. That, after all, is the essence of human ingenuity and genius, just as Xerox and Kodak were once considered the epitome of modern science and creativity. It is but a matter of time before the generation of Jobs, Wozniak, and Zuckerberg will be replaced by a new one of genius creativity.

---

[3] In author's records.

Although the telephone enables conversation when participants are physically separate from each other, it does not match the literally unlimited ability of social media to connect millions simultaneously, regardless of physical location. In December 1989 East Germans starved for democracy and freedom brought down the Berlin Wall. Their actions dramatically facilitated the end of Communism. The Internet represents, by analogy, the absolute destruction of tangible and intangible walls enabling communication anytime, anywhere. As Tahrir Square made remarkably clear in 2011, social media can bring a regime, seemingly intractable and impervious, to its knees. The consequences of regime change facilitated, if not initiated, by social media remains an open question. Nevertheless its speed, range, and impact poses extraordinary challenges for regimes accustomed to controlling information and its flow. As the Arab Spring made dramatically clear, repressive regimes were no match for the social media; in many ways, the fight was over before it began. It was, in retrospect, no match whatsoever.

The pattern repeats itself of slow-footed, not particularly nimble regimes caught off guard by the speed and reach of the social media; witness the dramatic demonstrations throughout Russia in the aftermath of clearly fraudulent elections. It is not by chance that regimes such as Iran, Syria, North Korea, and China make concerted efforts to either prevent or limit Internet access. The Internet/social media is the preferred means of communication for government protesters; the results have been clear in the recent past few years. The ability of protestors to circumvent government restriction and repression reflects ingenuity and determination enabling social media to be a critical change agent.

Nevertheless, the cliché "double-edged sword" clearly applies to the Internet and social media for the Internet can facilitate criminal acts that endanger society and individuals alike. There is little doubt that use of the Internet can be highly nefarious. In that vein, extremists maximize the extraordinary communication opportunities provided by the Internet, whether for recruiting, message sending, or instructional purposes. Extremists avail themselves of the largely unregulated nature of the Internet granting literally unlimited access both to information and the public. Extremists use the Internet to post graphic pictures of beheadings, provide detailed instruction on how to build bombs, and communicate for operational and other purposes. The Internet provides an open forum that significantly enhances the scope of extremist organizations posing significant challenges to law enforcement and national security officials.

As the number of extremist-related websites reflects, the Internet and social media have become important tools for extremist organizations. Conversations with security officials in the United States, Europe, and Israel consistently highlight the extraordinary challenges posed in seeking to both monitor the existing websites and to "connect the dots" between different websites and their content. With respect to understanding the reach of the Internet—particularly its harmful use—security officials with whom

I met[4] repeated a common refrain: they were slow to appreciate the power and reach of the Internet, and experienced frustration from being behind the proverbial "eight ball" in comparison to extremist organizations. As highlighted by the discussion below, law enforcement officials mandated with combating child pornography express similar frustration.

As has been made abundantly clear the Internet is used to transmit, facilitate, and enable child pornography.[5] To date, law enforcement efforts regarding child pornography have focused on how the Internet facilitates its dissemination.[6] The relationship between the Internet and child pornography highlights how the former readily facilitates criminal activity. The question is: what should and has the state done to proactively prevent the clear harm posed by child pornography? The question, obviously, is relevant to extremist organizations that endanger society.

In the United States, laws focus on those directly involved in viewing, distributing, or producing child pornography. To that extent, prosecutions emphasize possession, possession with the intent to disseminate,[7] production, and knowingly allowing your child to participate in producing child pornography if you are the child's parent or guardian.[8] Shows such as *How to Catch a Predator*[9] highlight that law enforcement agencies in the United States have formed special task forces intended to combat production and dissemination of child pornography. However, law enforcement officials are outnumbered, out-resourced, and undertrained.[10]

Harm posed by child pornography could be mitigated were Internet Service Providers (ISPs) held accountable for website content. To that end, the US Congress passed a number of measures, including the Child Protection and Sexual Predator Punishment Act of 1998.[11] According to Section 113 of this legislation, when ISPs become aware of child pornography they are required to report its content to the National Center of Missing and Exploited Children.[12] Failure to meet reporting requirements results in fines, arguably a "light" sentence that does not engender cooperation. According to the Act and the U.S. Court of Appeals Fourth Circuit ISPs are not required to monitor websites on their

---

[4] In Israel, Netherlands, Norway, and the United Kingdom.

[5] Net Blamed for Rise in Child Porn, BBC News (Jan. 12, 2004), http://news.bbc.co.uk/2/hi/technology/3387377.stm.

[6] Julian Fantino, Child Pornography on the Internet: New Challenges Require New Ideas, Police Chief Mag., Dec. 2003, available at http://www.policechiefmagazine.org/magazine/index.cfm?fuseaction=display_arch&article_id=158&issue_id=122003.

[7] If law enforcement finds an individual in possession of three or more copies of the same material there is possession even if intent to distribute cannot be proved.

[8] See generally Everson Law LLC, available at http://www.criminal-defense-attorney.info/lawyer-attorney-1296928.htm (last visited Aug. 17, 2013)

[9] A former show on Dateline NBC.

[10] See John Gallaugher, *What's Their Motivation?*, available at http://catalog.flatworldknowledge.com/bookhub/reader/8023?e=fwk-38086-ch13_s02 (last visited Aug. 17, 2013).

[11] Protection of Children from Sexual Predators Act of 1998, PL 105–314, Oct. 30, 1998, 112 Stat 2974.

[12] See *Reporting Child Pornography*, CYBERTELECOM, http://www.cybertelecom.org/cda/cppa.htm (last visited Aug. 17, 2013).

servers for child pornography; rather, action must be taken only when the ISP acquires knowledge of the pornography.[13] "[N]othing in this section may be construed to require a provider of electronic communication services or remote computing services to engage in the monitoring of any user, subscriber, or customer of that provider, or the content of any communication of any such person."[14]

In an effort to better understand the reluctance of administrators to limit the content of websites that post on their domains, I contacted administrators that host virulently anti-Semitic websites. The administrators with whom I spoke indicated an adamant refusal to limit the content posted, basing their rationale on First Amendment principles.[15] When I suggested websites hosted on their domain were potentially harmful, both administrators responded First Amendment protections were intended to protect unpopular perspectives and, therefore, limiting the reach of controversial positions would violate the spirit and letter of the law.[16] In accordance with Supreme Court precedent, US law enforcement and national security officials understand First Amendment protections prevent prosecuting Americans holding extremist beliefs. [17] In *Reno v. ACLU* the Court extended First Amendment protections to the Internet striking down portions of the 1996 Decency Act that prohibited "indecent" online communication. The Supreme Court reaffirmed these protections in *ACLU v. Ashcroft* holding any limitation on Internet speech, specifically non-obscene speech, unconstitutional.

However, and the caveat is particularly relevant in the extremism discussion: the Internet enables interaction and communication that, potentially, endangers society. Addressing the relationship between extremism and the Internet requires focusing on the following: (1) identification of extremist Internet websites; (2) how the Internet facilitates recruitment, message distribution, and coordination of extremists and extremism; and (3) whether the Internet can be used to counter extremism. Simply put, the Internet is a powerful facilitator for the exchange of views and significantly enhances the ability to organize and disseminate extremist views and goals. According to a recently conducted study, between 1996 and 2006 terrorist websites grew from fewer than 100 to more than 5,000.[18] An additional study highlights the dramatic rise in cyberterrorism despite efforts

---

[13] Protection Act, *supra* note 11; United States v. Richardson, 607 F.3d 357 (4th Cir. 2010).

[14] Richardson, 607 F.3d 357.

[15] For a different perspective, see Dominic Basulto, *Is the Internet an Inalienable Right?*, BIGTHINK (June 30, 2011, 9:48 PM), http://bigthink.com/ideas/39105.

[16] For a different response, see James Delahunty, *Apple Removes "ThirdIntifada" Application*, AFTERDAWN (June 25, 2011, 10:17 AM), http://www.afterdawn.com/news/article.cfm/2011/06/25/apple_removes_thirdintifada_application.

[17] Mark Hosenball, *Focus on Violent Extremists Hampered by US laws, Political Pressure*, REUTERS (Aug. 10 2012, 4:58 AM), http://in.reuters.com/article/2012/08/09/usa-security-extremists-idINL2E8J8HC620120809.

[18] Marie Wright, *Technology and Terrorism: How the Internet Facilitates Radicalization*, FORENSIC EXAMINER, *available at* http://www.theforensicexaminer.com/archive/winter08/7/ (last visited Jan. 10, 2013).

to curb its growth; according to this study there are approximately 7,000 terrorist-related websites.[19] Even more startling than the magnitude of these websites is the information available to the interested public. Although some may merely espouse terrorist views, others "offer tutorials on building bombs, sneaking into Iraq, setting improvised explosive devices (IEDs), and killing U.S. soldiers, and are used to host videos and messages to expand recruitment and fundraising efforts. Some even offer video games where users as young as seven can pretend to be warriors killing US soldiers."[20] The Internet, as facilitator of extremist ideas, is akin to an "echo chamber" whereby individuals with similar opinions are able to engage in closed dialogue for the express purpose of fostering their particular belief in an unencumbered manner to a, literally, endless audience. In that vein, the power of the Internet as an extraordinary facilitator of the exchange of views and enhancer of the ability to organize and further extremist views is unparalleled. It is also, frankly, dangerous.[21]

Western countries have debated whether to impose greater restrictions on Internet speech. These debates often follow in the wake of terrorist attacks. For example, in France Mohamed Merah carried out several attacks that resulted in the deaths of French paratroopers, Jewish schoolchildren, and a rabbi. It later emerged from the investigation that Merah had been consulting jihadist websites and visited Pakistan prior to the attacks. In the aftermath of these attacks, President Sarkozy made it illegal to visit or produce websites that encourage terrorism or hate crimes.[22]

The Internet is an ideal means of communication for terrorist organizations as it offers:

- Easy access;
- Little or no regulation, censorship, or other forms of government control;
- Potentially huge audiences spread throughout the world;
- Anonymity of communication;
- Fast flow of information;
- Inexpensive development and maintenance of a web presence;
- Multimedia environment (the ability to combine text, graphics, audio, and video, and to allow a user to download films, songs, books, posters, etc.);
- Ability to shape coverage in the traditional mass media, which increasingly use the Internet as a source for stories.

---

[19] Charles Hoskinson, *W.H. Online Counterterrorism Woes*, POLITICO (Oct. 19, 2011), http://www.politico.com/news/stories/1011/66401.html.

[20] Wright, *supra* note 18.

[21] Cassandra Vinograd, *Most Radicalism Linked to Intereet, Say UK Lawmakers*, MSNBC (Feb. 5, 2012: 7:26 PM), http://www.msnbc.msn.com/id/46274740/ns/technology_and_science-security/t/most-radicalism-linked-internet-say-uk-lawmakers/#.UO-NxYnjmoc.

[22] Dara Kerr, *France Criminalizes Citizens Who Visit Terrorist and Hate Web Sites*, CNET (Mar. 22, 2012, 6:10 PM), http://news.cnet.com/8301-1023_3-57402958-93/france-criminalizes-citizens-who-visit-terrorist-and-hate-web-sites/..

I. General Overview of Extremist Websites

The advantages of the Internet, according to Professor Gabriel Weimann, have not gone unnoticed by extremist organizations, no matter their political orientation. Today most extremist organizations have websites, and may have more than one in different languages serving different functions. The following list gathered by Weimann highlights the range of terrorist organizations world wide that maintain websites:

- The Middle East: Hamas (the Islamic Resistance Movement), the Lebanese Hezbollah (Party of God), the al Aqsa Martyrs Brigades, Fatah Tanzim, the Popular Front for the Liberation of Palestine (PFLP), the Palestinian Islamic Jihad, the Kahane Lives movement, the People's Mujahedin of Iran (PMOI-Mujahedin-e Khalq), the Kurdish Workers' Party (PKK), and the Turkish-based Popular Democratic Liberation Front Party (DHKP/C) and Great East Islamic Raiders Front (IBDA-C).
- Europe: the Basque ETA movement, Armata Corsa (the Corsican Army), and the Irish Republican Army (IRA).
- Latin America: Peru's Tupak-Amaru (MRTA) and Shining Path (Sendero Luminoso), the Colombian National Liberation Army (ELN-Colombia), and the Armed Revolutionary Forces of Colombia (FARC).
- Asia: al Qaeda, the Japanese Supreme Truth (Aum Shinrikyo), Ansar al Islam (Supporters of Islam) in Iraq, the Japanese Red Army (JRA), Hizb-ul Mujehideen in Kashmir, the Liberation Tigers of Tamil Eelam (LTTE), the Islamic Movement of Uzbekistan (IMU), the Moro Islamic Liberation Front (MILF) in the Philippines, the Pakistan-based Lashkare- Taiba, and the rebel movement in Chechnya.

The typical content of extremist organizations consists of a history of the organization and its activities; a detailed review of its social and political background; accounts of its notable exploits; biographies of its leaders, founders, and heroes; information on its political and ideological aims; fierce criticism of its enemies; and up-to-date news. Weimann notes:

Despite the ever-present vocabulary of "the armed struggle" and "resistance," what most sites do not feature is a detailed description of their violent activities. Even if they expound at length on the moral and legal basis, the legitimacy of the use of violence, most sites refrain from referring to the terrorists' violent actions or their fatal consequences—a reticence presumably inspired by propagandist and image-building considerations. Two exceptions to this rule are Hezbollah and Hamas, whose sites feature updated statistical reports of their actions ("daily operations") and tallies of both "dead martyrs" and "Israeli enemies" and "collaborators" killed.[23]

Weimann explains that the typical content of these sites suggests three different target audiences.

1. **Current and potential supporters.** Terrorist websites make heavy use of slogans and offer items for sale, including T-shirts, badges, flags, and videotapes and audiocassettes, all evidently aimed at sympathizers. Often, an organization will target its local supporters with a site in the local language and will provide detailed information about the activities and internal politics of the organization, its allies, and its competitors.

2. **International public opinion.** The international public, who are not directly involved in the conflict but who may have some interest in the issues involved, are courted with sites in languages other than the local tongue. Most sites offer versions in several languages. ETA's site, for instance, offers information in Castilian, German, French, and Italian; the MRTA site offers Japanese and Italian in addition to its English and Spanish versions; and the IMU site uses Arabic, English, and Russian. For the benefit of their international audiences, the sites present basic information about the organization and extensive historical background material (material with which the organization's supporters are presumably already familiar). Judging from the content of many of the sites, it appears that foreign journalists are also targeted. Press releases are often placed on the websites in an effort to get the organization's point of view into the traditional media. The detailed background information is also very useful for international reporters. One of Hezbollah's sites specifically addresses journalists, inviting them to interact with the organization's press office via email.

3. **Enemy publics.** Efforts to reach enemy publics (i.e., citizens of the states against which the terrorists are fighting) are not as clearly apparent from the content of many sites. However, some sites do seem to make an effort to demoralize the enemy by threatening attacks and by fostering feelings of guilt about the enemy's conduct and motives. In the process, they also seek to stimulate public debate in their enemies' states, to change public opinion, and to weaken public support for the governing regime.

---

[23] Gabriel Weimann, *How Modern Terrorism Uses the Internet*, 8 J. INT'L SEC. AFF. (Spring 2005), *available at* http://www.securityaffairs.org/issues/2005/08/weimann.php.

II. How Extremist Groups Use the Internet

Over the past several years, extremist groups have regularly used the Internet in accordance with the particular aims and goals of the organization. Like other Internet users, a major goal of the organization is to communicate, recruit, plan and coordinate, network, fundraise, gain publicity, and promote propaganda. An important example of online content that employs many of these goals is the online magazine *Inspire* produced by al-Qaeda supporters.

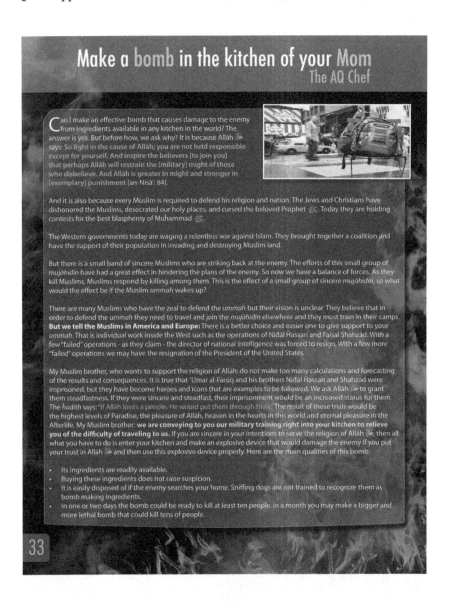

Seven different version of this magazine are produced in English, none in Arabic. Analysis of the substance of this magazine suggests the content is not directed at existing members or supporters but rather potential recruits. The magazine is impressive as it includes 100–150 pages of quality pictures, stories, and songs. However, unlike other magazines, *Inspire's* content includes bomb-making recipes (see Image 2) and public key encryption systems.

In addition to their English magazines, al-Qaeda also produces more technical magazines. One of these is the Arabic-language *Technical Mujahideen* that provides detailed information regarding how to protect information on a computer if seized by law enforcement agencies.

Extremist groups clearly benefit from the easy access and the limited restrictions that are the essence of the Internet. The numbers speak for themselves: as previously indicated, from 1996 to 2006 terrorist websites grew from fewer than 100 to over 5,000, and this number has at least doubled in the past six years.[24] To that end, the power of the Internet as an extraordinarily effective transmitter of information is, literally, unparalleled and limitless. Although the positive aspects of the Internet, whether in daily communication or in times of crisis, are clear, nefarious use is equally obvious. As the discussion in this chapter illustrates the Internet is essential to criminals as highlighted by the example of child pornographers and extremists alike. The failure of Congress to more aggressively address this issue coupled with the deep reluctance of administrators to proactively limit website content has left the Internet ripe for the picking by criminals and extremists alike.

---

[24] Wright, *supra* note 18.

6

CONTEMPORARY SOCIAL TENSIONS (i.e., ECONOMIC CRISES, BREAKDOWN OF TRADITIONAL FAMILY STRUCTURE)

I. Introduction

Addressing contemporary social tensions—the topic of this chapter—requires focusing on a number of issues, particularly the economy, immigration, and gender issues relevant to religion. The economic crisis that has struck both the United States and Europe ("Eurozone") has raised profound questions with respect to Europe's future.[1] These questions address not only the future of the European Union but also whether European nations will be able to honor their financial obligation in the context of social benefits and the welfare state. These are not trivial questions; they are essential to understanding extremism and the danger it poses to society.

Hand in hand with the economic crisis is the question of immigration to Europe; the spotlight naturally focuses on immigration from North Africa and Turkey.[2] Discussions with a broad range of European academics, policymakers, and security officials suggest that contemporary social tensions are particularly acute with respect to immigration from North Africa. Those discussions highlight a powerful connection between the

---

[1] Tim Lister, *The Future of Europe: 3 Scenarios*, CNN (June 18, 2012, 11:23 AM), http://www.cnn.com/2012/06/15/world/europe/europe-future/index.html?hpt=hp_c1.

[2] For a thorough and objective analysis, please see *Muslims in Europe: Promoting Integration and Countering Extremism*, CONGRESSIONAL RESEARCH SERVICE (Sept. 7, 2011), http://www.fas.org/sgp/crs/row/RL33166.pdf (last viewed June 17, 2012).

economic crisis and immigration; in many ways, the two are inexorably linked both in reality and perception.[3]

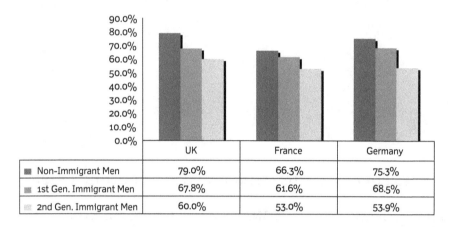

	UK	France	Germany
■ Non-Immigrant Men	79.0%	66.3%	75.3%
▨ 1st Gen. Immigrant Men	67.8%	61.6%	68.5%
▨ 2nd Gen. Immigrant Men	60.0%	53.0%	53.9%

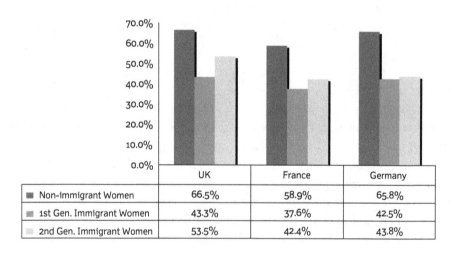

	UK	France	Germany
■ Non-immigrant Women	66.5%	58.9%	65.8%
▨ 1st Gen. Immigrant Women	43.3%	37.6%	42.5%
▨ 2nd Gen. Immigrant Women	53.5%	42.4%	43.8%

Employment Rates[4]

---

[3] *See generally* Soeren Kern, *Islam in Germany: "Germany Does Away with Itself,"* RIGHTSIDE NEWS (June 16, 2012, 6:07 AM), http://www.rightsidenews.com/2012061616432/world/geopolitics/islam-in-germany-qgermany-does-away-with-itselfq.html; Jorn Madslien, *Norway's Far Right Not a Spent Force*, BBCNEWS, http://www.bbc.co.uk/news/world-europe-14260195 (last updated July 23, 2011); Robert Bridge, *Rise of Right-Wing Extremism Rattles Europe*, RT (July 25, 2011, 7:03 PM), http://rt.com/politics/norway-extremism-russia-multiculturalism/; Sylvia Poggioli, *Norway Questions Its Tolerance of Extremisism*, NPR (July 26, 2011), http://www.npr.org/2011/07/26/138696308/norway-questions-its-tolerance-of-extremism.

[4] Yann Algan, Christian Dustman, Albrecht Glitz & Alan Manning, *The Economic Situation of First and Second-Generation Immigrants in France, Germany and the United Kingdom*, 120(542) ECON. J. f4–f30 (2010), *available at* http://ideas.repec.org/a/ecj/econjl/v120y2010i542pf4-f30.html.

At its core this chapter examines the very nature of society in an effort to provide a snapshot regarding tensions between society and extremist groups and individuals. This is largely a descriptive chapter aimed at addressing significant domestic issues that define contemporary society. The chapter is based on numerous interviews with a broad range of both subject matter and country-specific experts conducted in Holland, Norway, the United Kingdom, and Israel.

The four countries confront complicated intersections and forks in the road that require thoughtful resolution with one eye focused on today, the other on tomorrow. The complexity and tension belie what Steven Pinker has suggested regarding the decline of violence.[5] Because of the manner in which extremism poses dangers to society, analyzing the nature of its impact requires examination beyond empirical data. That is, although empirical data may reflect a decrease in violence, extremism's impact on society extends beyond specific acts of violence, whether against individuals or groups.

By way of example: the demands by Israeli Orthodox Jews for gender discrimination on public transportation led the Israeli Supreme Court in the seminal case regarding separation on buses between the sexes to ask "Have we gone back to the days of Rosa Parks?"[6] The harassment, humiliation, and verbal abuse directed at women who either sat in the front of a bus or whose attire was deemed insufficiently modest are but examples of values predicated on extremist interpretation of religiosity.

Essential to the discussion is recognition that extremism does not *inherently* endanger society; the question is in its manifestation and implementation. Thoughts alone do not pose a risk to society or specific individuals. However, when those thoughts are translated into action society must protect itself. However, much disagreement exists regarding the distance between potential harm and actual harm; defining that distance is essential to determining when society can impose limits on otherwise guaranteed rights and freedoms.

These questions served as the basis for discussions in the four countries. As might be expected, responses and dialogue varied greatly depending on present tensions in each country, its history, and the particular perspective of the interlocutor. Disagreement was, naturally, voiced whether extremism poses a danger; furthermore, among those who view extremism as posing a danger, opinions ranged widely regarding how and when to minimize its impact.

II. Holland

A leading Dutch journalist starkly posed the question: what is Dutch society today?[7] My interlocutor suggested the key issues in understanding the relationship between

---

[5] Steven Pinker, The Better Angels of our Nature: Why Violence Has Declined (2011).
[6] HCJ 746/07 Naomi Regan v. Ministry of Transportation, http://elyon1.court.gov.il/files_eng/07/460/007/t38/07007460.t38.htm (last visited Aug. 17, 2013).
[7] Private conversation (records in author's files).

traditional Dutch society and the immigrant population requires focusing on education, housing, crime rates, and employment. He suggested—as others have—that Europe today is largely composed of "parallel societies."[8] In raising the specter of parallel societies the focus is, in the Netherlands, on Moroccan and Turkish on first- and second-generation immigrants to Holland. In the context of social tensions, a critical question is one of allegiance and identity; according to a leading Dutch academic, Moroccan youth identify with Islam whereas Turkish youth identify with Turkey.[9]

Jean Tillie and Marieke Slootman's research regarding the radicalization of Moslem youth in the Netherlands is particularly insightful:

> Muslims differ from the average resident of Amsterdam especially in the two core convictions. Muslims are three times more likely to consider their religion superior to others than the Christians in Amsterdam, and they are more likely than the average Amsterdammer to find the debate about Islam is conducted in a negative manner. These differences indicate a gap between many Muslims, especially Moroccans, and the average Amsterdammer in their religious beliefs (or at least in the manner these beliefs are formulated) and in their perception of the social discourse. Turkish Muslims agree with the average Amsterdammer in their perceptions of the debate about Islam although they are in general more orthodox than Moroccans. Differences within society are in themselves not harmful, and it is not surprising that Moroccans, who are often the subject of negative news coverage, perceive the debate about Islam as negative. Moroccans are also more inclined to act to influence the debate. These differences seem relevant to us, because contrasts with the rest of society can lead to a mutual feeling of discord and of not being understood.[10]

This research is particularly relevant for it highlights that alienation from mainstream society significantly facilitates the ability of extremists to prey on disaffected youth, contributing to their radicalization. In discussing immigration in the context of extremism, the question is the degree of integration of the immigrant into the larger society. That question, however, works both ways: to what extent does traditional Dutch society welcome immigrant values, mores, and norms? Professor Paul Scheffer book, *Immigrant Nations*, is particularly insightful regarding issues addressed in this chapter. Similar to Professor Minow's article regarding tolerating intolerance[11] Professor Scheffer writes:

> It's clear that in times of large-scale immigration tolerance is put to the test. Innumerable people have arrived in the Netherlands after growing up in unfree

---

[8] See discussion in Chapter Three.

[9] Private conversation (records in author's notes).

[10] Marieke Slootman & Jean Tillie, *Processes of Radicalisation: Why Some Amsterdam Muslims Become Radicals*, Inst. for Migration and Ethnic Studies, Univ. of Amsterdam (Oct. 2006), *available at* http://dare.uva.nl/document/337314.

[11] See Chapter One.

societies. Sometimes, conservative Muslims express beliefs that were commonplace some 40 years ago, but that doesn't make them any less disturbing in the here and now. This was clearly demonstrated by a case known to the Dutch as the el-Moumni affair. A Rotterdam imam at the An-Nasr mosque, who had been banned from preaching in Morocco because of his radical beliefs, caused a huge stir when he delivered a sermon in which he said of homosexuality, among other things: "If this sickness spread, everyone will be infected and that could lead to us dying out."[12]

Furthermore, according to Scheffer:

The Dutch now find themselves with a new religious community in their midst, and this time history, language and the constitution can't be assumed to serve as ties that will mitigate division. In the past it was possible to find shared points of reference....The extent to which the Dutch underestimate the command of a common tongue as one of the essential sources of mutuality available in their fragmented country is remarkable....In the Netherlands today, the Dutch language cannot be taken for granted as a shared vehicle, given many immigrants' limited proficiency in it.[13]

In quoting August Hans den Boef, Scheffer points out that "Integration via the mosque means integration within religious communities that are divided along national and regional lines and led by their conservative male segments, which largely consist of people from tribal cultures who have little education. In Dutch Muslim communities most children attend black schools, or Islamic schools that are an extension of the mosque."[14]

With respect to social tensions in the context of immigrant communities, Scheffer writes:

A nation that enjoys freedom of religion can make room for Islam only on condition that the vast majority of Muslims accept their duty to defend that same freedom for people with whom they fundamentally disagree. This attitude is lacking in many mosques, where the principles and institutions of liberal democracy are questioned and in some cases rejected. Governments have looked away for a long time, not wanting to cause conflict....Research shows that in general young Muslims in the Netherlands have the same views about democracy as their counterparts in the rest of the population. Only when it comes to freedom of expression do significant differences emerge: no more than a small minority of Turkish and Moroccan young people are in favor of press freedom if it means a religion can be ridiculed. This is another indication that the integration of Islam by the pillarization route will be

---

[12] Paul Scheffer, Immigrant Nations 121 (2011).

[13] *Id.* at 125.

[14] *Id.* at 127.

less easy than it was in the case of religions required to hold their own for many years in open rivalry in a democratic environment.[15]

In this vein, research by Ineke Roex, Sjef van Stiphout, and Jean Tillie is of particular importance: "Sensitivity to radicalism and extremism is higher among orthodox Dutch Muslims. Their tolerance towards a multi-religious society is lower, they think that Dutch women have too much freedom, they politically participate less in society, they identify less with The Netherlands and, most importantly, they think, more than other groups, that violence is a legitimate means for religious goals."[16]

According to this study, "13 per cent of the Islamic schools in The Netherlands is connected to a salafist organization. Given the size of the salafist community this is a strong overrepresentation."[17] Important to recall that Salafism refers to a particularly strict form of Islam,[18] perceived by some to pose a danger to Western society and its institutions.[19] Herein lies a particular tension: "the European Convention on Human Rights (ECHR) protects religious freedom, and the right to hold and to manifest belief, as well as the authority of the state to limit the exercise of the right to manifest religion."[20]

In 1994 the European Court of Human Rights (Strasbourg) held:

"Freedom of thought, conscience and religion is one of the foundations of a 'democratic society' within the meaning of the Convention. It is, in its religious dimension, one of the most vital elements that go to make up the identity of believers and their conception of life, but it is also a precious asset for atheists, agnostics, skeptics and the unconcerned. The pluralism indissociable from a democratic society, which has been dearly won over the centuries, depends on it."[21] Nevertheless, the state has the right to limit or restrict the manifestation of religion with the caveat that the restriction serve a legitimate purpose and not be deemed arbitrary. As Professor Doe writes "Interference justified by reference to *public safety and health* [emphasis in original] indicate well the inferiority of the right to manifest religion in the hierarchy of social values. The pattern across Europe is that the threshold to establish the aim of public safety and health is not high."[22]

---

[15] *Id.* at 128.

[16] *See* Ineke Roex, Sjef van Stiphout & Jean Tillie, *Salafisme in Nederland*, Instituut voor Migratie-en Etnische Studies at viii (2010).

[17] *Id.* at vii–viii.

[18] *See generally An Introduction to the Salafi Da'wah*, available at http://www.qss.org/articles/salafi/text.html (last visited Jan. 11, 2013).

[19] *Germany Hunts Down Radical Islamist Salafies with Mass Police Raids*, NAT. TURK (June 15, 2012), http://www.nationalturk.com/en/germany-hunts-down-radical-islamist-salafis-with-mass-police-raids-19750.

[20] NORMON DOE, LAW AND RELIGION IN EUROPE: A COMPARATIVE INTRODUCTION 17 (2011).

[21] Kokkinakis v. Greece, 260 Eur. Ct. H.R. ¶ 16 (1993) (cited in DOE, *supra* note 20, on page 43).

[22] DOE, *supra* note 20.

There is powerful tension between secular society and religious society; in examining contemporary social tensions the question is whether they can coexist under one umbrella. The question is posed not with respect to mainstream, moderate faith but rather extremist faith that places civil law secondary to religious law. The tension is to what extent should otherwise protected rights be honored by the state when they challenge, if not endanger, public order and offend group and personal sensitivities. The tension is significantly exacerbated in the context of immigration and alienation reinforced by an economic crisis that undermines society's stability and structure.[23]

According to Tillie and Slootman:

Feelings of deprivation are widespread among Muslims in the Netherlands. This feeling is fed by the current tone of debate. Although some feel victimised, there is a certain degree of actual socio-economic deprivation. For example, there has been an increase in the percentage of students from immigrant backgrounds who go on to higher education, from approximately a sixth in 1996 to around a quarter in 2002, but this is still far below the half of all students from a Dutch background who register for higher education. Secondary school drop-outs are also more common among young people with immigrant backgrounds. We have already seen that the Muslims in Amsterdam are relatively low educated compared to the native-born Dutch When we look at unemployment statistics, we see an equally pessimistic image. In Amsterdam, 6 percent of the native-born Dutch working population is unemployed, compared with 16 percent of the Turks and 28 percent of the Moroccans.

The situation of the Turks has improved since 1997, but that of the Moroccans has deteriorated. Both the first and the second generation of immigrants are disappointed in the opportunities they have in the Netherlands....The first generation guest workers are mostly dissatisfied with their own housing situation and their financial position. They are also disappointed that their children do not have the social and economic opportunities they had hoped for. The younger generation, who see their future in the Netherlands, experiences stigmatisation and discrimination in their daily lives. Young men are turned away at clubs and cafés, and young women with covered heads are insulted. These young people feel as though they must work twice as hard as young native-born Dutch people to earn the same recognition at school or work. Especially the idea that there are insufficient internships available for young immigrants leads to frustration and anger. The young people feel (increasingly) discriminated against and alienated.[24]

---

[23] For discussion regarding Norway see *Committee on the Elimination of Racial Discrimination,* UN (Mar. 11, 2011), *available at* http://reliefweb.int/sites/reliefweb.int/files/resources/FDF662F16DB156F385257 853006165FB-Full_Report.pdf.

[24] Slootman & Tillie, *supra* note 10.

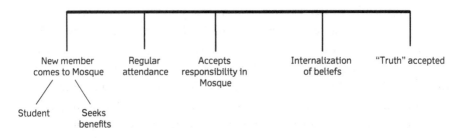

Process of Radicalization[25]

With respect to second-generation radicalization, Tillie and Slootman note:

> Due to the disappearance of the national-ethnic ties and the contact with Dutch society, many young people seek their own version of Islam, pure and free from the superficial Moroccan traditions of their parents. This way the children can take their own respectable place in the community. Parents are often labeled as ignorant by their own children. Some of these developments are approved of by parents because they wish to see that their children take religion seriously, but some find the young people are becoming too strict. These parents then begin to fear that their children are putting too much distance between themselves and Dutch society, limiting their social options and opportunities.[26]

On the issue of self-identification, Tillie and Slootman comment:

> In our conversations with the interview subjects, we learned that young people increasingly identify themselves with their religion. They call themselves "Muslim" more often. This was noticed by Buijs, Demant and Hamdy. This trend towards identifying oneself as a Muslim is not only an individual self-identification, but also a result of labelling by others. In Dutch society, there is still a split between immigrants and the native-born Dutch—the terms "allochtone" and "autochtone", implying language skills and not ethnic background, are used frequently in the Dutch media and illustrate this division, increasingly formulated as Islamic versus non-Islamic. In so doing, a "Muslim category" is created, especially by the media. Muslims are often spoken of as a group, in the Netherlands as well as internationally. Individuals with a Mediterranean appearance are increasingly identified as Muslim. Through this division, Muslims increasingly feel as if they are second-class citizens, which creates a Muslim identity that supersedes national-ethnic lines. Islam is re-appraised as a religion and gains importance as a signifier of identity. This reinforcing of the Muslim

---

[25] Chart created by Nadav Czerninski.
[26] *Id.* at 51.

identity satisfies the need for belonging and acceptance: it offers stability and is a source of self-confidence, and from there it can feed a feeling of superiority over those (non-Muslims) towards whom one feels disadvantaged. This leads many to identify with the worldwide Muslim population, the umma.[27]

Marginalization from mainstream society often leads to radicalization among young immigrants and natives alike. A report by the European Commission's Expert Group on Radicalization explained:

At the global level, polarising tendencies and radicalisation processes can be witnessed within many religious, ethnic and cultural population aggregates. Within this global mood that is also characterised by widespread feelings of inequity and injustice a very acute sense of marginalisation and humiliation exists, in particular within several Muslim communities worldwide as well as among immigrant communities with a Muslim background established in European countries. These perceptions and feelings are often underestimated by Western observers. Today's religious and political radicalisation should however not be confounded.

The former is closely intertwined with identity dynamics, whereas the latter is boosted by the aforementioned feelings of inequity whether real or perceived. Both expressions of radicalisation processes are thus the result of very different individual and collective dynamics.

The widespread feeling of humiliation and uncertainty basically rests upon a whole array of widely diverging specific local circumstances. As in the past, it offers fringe groups an opportunity to justify their recourse to terrorism.[28]

III. Norway

Anders Breivik targeted the future generation of the Labor Party, young people at the vanguard of what he detests: a more multicultural, ethnically, and religiously integrated Norway.[29]

Following the horrific attacks that left 77 dead in Norway, many European leaders have been asking questions about the dangers of right-wing radicalization in the region. In recent years European Union member countries have seen growing support for right-wing populist groups but the attacks confessed to by Anders Behring Breivik took their anti-Islam, xenophobic ideology to an entirely new and deadly level.

---

[27] *Id.* at 54.

[28] *Radicalisation Processes Leading to Acts of Terrorism*, EUR. COMM., May 15, 2008, *available at* http://www.rikcool saet.be/files/art_ip_wz/Expert%20Group%20Report%20Violent%20Radicalisation%20FINAL.pdf.

[29] Eric Westervelt, *Norway "Still Shattered" as Extremist Goes on Trial*, NPR (Apr. 15, 2012, 6:02 AM), http://www.npr.org/2012/04/15/150661728/norway-still-shattered-as-extremist-goes-on-trial.

In hopes of preventing similar events, the EU interior ministers and the European law enforcement agency Europol pledged to review the dangers posed by far-right extremists within the 27 member states. The topic of radicalization was tacked on to the agenda for the late September 2011 meeting of the Justice and Home Affairs Council, to which non-EU member Norway was also invited. During that same month, a EU anti-radicalization network, set in motion the previous year, was able to take up its work.

In a blog entry announcing the new measures, European Commissioner for Home Affairs Cecilia Malmström referred to Breivik's 1,500-page online manifesto:[30] "I have many times expressed my concern over xenophobic parties who build their unfortunately quite successful rhetoric on negative opinions on Islam and other so-called threats against society," she wrote. 'This creates a very negative environment, and sadly there are too few leaders today who stand up for diversity and for the importance of having open, democratic and tolerant societies where everybody is welcome.' "[31]

In June 2012 I spent the better part of a week in Norway meeting with a wide range of Norwegian academics, thought leaders, law enforcement/national security officials, and politicos.[32] Some of those I met with testified at Breivik's trial; others had followed it to varying degrees of intensity and interest. One individual was acquainted with a survivor of the attack and had mutual friends with one victim. If not for Breivik, research relevant to this book project would not have taken me to Norway; that assessment very much resonated with my interlocutors.

There was wide agreement that incorporating Norway in a discussion regarding contemporary extremism was appropriate and relevant. The Norwegians with whom I met conveyed a heavy heart resulting from the horrific results of Breivik's attack and shock to their understanding of traditional Norwegian mores and norms. Across the board rejection was expressed that Breivik was insane; consensus was universally articulated that Norwegian society must acknowledge homegrown extremism exists in its midst. The common refrain was that were Breivik not an ethnic Norwegian[33] the question of his sanity would not have been raised either by the court or prosecutor. In other words, internalizing that a right-wing ethnic Norwegian extremist murdered 77 fellow ethnic Norwegians poses enormous challenges for Norwegian society.

On the other hand, hyperbole must be avoided; Breivik evidentially acted alone, and his actions have not led others to commit to similar acts.[34] Unlike terrorist organizations

---

[30] See Breivik's Manifesto, *available at* http://www.breiviksmanifesto.com/ (last visited Jan 11, 2013).

[31] *EU Declares Fight against Right-Wing Extremisim*, SPIEGEL (July 27, 2011), http://www.spiegel.de/international/europe/after-norway-eu-declares-fight-against-right-wing-extremism-a-776985.html. For a thoughtful discussion regarding the dangers of unlimited free speech, see Sindre Bangstad, *Whatever Happened to Norway's Incitement Laws?*, INST. OF RACE RELATIONS (Oct. 20, 2011), http://www.irr.org.uk/news/whatever-happened-to-norways-incitement-laws/.

[32] Notes of all conversations in author's records.

[33] Ethnic Norwegians here mean "native."

[34] These lines are accurate as of Jan. 13, 2013.

such as al-Qaeda, Hamas, IRA, and the Tamil Tigers, Breivik is a lone wolf, closer to Timothy McVeigh[35] and the Unabomber[36] than to Osama bin Laden. Breivik's manifesto, largely a cut and paste of innumerable articles, blogs, commentary, and writings of others posits that Norwegian leaders have surrendered to "cultural Marxism," which endangers contemporary Norway. A careful reading of the manifesto and discussions with Norwegian thought leaders indicates that "cultural Marxism" is, in essence, an euphemism for "multiculturalism," with the clear target immigrants, particularly Moslems. In other words, Breivik accuses Norway's leaders of capitulating to Islam and in doing so endangering the state as it presently exists.

Breivik references the Norwegian government in World War II established by the Nazis after German occupation of Norway. In other words, contemporary Norwegian leadership is the modern day Quisling; the reference is to the Norwegian, Vidkun Quisling, who collaborated with the Nazis by heading a puppet government.[37] According to the manifesto, modern-day Norwegian leadership, much like Quisling, is collaborating with an external force. Quisling collaborated with Nazi Germany, whereas modern-day Norwegian leaders are collaborating with Islam; in other words, similar to the Nazi occupation that threatened Norway, occupation by Islam endangers modern Norway. According to Breivik, the fault both in words and deeds lies with Norwegian leadership rather than with the immigrants themselves; the latter are the beneficiaries of the former's policies. It is for that reason that Breivik's attacks were directed at present and future Norwegian leadership.

On Friday July 22, 2011, a car bomb detonated in downtown Oslo blowing out windows in the prime minister's office and damaging the oil and finance ministries; as a result of this attack 8 people were killed and 290 wounded. According to multiple sources the late hour (3:27 PM) of the attack minimized the loss of life. After detonation of the bomb, Breivik drove to Utoeya Island, the site of a Labor Party youth camp. Traveling by ferry, dressed in a police uniform and heavily armed, Breivik immediately opened fire upon arrival on the island. Logistical difficulties encountered by Norwegian law enforcement officials enabled Breivik to conduct his attack largely undisturbed for over an hour. When police arrived, Breivik immediately surrendered; his casualties numbered 69 killed, 33 wounded.[38] Over the course of three hours Breivik's two attacks resulted in 77 deaths and over 300 wounded.

---

[35] *See generally* Ted Ottley, *Timothy McVeigh & Terry Nichols: Oklahoma Bombing*, TRUTV, http://www.trutv. com/library/crime/serial_killers/notorious/mcveigh/dawning_1.html (last visited Jan. 13, 2012).

[36] *See generally* Ted Ottley, *Ted Kaczynski: The Unabomber*, TRUTV, http://www.trutv.com/library/crime/terrorists_spies/terrorists/kaczynski/1.html (last visited Jan. 11, 2013).

[37] Vidkun Quisling, Britannica, *available at* http://www.britannica.com/EBchecked/topic/487555/Vidkun-Quisling (last visited Aug. 17, 2013).

[38] For a timeline of the attacks see *Timeline: How Norway's Terror Attacks Unfolded*, BBCNews, http://www.bbc. co.uk/news/world-europe-14260297 (last updated Apr. 17, 2012).

As quickly became apparent, Breivik's attacks were neither spontaneous nor impulsive; rather, the manifesto and his actions on July 22 reflect careful planning, significant attention to detail, and rigorous self-discipline that enabled a gathering of materials necessary for both attacks. Breivik's statements at his trial before the Oslo District Court confirmed his intensity and depth of planning, the motivation for the attack, the defining of the victims as traitors, and his complete lack of remorse.[39] In addition, Breivik had planned on capturing and beheading former Norwegian Prime Minister Gro Harlem Brundtland who was also on the island; however, technical difficulties forced him to abandon this idea.[40] Conversations with Norwegian security officials confirmed that Breivik flew under the radar of the intelligence community and was, therefore, able to prepare, unabated, over the course of a number of years.[41]

Breivik's claim to belong to a secret organization modeled on the medieval Christian military order the Knights Templar has not been substantiated. Similarly, evidence supporting his claims to have links with far-right British groups has not been found. Conversations with Norwegian subject matter experts, including those who testified before the Oslo District Court as expert witnesses, confirmed Breivik's self-assessment: Breivik was motivated by extreme right-wing ideology that, in the context of a civil war, seeks to protect Norway from multiculturalism, traitors, and Moslems.

Given that Breivik assumed responsibility for his actions of July 22, 2011, one of the most important questions before the court was determing his sanity. An initial psychiatric evaluation determined he was insane, suffering from paranoid schizophrenia and therefore not responsible for his actions; however, subsequent psychiatrist evaluations concluded Breivik is not psychotic and must be held accountable for his actions.[42] While the prosecution asked the court to find Breivik insane, Breivik requested the court find him sane but acquit on the grounds he was protecting Norway from those supporting and facilitating Islamic immigration.[43] The question of Breivik's sanity is of paramount importance: if found insane then his actions can be dismissed as those of a psychotic, whereas if the Court finds him sane, Norwegian society is confronted with powerful and troubling questions regarding its makeup and character. A public opinion poll found that 74 percent of the Norwegian public believes Breivik mentally competent to be sentenced to prison.[44]

---

[39] *Anders Brevik Details Norway Massacre Plans, Cite Al-Qaeda Inspiration*, WASH. POST (Apr. 20, 2012), http://www.washingtonpost.com/world/exclude/anders-breivik-details-norway-massacre-plans-cites-al-qaeda-inspiration/2012/04/2.

[40] Karen Kissane, *Breivik Reveals Chilling Plan to Behead PM*, SMH (Apr. 20, 2012), http://www.smh.com.au/world/breivik-reveals-chilling-plan-to-behead-pm-20120419-1xaib.html.

[41] Private conversations (notes in author's records).

[42] *Prosectors in Norway Call for Breivik Insanity Verdict*, BBCNEWS http://www.bbc.co.uk/news/world-europe-18530670 (last updated June 21, 2012).

[43] Balazs Koranyi, *Prosecutors Want Mass Killer Breivik Ruled Insane*, REUTERS (June 21, 2012), http://www.reuters.com/article/2012/06/21/us-breivik-trial-idUSBRE85K0TT20120621.

[44] Julia Gronnevet & Karl Ritter, *Norway Prosecutors Assert Breivik Insane*, YAHOO! (June 21, 2012), http://news.yahoo.com/norway-prosecutors-assert-breivik-insane-184515198.html.

The question of Breivik's sanity goes far beyond Breivik himself; it cuts to the core of homegrown right-wing extremists "living in our midst." The overwhelming majority of individuals whom I met responded similarly when queried about their initial reaction to the news reports regarding the bombing (not the island attack): "I was stunned al-Qaeda had come to Norway" was the standard response.[45] However, when hearing reports regarding the second (island) attack, my interlocutors explained they gradually realized the attacker must be an ethnic Norwegian. This was predicated on an assumption al-Qaeda would not deliberately attack a Labor Party youth organization convening on Utoeya Island for their annual meeting. The initial reaction is similar to one expressed by many, including recognized experts, in the immediate aftermath of the Oklahoma City bombing.[46]

The difference between Breivik's two attacks contributed to the very different responses. The first attack—a car bomb—is similar to innumerable acts of terrorism committed worldwide over decades. It is for that reason that many expressed the sentiment "al-Qaeda in Norway." However, the second attack required specific information pertaining to the youth party convention; committing the island attack was conditioned on obtaining information regarding ferry crossings that strongly suggested an act committed by an ethnic Norwegian.

Regarding Breivik, the commentary below by a Norwegian academic concisely summarizes the legal, moral, political, and cultural dilemma facing contemporary Norwegian society:

> The case raises a profound moral-philosophical question for Norwegian society: Are we prepared in a thoroughly secularized society to accept and face up to the existence of evil in our midst, or must evil perpetrated by white ethnic Norwegians always be rendered as an articulation of mental illness? There is a precedent with regard to this in Norwegian courts: When non-white Norwegians kill their partners or wives, it is always rendered through the lens of "culture" or "religion"; when white Norwegians do the same it is always cast by the Courts and public as expressions of mental illness.[47]

This was not the first time right-wing extremists have committed violent acts in Norway:

> On January 26 2001, fifteen year old Benjamin Labarang Hermansen was brutally stabbed to death in the eastern suburb of Holmlia in Oslo by three young neo-Nazis. Hermansen had been born to a Norwegian mother and a Ghanaian father. Joe Erling Jahr (20), Ole Nicolai Kvisler (22) and Veronica Andreassen (18)

---

[45] Notes in author's records; *see also* Oyvind Strommen, *Violent "Counter-Jihadism,"* FOREIGN AFFAIRS (July 27, 2011), http://www.foreignaffairs.com/articles/67999/oyvind-strommen/violent-counter-jihadism.

[46] *See generally* John F. Sugg, *Steven Emerson's Crusade*, FAIR (Jan 1, 1999), http://fair.org/extra-online-articles/steven-emersons-crusade/.

[47] Excerpt from email sent to author (full text in author's records).

were eventually charged with the murder. Jahr and Kvisler were sentenced to 18 and 17 years in prison, whereas Kvisler's girlfriend Andreassen was sentenced to 3 years in prison as an accomplice to the murder. The three had set out from a council flat in in the nearby eastern suburb of Bøler armed with knives on the day of the murder, intending to "to attack immigrants."[48]

The background for Hemansen's murder:

On 19 August 2000, a group known as the Boot Boys organized a march in commemoration of the Nazi leader Rudolf Hess. Some 38 people, wearing "semi-military" uniforms, some with their faces covered participated. One of the central Boot Boys figures made a speech, in which he stated:

We are gathered here to honor our great hero, Rudolf Hess, for his brave attempt to save Germany and Europe from Bolshevism and Jewry during the Second World War. While we stand here, over 15,000 Communists and Jew-lovers are gathered at Youngstorget in a demonstration against freedom of speech and the white race. Every day immigrants rob, rape and kill Norwegians, every day our people and country are being plundered and destroyed by the Jews, who suck our country empty of wealth and replace it with immoral and un-Norwegian thoughts. We were prohibited from marching in Oslo three times, whilst the Communists did not even need to ask. Is this freedom of speech? Is this democracy?...Our dear Führer Adolf Hitler and Rudolf Hess sat in prison for what they believed in, we shall not depart from their principles and heroic efforts, on the contrary we shall follow in their footsteps and fight for what we believe in, namely a Norway built on National Socialism..." The Nazi salute was made and "Sieg Heil" shouted.[49]

Boots Boy leader Terje Sjoli was convicted on charges of racism and anti-Semitism; on appeal, the conviction was overturned by the Norwegian Supreme Court. In 2004 the decision was appealed to the UN Committee on the Elimination of Racial Discrimination, which issued an unusually strong opinion against the Norwegian Supreme Court. In their appeal the petitioners—the Jewish community of Oslo and the Norwegian Antiracist Center—contended they were victims of violations by the state party of articles 4 and 6 of the Convention.[50]

---

[48] *See generally* Sindre Bangstand, *After Anders Breivik's Conviction, Norway Must Confront Islamophobia,* GUARDIAN (Aug. 28, 2012), http://www.guardian.co.uk/commentisfree/belief/2012/aug/28/anders-breivik-norway-islamophobia-muslims; *see also Newo-Nazis Held for Oslo "Racist" Murder,* BBCNEWS (Jan 29, 2001), http://news.bbc.co.uk/2/hi/europe/1142780.stm; Steve James, *Mass Protests against Racist Murder in Norway,* WSWS (Feb. 11, 2001), http://www.wsws.org/articles/2001/feb2001/norw-f13.shtml.

[49] *See* Committee Elimination of Racial Discrimination, *available at* http://www.unhchr.ch/tbs/doc.nsf/0/bof 01303db356e96c125714c004eb10f?Opendocument (last visited Jan 11, 2013).

[50] Articles 4 reads: States Parties condemn all propaganda and all organizations which are based on ideas or theories of superiority of one race or group of persons of one colour or ethnic origin, or which attempt to

The thrust of their petition is that they were "not afforded protection against the dissemination of ideas of racial discrimination and hatred, as well as incitement to such acts, during the march of 19 August 2000; and were not afforded a remedy against this conduct, as required by the Convention."[51] The Committee's final recommendation in its opinion is that "the State party take measures to ensure that statements such as those made by Mr. Sjolie in the course of his speech are not protected by the right to freedom of speech under Norwegian law."[52]

However, the Boot Boys was not the first extreme right-wing xenophobic anti-immigration group in Norway;[53] the White Election Alliance party was established in 1993. Important to recall is that previous anti-immigrant resistance movements were largely dominated by World War II resistance heroes; in that vein, from an ideological–philosophical perspective Breivik represents a new resistance movement best described as the new Crusaders fighting the third attempt by Islam to conquer Europe with the assistance of both internal and external collaborators. Although the electorate resoundingly rejected the White Election Alliance party, its campaign drew attention to the "immigrant question" and particularly the role, place, and legitimacy of immigrants in Norwegian society. The Alliance was a legitimate political party, fully engaged in the political process in direct contrast to the Boot Boys who were "more of a hooligan

---

justify or promote racial hatred and discrimination in any form, and undertake to adopt immediate and positive measures designed to eradicate all incitement to, or acts of, such discrimination and, to this end, with due regard to the principles embodied in the Universal Declaration of Human Rights and the rights expressly set forth in article 5 of this Convention, *inter alia*:

(a) Shall declare an offence punishable by law all dissemination of ideas based on racial superiority or hatred, incitement to racial discrimination, as well as all acts of violence or incitement to such acts against any race or group of persons of another colour or ethnic origin, and also the provision of any assistance to racist activities, including the financing thereof;

(b) Shall declare illegal and prohibit organizations, and also organized and all other propaganda activities, which promote and incite racial discrimination, and shall recognize participation in such organizations or activities as an offence punishable by law;

(c) Shall not permit public authorities or public institutions, national or local, to promote or incite racial discrimination; Article 6 reads: States Parties shall assure to everyone within their jurisdiction effective protection and remedies, through the competent national tribunals and other State institutions, against any acts of racial discrimination which violate his human rights and fundamental freedoms contrary to this Convention, as well as the right to seek from such tribunals just and adequate reparation or satisfaction for any damage suffered as a result of such discrimination.

[51] Committee on the Elimination of Racial Discrimination, *supra* note 50.

[52] *Id.*

[53] For a discussion of this issue, see http://www.tau.ac.il/Anti-Semitism/asw98-9/norway.htm (last visited July 4, 2012).

group than a political movement."[54] White Election Alliance leader Jack Erik Kjuus, who advocated the forced sterilization of adopted children and foreigners married to Norwegians, was convicted in 1997 of racism; the Norwegian Supreme Court upheld his conviction.[55]

The White Election Alliance originated as a joint list for the 1993 general election for two registered political parties, both led by Jack Erik Kjuus. One of the participants were *Hjelp fremmedkulturelle hjem* [Help the aliens go home], a party originally formed in 1973 under the name *Ensliges parti* [The singles' party]. The other party, *Stopp innvandringen* [Stop immigration] was registered by Jack Erik Kjuus in 1988.

"Stop Immigration" was originally the heading of an advertisement put in the newspaper *Aftenposten* by Jack Erik Kjuus, then posing as leader of a *Tverrpolitisk velgerforbund* [Association of electors across the political spectrum]. The Association called for a referendum on a proposition recommending a total halt to granting refugees asylum. A complaint was filed against Kjuus and *Aftenposten* by the Antiracist Centre (ARC) for violation of the Penal Code Article 135a, known as the "racism article". The prosecution decided to drop the case. Chief Superintendent Anne Marie Aslakrud at the Oslo Police Department wrote in her recommendation to the Prosecution that the advertisement "ikke er rettet mot asylsøkerne, men (…) er en kritikk mot norsk innvandringspolitikk." [is not directed at the refugees, but (…) is a criticism against Norwegian immigration policies] The ARC complained to the Director General of Public Prosecutions, who found no reason to reverse the decision.

Following a campaign with immigration issues as a central topic, Stop Immigration was the choice of fewer than 9000 voters in the 1989 elections. In relative numbers, this means 0,3 percent of the electorate, the best result for any of Kjuus' parties in general elections ever. In the local elections of 1991, Frank Hove was elected to the City Council of Drammen. Re-elected in 1995, he is the only representative of Stop Immigration with some measure of political success. In the general elections of 1993, the support for Stop Immigration was down to fewer than 2000 votes and in 1997 fewer than 500.

The Alliance participated in the general election in the counties of Akershus, Oslo and Buskerud, and received a total of 463 votes. The Fatherland Party ran in all counties, and achieved fewer than 4000 votes altogether.[56]

---

[54] Email received from Norwegian subject matter expert (in author's records).
[55] *See* Youth, Racist Violence and Anti-racist Responses in the Nordic Countries, *available at* http://www.nuo-risotutkimusseura.fi/julkaisuja/virtanen/3/4.html (last visited Jan. 13, 2013).
[56] Eric Lundeby, Free Speech and Political Exclusion (2000) (PhD thesis, University of Oslo), *available at* http://www.lundeby.info/EL%20Free%20Speech%20Dissertation.pdf.

A. GAINING PERSPECTIVE

During my visit to Oslo I met with a senior security official;[57] during the course of our two-hour conversation we discussed a wide range of security-related issues focusing on Breivik, right-wing extremism, and immigration to Norway. The official was candid regarding the intelligence community's failure to recognize Breivik as a threat. When I expressed surprise at certain aspects of the operational response to the island attack, the official noted that circumstances notwithstanding—the island is 38 km/24 miles from Oslo, road conditions were less than ideal, only one police helicopter was available, initial responders were focused on the Oslo bombing, and the first boat available to police nearly sank—the police response was in accordance with procedures and guidelines.

Although not underestimating the extraordinary impact of Breivik's attack the official was unhesitating in stating Islamic extremism poses the most pressing threat facing Norway today.[58] In doing so the official noted the vulnerability of both larger society and moderate Moslems to Moslem extremists who use sharia to hinder integration by encouraging radicalization. The official noted that at public high school prayer meetings extremist Islamic views are articulated; in that vein the official expressed concern regarding the possible creation of a parallel society if state authorities and laws are not perceived as legitimate.[59] Regarding parallel society, the official emphasized the existence of insular communities in Oslo and public schools with Norwegian citizens[60] but not ethnic Norwegian teachers.[61]

In identifying Islamic extremism as posing the most significant danger to Norwegian society the official was not gainsaying the obvious threat posed by right-wing extremist ethnic Norwegians, for the results of July 22, 2011 are undeniable regarding their impact and harm. However in distinguishing between Islamic extremism and Norwegian right-wing extremism the official emphasized that Breivik was a classic "lone wolf" with no organization, either in Norway or the United Kingdom, supporting, facilitating, or abetting him.[62] This in contrast to Islamic terrorism that in the overwhelming majority of instances is committed by terrorist organizations, whether international or domestic in orientation.[63] A caveat is required: while emphasizing the threat posed by Islamic

---

[57] Name and position in author's records.

[58] In earlier conversations I asked Dutch and Israeli security officials what single attack causes them to lose sleep at night. For the former an attack on MP Wilders; for the latter, an attack on an ELAL (Israel's national airline) plane.

[59] *See* Chapter Three.

[60] Reference is to children of immigrants

[61] For further discussion regarding schools in Europe today, see SCHEFFER, *supra* note 12; "ethnic Norwegians" refers to those who have been in Norway for generations.

[62] Breivik claimed to belong to a secret organization modeled on the medieval Christian military order the Knights Templar and that he was in contact with like-minded individuals in the United Kingdom; neither claim has been substantiated.

[63] AMOS GUIORA, GLOBAL PERSPECTIVES ON COUNTERTERRORISM (2007).

extremism—as compared to right-wing extremism—the security official noted that, presently, the number of Moslem extremists in Norway is limited.

In differentiating between the two categories, the official suggested that right-wing extremists are, broadly speaking, marginalized individuals with a weak ideology[64] whereas Islamic extremist terrorism is the result either of incitement by imams or self-radicalization by the actor. In many ways, Breivik's actions are akin to the latter: he largely self-radicalized though his ideology was influenced by a number of individuals, in particular the blogger Fjordman.[65] While Breivik represents a new phase, perhaps "latest incarnation" is the better term, of right-wing xenophobia in Norway, the security official does not believe Breivik's actions will motivate others to follow in his footsteps. The evaluation is based on a professional assessment of intelligence and open-source information; nevertheless, it represents an important perspective in determining future threats and how to effectively prevent an attack and minimize its impact if proactive measures were not successful.

Perhaps the two threats—Islamic extremism and right-wing extremism—are more connected than initially apparent. In justifying his actions, Breivik claimed Europe is under attack from two distinct forces, Moslem immigrants and traitorous capitulating governments. Nevertheless, extremist members of that immigrant community are identified as *the* threat, though an ethnic Norwegian attacked other ethnic Norwegians he accused of capitulating to the very immigrants identified by the security official as posing the most significant threat to Norway.

To better understand the tensions and threats confronting Norwegian society it is necessary to examine three core issues: limits of free speech,[66] the extent of integration, and the role of immigrants in Norwegian society.[67] Immigration to Norway can be divided into two distinct categories: cultural immigrants from Sweden and Denmark and job seekers from Pakistan, Turkey, and Morocco. A large portion of immigrants from the latter category is able to gain entrance into Norway via family reunification. Family reunification means that a family member abroad is reunited with one or more members of his or her family already living in Norway. Residence permits in connection with family reunification are granted primarily to spouses or children under 18 years of age. In order for a person abroad to be entitled to family reunification, that person must be a close relative of the person in Norway with whom reunification is being sought. In special cases, cohabitants, parents, and other close relatives may be granted residence permits or

---

[64] A careful reading of Breivik's manifesto suggests the label of weak ideology is not applicable in his case.

[65] "Fjordman" is the pseudonym of Peder Are Nøstvold Jensen, who is a Norwegian far-right anti-Islamic blogger; Jensen writes extensively on the blog Gates of Vienna, http://gatesofvienna.blogspot.co.il/ (last visited July 5, 2012).

[66] See Chapter Seven.

[67] For an informative discussion regarding integration in Europe, see RINUS PENNINX, DIMITRINA SPENCER & NICHOLAS VAN HEAR, MIGRATION AND INTEGRATION IN EUROPE: THE STATE OF RESEARCH (2008), *available at* http://www.norface.org/files/migration-COMPAS-report.pdf.

work permits in Norway on the grounds of family reunification. The definition of the term "close relatives" in Norway often comprises fewer people than is the case in other countries. If conditions for family reunification are satisfied, work permits are usually granted to persons over 18 years of age, regardless of whether they have received a specific job offer. A work permit granted on the grounds of family reunification usually gives the holder general access to work not limited to a specific job or work place.

Regarding recent immigrants from Poland and the former Yugoslavia, their categorization is unclear. Subject matter experts suggest "cultural immigrants" is a more appropriate term though many of these immigrants are job seekers akin to immigrants from non-European countries.[68] However, Breivik's reference to immigrants is limited to Moslems; the Third Crusade is in direct response to his conviction that Moslems are seeking to conquer Europe.

On February 22, 2011, the U.N. Committee on the Elimination of Racial Discrimination heard the Norwegian delegation's response to the 19th and 20th periodic reports of Norway regarding implementation of the provisions of the International Convention on the Elimination of all Forms of Racial Discrimination:

> In preliminary concluding observations, Régis de Gouttes, the Committee Expert who served as country Rapporteur for the report of Norway, referred to issues of national legislation and the position that the Committee would like allotted to its recommendations in Norwegian domestic law. He also mentioned policies dealing with refugees, asylum seekers and migrants in Norway and expressed his concerns about the requirement of learning the Norwegian language, detention of unidentified individuals, access to jobs, medical care, education, interpretation services...[69]

In response the Norwegian delegate, Tora Aasland, Minister of Education and Research and Acting Minister of Children, Equality and Social Inclusion focused on the following issues:

> The delegation leader said that Norwegian society was seen as homogenous despite the fact that immigrants and their children made up 11 per cent of the population. There were five national minorities living in Norway with people with backgrounds and roots from more than two hundred different countries and independent

---

[68] It is important to note that non-Norwegian Europeans (from Denmark and Sweden) are similarly job seekers (as an anecdote, a waiter from Denmark explained that economics and employment opportunities brought him to Norway).

[69] See *Committee on the Elimination of Racial Discrimination Considers Report of Norway*, UNOG (Feb. 22, 2011), http://www.unog.ch/80256EDD006B9C2E/%28httpNewsByYear_en%29/1CEB5B55C2F5DB19C12 5783F004D000E?OpenDocument.

regions. This diversity was not only seen as a strength, it also contributed to Norway's economic growth and cultural enrichment. This was also a challenge to the government as the society was not immune to prejudice and xenophobia with people victims of stigmatization and discrimination. She stressed that integration policies were based on the fundamental values of Norway and included freedom of opinion and expression, gender equality, equal treatment and the right to marriage and choice of spouse.[70]

In the committee's final preliminary comments the following prescient warning was sounded:

The Rapporteur asked about instances of xenophobia and racist ideas by political leaders and media which might lead to racial violence and how the State could combat this. Mr. de Gouttes also talked about the discrimination experienced by minority groups. These were issues which would or should be included in the committee's final report.[71]

IV. Israel Today

Israel is at a crossroads on a number of critical issues. Particularly important for our purposes are two separate issues: the relationship between the state and Orthodox Jews and the future of Jewish settlements in the West Bank. The first issue is purely domestic in nature while the second has clear domestic and international ramifications and implications.[72] The two issues are at the core of the contemporary Israeli debate. Regarding

---

[70] *Id.*

[71] See the 19th and 20th Reports found here: http://daccess-dds-ny.un.org/doc/UNDOC/GEN/G10/437/39/ PDF/G1043739.pdf?OpenElement   http://www.unog.ch/80256EDD006B9C2E/%28httpNewsByYear_ en%29/1CEB5B55C2F5DB19C125783F004D000E?OpenDocument (last visited Jan. 11, 2013).

[72] The overwhelming majority of the international community's criticism of Israel is focused on Israel's occupation of the West Bank and Gaza Strip (result of the 1967 Six-Day War) and the Jewish settlements built in both areas subsequent to the war. Whereas Israel unilaterally disengaged from Gaza in 2004, the Palestinian Authority (PA) assumed power in Palestinian cities in the West Bank (the PA does not exercise control or power over Jewish settlements in the West Bank), and HAMAS controls the Gaza Strip (resulting from elections). The international community focus on the West Bank is largely restricted to these two issues. Although discussion regarding the legality/illegality of Jewish settlements in the West Bank is beyond the scope of this book, its relevance to both the domestic political debate in Israel and Israel's standing—if not growing isolation—in the world today is beyond dispute. The following is but an example: in 2012 Prime Minister Netanyahu, at the urging of settlement leaders, appointed a committee comprised of legal scholars to examine the status of the West Bank. This committee, chaired by former Supreme Court justice Edmund Levy, was convened largely with the intent to counter the Sasson Report, written by Talia Sasson, a former senior Ministry of Justice official; the Sasson Report commissioned by then Prime Minister Sharon concluded state funds had been diverted to building West Bank settlements and outposts that violated Israeli law. The Prime Minister's Office acknowledged that Netanyahu received the Report two weeks after Justice Levy presented the prime

the Orthodox community, the question is whether, broadly speaking, secular and religious-nationalist[73] Israelis will continue to bear the financial and military burden from which the Orthodox are, largely, excused. Regarding settlements, the question is directly related to resolution of the Israeli–Palestinian conflict and whether an independent Palestinian state will be established in the West Bank.

The essence of extremism of Israel is directly related to both issues: increasingly strident voices in the Orthodox community are demanding separation between the sexes and are actively engaged in rejecting calls for an equal burden.[74] As discussed below, the term "state within a state" is particularly appropriate in describing the relationship between Orthodox Jews and Israeli society; extremism is inherent to the debate in the context of how this troubling paradigm is understood and manifested by certain voices in the Orthodox community. With respect to the religious nationalist community the questions regarding settlements, the Israel–Palestinian peace process, and the West Bank are neither ephemeral nor abstract. Quite the opposite: the future of the West Bank and of Jewish settlements[75] raises profound religious, existential, and political concerns and questions for religious nationalist Jews.[76] As repeatedly demonstrated, extremists in the religious nationalist camp are strident in voice and violent in action. Israeli authorities have confronted religious nationalist violence for over 30 years: murderous acts of the Jewish Underground,[77] the assassination of Prime Minister Rabin,[78] and attacks against both Palestinians living in the West Bank and IDF soldiers stationed there.

While Rabin was the target of unmitigated, venomous incitement articulated by rabbis and right-wing politicians religious nationalist extremists have engaged in violent action for decades. In large part the state has turned a blind eye; Rabin paid the ultimate price for a reality whereby one sector of the population perceives itself as beholden to the Almighty rather

---

minister with the Report (June 2012); the reason for the delay was grave concern regarding how the international community would react to the Report which concluded Israel was not an occupier in the West Bank and that the settlements are legal. International attention and condemnation were immediate; *see* Isabel Kershner, *Validate Settlements, Israeli Panel Suggests*, N.Y. TIMES, July 9, 2012, http://www.nytimes.com/2012/07/10/world/middleeast/israeli-panel-says-west-bank-presence-is-not-occupation-and-recommends-approval-of-jewish-settlements.html?_r=2&emc=tnt&tntemail1=y; *Wrong Time for New Settlements*, N.Y. TIMES, July 10, 2012, http://www.nytimes.com/2012/07/11/opinion/wrong-time-for-new-settlements-in-the-west-bank.html?ref=opinion.

[73] I use the term "religious nationalist" rather than "nationalist religious," reflecting direct translation of the political party that historically represented this sector: Meflaga Da'tit Leumit (Religious Nationalist Party).

[74] This is a direct translation of the term used by protestors demanding a draft of all Haredim to the IDF; perhaps a more accurate translation is "shared burden" between the Haredim and the rest of Israeli society. It is an open question to what extent the demand for "equal burden" includes Israeli Arabs who are not drafted to the IDF but can volunteer to do so.

[75] Whether built with permission (referred to legal) or without authorization (referred to as illegal settlements).

[76] The issue, similarly, raises many questions for secular Jews opposed to the continued building of settlements in the West Bank and/or who favor a two-state solution to the conflict.

[77] Early–mid 1980s.

[78] November 4, 1995.

than to state law. Tragically, Israeli governments—right and left alike—have failed to directly address this deliberate delegitimization. In the context of examining religious nationalist Jewish extremism, the questions are whether an assassination of a prime minister who orders the dismantling of Jewish settlements is deemed legitimate by rabbis, would IDF soldiers dismantling settlement be attacked, and would Islamic holy sites be attacked.[79]

History has shown that religious extremists in Israel attack both Jewish[80] and Palestinian[81] targets. Therefore, warnings issued by rabbis and settler leaders regarding violence that may ensue in the face of possible withdrawal from the West Bank must be treated with the utmost seriousness by the Israeli security and intelligence community.[82]

Orthodox Jews who largely do not serve in the Israel Defense Forces are the beneficiaries of an extraordinary political arrangement whereby the majority of adult males do not work. This in direct contrast to religious nationalist Jews who serve in the IDF and directly contribute to the Israeli economy, akin to secular Jews. In the main, Orthodox Jews vote for Orthodox political parties whereas religious nationalist Jews vote for right-wing political parties committed to the continued building of settlements in the West Bank. Focusing on specific issues will facilitate understanding of Israeli society: the issues that will draw our attention are West Bank settlements, the "equal burden" with respect to employment and military service, and gender discrimination in Orthodox Jewry.

In a crux, religious nationalist Jews want the continued building of settlements in the West Bank; extremists among them view any negotiated settlement with Palestinians resulting in dismantling of settlements as an act of treason. This view is predicated on a belief that according to the Old Testament the West Bank is God-given to the Jewish people. Extremist rabbis issue proclamations, give sermons, and write books that incite; in addition to incitement against Rabin, rabbis have pushed the limits of free speech with respect to incitement against homosexuals, Israeli-Arabs, and Palestinians. As discussed in Chapter Seven, free speech protections in Israel extend to speech that would be subject to prosecution in other countries.

The intelligence community's assessment is that were the government to return all or part of the West Bank to the Palestinians, whether unilaterally or in the context of a peace agreement, the decision would be met with violence. Targets of that assumed violence

---

[79] The Jewish Underground planned on blowing up the Dome of the Rock; according to experts such an action would have directly resulted in a regional war, if not more.

[80] For example, in February 1983 during a Peace Now demonstration urging Prime Minister Begin to adopt the findings of the Kahane Commission regarding Sabra and Shatila, a grenade thrown by Yona Avrushmi, a right-wing activist, murdered Emil Grunzweig; see Emil Grunzweig Peace Now, http://peacenow.org.il/eng/content/emil-grunzweig, (last visited Jan. 11, 2013).

[81] Ori Nir, *Short History of Israeli Right Wing Terrorism*, PEACE NOW (Nov. 13, 2009, 1:55 PM), http://peacenow.org/entries/short_history_of_israeli_right_wing_terrorism#.T_80a3AVxNo.

[82] *Jewish Terrorism Threat Grows in West Bank*, UPI (Dec, 21, 2011), http://www.upi.com/Top_News/Special/2011/12/21/Jewish-terrorism-threat-grows-in-West-Bank/UPI-83091324497138/.

would be IDF soldiers, Palestinians, and political leaders responsible for the policy.[83] The policy implemented by West Bank settlers is referred to as "price tag";[84] Ori Nir, spokesperson of Americans for Peace Now and former Washington bureau chief of *Haaretz*[85] describes it in the following manner:

> "Price Tag," also known as "Arvut Hadadit" (Mutual Responsibility), is a set of violent tactics employed by national-religious Israeli settlers in the West Bank to deter Israeli law enforcement authorities from removing illegally-built structures from West Bank settlements. The tactics employed include attacks on Palestinians and their property, as well as attacks on Israeli military and police officers. These tactics are designed to obstruct and deter law enforcement inside settlements, but their ultimate goal is to deter Israeli leaders from implementing a possible future Israeli-Palestinian peace agreement that entails removing Israeli settlements from the West Bank.[86]

In broad stokes, Prime Minister Netanyahu's right-wing coalition is perceived as a pro-settlement movement. However, settler leaders have voiced criticism of the government's decision to implement Israeli Supreme Court decisions regarding the dismantling of illegal Jewish settlements. In addition, acts of settler violence against Palestinians are not an infrequent occurrence; furthermore, and equally troubling, settlers responsible for acts of violence are rarely prosecuted.[87] This is in direct contrast to the robust response of Israel's intelligence community, law enforcement and IDF to Palestinian terrorism.[88]

Judaism is divided into two distinct categories: Ashkenazi Jews whose background is European, and Sephardic Jews who come from North Africa and the Middle East. The Ashkenaz Orthodox community is divided into different communities; the largest are Lita'im and Hasidim, the dominant are Gur, Viznitz, and Belz.[89] The original religious political parties in Israel were Mizrahi and Hapoel Mizrahi, which joined forces in the 1950s and formed the National Religious Party. In the early 1980s Rabbi Shach, the head of the

---

[83] In that context, Carmi Gilon, the former Head of Israel Security Agency (1994–1996) stated that a prime minister who decides to return the West Bank (in whole or in part) would be assassinated; Gilon, who resigned in the aftermath of the Rabin assassination (1995) made his comments in the documentary *Gatekeepers. See The Gatekeepers*, JFF, http://www.jff.org.il/?CategoryID=745&ArticleID=1340 (last visited Jan. 11, 2013).

[84] For a compilation of "price tag"–related attacks on Palestinian targets see http://peacenow.org/entries/price_tag_timeline#.T_8hNXAVwdU (last visited July 12, 2012); for a report regarding "price tag" as applied in Israel, in addition to the West Bank, see http://peacenow.org/entries/price_tag_terrorism_crosses_the_green_line#.T_8ivXAVxNo (last visited July 12, 2012).

[85] Israel's most important newspaper.

[86] Ori Nir, *Price Tag*, 44 CASE W. RES. J. INT'L L. 277 (2012).

[87] *See* Saed Bannoura, *Israel Fails to Prosecute Soldiers, Settlers, Who Attack Palestinians*, UNHRC (Sept. 25, 2012), http://www.imemc.org/article/64290.

[88] Eyal Gross, *Security for Israeli Settlers, Not for Palestinians*, HAARETZ, May 28, 2012, http://www.haaretz.com/opinion/security-for-israeli-settlers-not-for-palestinians-1.433069.

[89] Hassidic Jewry was established in Eastern Europe.

Litai'im, broke away from Gur and its political party, Agudat Yisrael, and created two new political parties: SHAS, a Sephardic Orthodox party and Degel HaTorah, an Ashkenazi Orthodox party. These distinct communities have different beliefs and varying degrees of orthodoxy dedicated to ensuring supremacy of their particular rabbi and community.

Over the past decades the Orthodox population in Israel has significantly grown; in 1977 there were 6 Orthodox members of the Knesset (Parliament), in 2012 there are 16. Commensurate with an increase in political power is an increasing stridency and extremism that affects both the state and society.

The overwhelming majority of Orthodox Jews live in self-enclosed communities, often-times in poverty or near-poverty, in Israeli cities, including Jerusalem, Modi'in Illit, Bnei Brak, and Bet Shemesh.[90] As a result of political arrangements predicated on mutual convenience Israeli governments, whether Likud[91] or Labor,[92] have institutionalized an infrastructure whereby adult Orthodox males study religious text rather than contribute to the larger society. As suggested by an Israeli subject matter expert, the worldviews of Orthodox Jews and the majority of Israeli society are strikingly distinct; the phrase "we do not live in the State of Israel but rather in the Land of Israel" concisely summarizes the relationship between Orthodox Jewry and the rest of society.[93]

For the Orthodox Jew, the individual has no control over his destiny; all decisions are God's. Orthodox Jews are not burdened by the complicated dilemmas that confront Israeli society for they do not participate in the larger national debate. The primary interaction between the Orthodox community and the political system is ensuring continued government financial support of institutions essential to their way of life.

What has significantly contributed to a system whereby one sector in the Jewish population has a higher birth rate and whose contribution to the workforce is significantly less than the rest of society is a two-tiered social benefit system. In 1977, then Prime Minister Begin implemented significant welfare payments for large families;[94] this legislation directly contributed to a Haredi birth rate significantly higher than that of secular and religious nationalist Jews. In addition, the Haredi birth rate was higher than that of the non-Jewish population.[95] In addition to benefit payments for families, non-working males whose way of life dictates they study religious text rather than work receive monthly allowances from

---

[90] NACHMAN BEN-YEHUDA, THEOCRATIC DEMOCRACY: THE SOCIAL CONSTRUCTION OF RELIGIOUS AND SECULAR EXTREMISM (2010).

[91] Right-wing Israeli political party. It was founded in September 1973 to challenge the Israel Labour Party, which had governed the country since its independence in 1948, and first came to power in 1977.

[92] Israeli social-democratic political party founded in January 1968 in the union of three socialist-labour parties. It and its major component, Mapai, dominated Israel's government from the country's independence in 1948 until 1977, when the rival Likud coalition first came to power.

[93] Private conversation (notes in author's records).

[94] See what is known as the "Large Families Law."

[95] Israeli-Arabs compromise approximately 20 percent of the Israeli population. *See Latest Population Statistics for Israel*, JEWISH VIRTUAL LIB. (Sept. 2012), http://www.jewishvirtuallibrary.org/jsource/Society_&_Culture/newpop.html.

the government.[96] Orthodox Jews comprise 10 percent of the Israeli population[97] with a birth rate of 6.5[98] as compared to 2.7 for secular Israelis[99] and 4.5 for Israeli-Arabs,[100] and an employment rate significantly below that of secular,[101] Arab-Israelis,[102] and religious-nationalist Jews.[103]

Political considerations led Prime Minister Ben Gurion in 1948 to agree that Orthodox Jews receive deferments;[104] when that decision was made, much criticized today, there were 600 male draft-age Orthodox Jews (out of a population of 600,000), whereas today there are 63,000 (Jewish population of almost 6 million).[105] In order to create a mechanism whereby Orthodox Jews would be drafted into the IDF, then Prime Minister Ehud Barak (2001) convened the Tal Commission.[106] The commission's suggestion that Orthodox males receive a deferment until the age of 22, at which point they could decide whether to serve or learn,[107] was adopted into law (2002). However, the government subsequently admitted the law did not satisfactorily resolve the question of induction of Orthodox Jews; proponents cited the establishment of a religious brigade within the IDF[108] as an indicator of successful implementation.

Nevertheless, the Israel Supreme Court struck down the law; the President (akin to Chief Justice) of the Court, Dorit Beinisch, wrote, "The law, which has already been found in violation of the right to equality as part of the right to dignity, does not meet the proportionality standard and is therefore unconstitutional."[109] The Court gave the government until August 1, 2012 to resolve the issue; failure to do so would result in automatic induction of all Orthodox Jews, a measure Orthodox rabbis and political parties deeply resist and oppose (In large part, the issue, to date, has not been resolved. This assessment is relevant to the date September 29, 2013).

---

[96] *See generally* Yair Ettinger, *Israel to Defend Special Welfare Payments to Yeshiva Students before High Court*, HAARETZ (Nov. 13, 2012, 3:49 AM), http://www.haaretz.com/news/national/israel-to-defend-special-welfare-payments-to-yeshiva-students-before-high-court.premium-1.477280.

[97] *See generally* Aaron Heller, *Israeli Draft Pits Secular Jews vs. Ultra-Orthodox*, HUFFINGTON POST (July 7, 2012, 3:09 PM), http://www.huffingtonpost.com/2012/07/07/israeli-draft-pits-secular-orthodox-jews_n_1655909.html.

[98] A. Hleihel, *Fertility among Jewish and Muslim Women in Israel, by Level of Religiosity, 1979–2009* (2011). Working Paper Series, No. 60, Jerusalem: Israel Central Bureau of Statistics (in Hebrew).

[99] See facts and figures from Taub Center for Social Policy Studies in Israel (2009), *available at* http://taubcenter.org.il/.

[100] *Id.*

[101] *Id.*

[102] *Id.*

[103] *Id.*

[104] Ofer Aderet, *Battle over Haredi Draft Is Decades old*, HAARETZ, Nov. 7, 2012, http://www.haaretz.com/news/national/battle-over-haredi-draft-is-decades-old.premium-1.450291.

[105] Israeli Arabs are not drafted to the IDF but may volunteer to serve; according to a news report (July 8, 2012; Gali-Tzahal Radio) 2,400 Israeli Arabs volunteer (2012) as compared to 240 in 2006.

[106] Justice Zvi Tal sat on the Israeli Supreme Court.

[107] Orthodox Jews study religious text in yeshivot.

[108] Nahal Haredi.

[109] Aviad Glickman, *High Court Rules against Extending Tal Law*, YNET (Feb. 22, 2012, 12:53 AM), http://www.ynetnews.com/articles/0,7340,L-4193034,00.html.

A. ORTHODOX JEWRY AND WOMEN

Orthodox Jewry in Israel is, according to experts,[110] more extreme than in the past. Although a number of issues reflect the increasing extremism two examples will be highlighted: separation of men and women on public transportation and on sidewalks in religious neighborhoods. Religious texts do not justify either measure; rather, both are the result of Orthodox rabbis articulating extremist interpretation of religious text. Both result in sexual discrimination based on extremist interpretation of religious text that directly affects the rights and status of Orthodox women. The measures reflect a hardening of interpretation regarding gender and the status of women.

Although Orthodox Jewry, like other faiths, emphasizes modesty, there is a sharp distinction between clothing guidelines and clearly discriminatory measures against women. Measures directed at women reflect what has been described as a "new religion unrelated to traditional Judaism":[111] It is a religion where "kosher is not kosher enough,[112] conversions to Judaism can be annulled, traditional female modesty is insufficient, and separation of men and women is demanded with the exception of within the privacy of the home."[113] One commentator observed the extremism process reflects concern, if not fear, from the increasing liberalism of the outside world. In particular, the perception among Orthodox Jews is that secular Israelis are seeking to penetrate the closed community, particularly through the Internet.

In the context of this enhanced concern regarding external penetration strident extremism gains legitimacy. The guiding hand of a leading rabbinical authority responsible for the increasing extremism is, apparently, not to be found. Rather, the enhanced extremism is the result of local initiative that increasingly sets the tone in the Orthodox communities. One of the realities of enhanced extremism in a closed community is the inevitable "competition" with respect to articulating and implementing increasingly extreme measures. The move to separate women from men on public transportation, for instance, was not the result of a decision by a leading rabbi; rather it was, literally, a grassroots movement that snowballed and took on a life of its own.

In its ruling on the segregation of women and men on buses, the Israel Supreme Court sitting as the High Court of Justice held that coerced segregation is illegal. The passage below, directly citing the High Court of Justice, is admittedly long; however, this is necessary in order to fully appreciate the complexity and depth of the issue both legally and practically. From the tone and tenor of the ruling it is clear that the Supreme Court justices sought to convey not only their opposition predicated on the law to the

---

[110] Notes, names, emails, and records of interviews with subject matter experts in author's files.

[111] Private conversation (notes in author's records).

[112] In an increasing number of restaurants in Jerusalem, a "kosher" certificate is no longer sufficient; rabbinical authorities are demanding a "Glatt" kosher certificate, which is both more expensive and requires greater dietary supervision.

[113] Private conversation (notes in author's records).

discrimination but also their deep philosophical concern, if not outrage, regarding the separation of men and women. The ruling, then, must be understood not only as an important legal document but, perhaps, more as yellow—if not red—flag regarding the very nature of the relationship between Orthodox Jewry and the state. This opinion cannot be understood as just "another ruling" for its significance must be understood in the broader context.

The reference to Rosa Parks is a direct message to decision makers and the public regarding the insidiousness of the separation of sexes. Justice Rubenstein is clearly equating the discrimination against Israeli women with the institutionalized discrimination against African Americans that was the essence of the Deep South. The ruling, then, is a clarion call to recognize not only the broader cost of extremism but also perhaps more importantly the direct harm to individuals forced to pay the price of discrimination should society choose to tolerate unmitigated intolerance.

The Petition filed at the beginning of 2007, concerns bus lines…in which men and women were customarily separated. This is how the Petitioners described the prevailing reality:

"For approximately nine years, the public transportation companies…have been operating bus lines which are called "*mehadrin* lines" [literally: "meticulous," for orthodox or ultra-orthodox Jews who meticulously observe the religious laws]. On these lines…women are required to board by the rear door and to sit in the back of the bus, whereas men board by the front door and sit in the front seats. In addition, the women passengers are required to dress modestly…Women who do not resign themselves to these coercive arrangements and attempt to oppose them…are humiliated and suffer severe verbal harassment, are made to leave the bus and are even threatened with physical violence."

The Petitioners argued that these arrangements violate the principle of equality, the constitutional right to dignity, and freedom of religion and conscience—and that they are employed with no authority under the law. In effect, after four years of litigation (reviewed below), no one today can dispute that the coercive, dictated reality described above is illegal.[114]

In the words of Justice Rubenstein:

To clarify the situation for anyone to whom the above statement is not clear, we will state: a public transportation operator—like any other entity under the law—is not entitled to tell, ask or instruct women where they should sit on a bus merely because they are women, or what they should wear, and they are entitled to sit anywhere

---

[114] HCJ 746/07 Naomi Ragen v. Ministry of Transportation, http://elyon1.court.gov.il/files_eng/07/460/007/t38/07007460.t38.htm (last visted Aug. 17, 2013).

they wish. Naturally, the same applies to men; however, for reasons that are not hard to understand, all the complaints refer to an insulting attitude toward women. When I go back and read the lines that were just emphasized above, I am amazed that it should have been necessary to write them in Israel in 2010. Have we gone back to the days of Rosa Parks, the African American woman who, in refusing to give up her bus seat for a white passenger in 1955, helped to end racial segregation on buses in Alabama, United States, in 1955?[115]

Is it really even necessary to state that it is forbidden to coerce or order a woman to sit in the back rows on the bus…? Is it really necessary to state that men who harass a woman who sits outside the intended area…thereby commit a forbidden act and are liable to criminal prosecution? Does not any rational person, whether secular, religious, or Haredi, understand this without explanation?[116] [all emphases in the original]

The description below best illustrates both the reality and impact of gender segregation based on religious extremism:

Must it really be said that an attack by men on a woman who deviated from the designated female seating area (as described in some of the affidavits that were filed) is prohibited, and is likely to lead to an action in criminal court? Is this not understood and self-evident to every decent person—secular, religious or ultra-Orthodox? In one of the affidavits that were appended to the Petition, the following description (with reference to 2004) appears:

The bus was completely empty of passengers. I chose to sit on a single seat at the front of the bus. When the bus began to fill up, several ultra-Orthodox men suddenly came up to me and insistently demanded that I get up from my seat and move to the back of the bus. I was utterly horrified. I answered that I did not see rules anywhere with regard to such an arrangement on the bus…

I was subjected to an incessant attack of verbal insults and physical threats; a large ultra-Orthodox man leaned over me and berated me quite loudly throughout the entire trip. Through all that time, the driver did not intervene…I felt as if I had been subjected to "psychological stoning", although I had not done anything wrong (affidavit by Petitioner 1).

Woe to the ears that hear this! And where is human dignity, "which supersedes [even] a Torah (Biblical) prohibition" (Babylonian Talmud, Brakhot, 19b). Can anyone say that this event was reasonable? In another affidavit, which refers to 2006, a National Servicewoman describes how, when traveling very late at night

---

[115] *Id.*

[116] *Id.*

(the bus left Jerusalem for Ofakim after 11:00 p.m.), she did not object to separating from her [male] traveling companion and sitting in the back rows. Nonetheless:

From where I was sitting in the back, I noticed one of the passengers speaking to the driver, and after that, an uproar began next to the driver...I understood that, as a woman, I was forbidden to approach the front of the bus myself. I called my partner, who was sitting in the front of the bus, on my mobile phone...My partner explained to me that passengers had spoken to the driver about how I was dressed. I should add that I was wearing a long-sleeved shirt and a skirt which came to just above the knees.

The uproar did not quiet down, and the driver turned to my partner and demanded that we get off the bus in the middle of the road, in the dead of night, "to avoid problems," in his words. Only after my partner passed me a long shirt, with which I was forced to cover my legs, did the uproar quiet down...The driver answered that this was Egged's declared policy and that no one may board the *"mehadrin* lines" in immodest attire (affidavit by Petitioner 2; emphases added—E.R.).

Even if we ignore the very fact of the gender separation, to which the female passenger was "resigned," can we resign ourselves, in Israel in 2010, to the sentence "I understood that, as a woman, I was forbidden to approach the front of the bus myself"? Or to a driver who wants—Heaven help us—to make passengers get off the bus in the middle of the road, in the dead of night, because he claims that the girl's attire does not comply with Egged's modesty rules? I would not like to think that money—the wish to profit by operating the lines in question—would mean everything; the sages have already said "The Lord said, 'The cry of Sodom and Gomorrah is great'—on account of the maiden" (Sanhedrin 109b). Another affidavit stated that even the Petitioner's proposal to cover her bare shoulders with additional clothing was not accepted by the passengers and the driver, and she was not allowed to board the bus (affidavit by Petitioner 5). Again: what about human dignity?".[117] [except as otherwise noted, all emphases in original]

With respect to the increasing extremism in the Orthodox community Justice Rubenstein wrote:

It should also be noted that the phenomenon of *"mehadrin* lines" has not always existed...buses was mixed, even in places where the population was largely ultra-Orthodox, such as Jerusalem and Bnei Brak. This is, therefore, a recent phenomenon...It is possible—as has been proposed in various articles—that this is part of a process of radicalization in ultra-Orthodox society.[118]

---

[117] *Id.*
[118] *Id.*

As reported in the Israel Action Research Institute annual report, segregation is not limited to public transportation; the report highlights gender segregation at funerals, government offices, health clinics, and sidewalks. As Justice Rubenstein noted these examples highlight a process best described as radicalization in the Orthodox community; the radicalization, which is devoid of a guiding hand has the practical import of discriminating against women in the name of religion. The lack of a guiding hand, however, does not diminish from the significance of the measures; in the name of religious extremism the community to which they belong actively discriminates against women. What is particularly troubling is the willingness of state officials to abide with extremism-based gender discrimination. The following example of how one community[119] in Israel celebrated the Jewish holiday of Simhat Torah is instructive:

> During the Simchat Torah celebrations in Mevasseret Zion at the end of the festival of Sukkot in 2011, which were sponsored by the local council, those present were asked to separate into two groups, one for men and one for women. Dozens of local residents left the event in protest. In a report on the event published in the local newspaper Kol Ha'ir on October 28, 2011, Mr. Arye Shamam, the head of the local council, was quoted as saying: "Even in a secular Jewish community, most of the population observe the religious laws in accordance with the accepted Orthodox practices, including the segregation of men and women in areas where Torah scrolls and rabbis are present. Since this was a religious event and we wanted the rabbis to participate, the approach I instructed was to enable everyone to live in peace with each other, so that those who wished to be in a segregated area had that opportunity. The segregation of women and men was only implemented in a small area where the Torah scrolls and rabbis were present, while the rest of the compound where the event took place had a mixed crowd for the enjoyment of those celebrating".[120]

With respect to segregated sidewalks:

> Ahead of the festival of Sukkot in 2011, posters were displayed around Jerusalem urging women not to enter Mea She'arim Street during the water libation celebrations, which form part of the festival. The announcement asked women to use alternative routes (such as Shivtei Israel Street) in order to reach their homes, "and thereby help avoid mingling." Reports on this subject in Haaretz and on the Kikar Hashabbat website noted that the Toldot Aharon Hassidic sect was spending a

---

[119] In the name of full disclosure, I reside in the referenced community, Mevassert Zion; although my family did not attend the event there is little doubt we would have, along with others, walked out.

[120] *Ragen, supra* note 114, at 38.

large amount of money in order to hire stewards who would be stationed on the streets in order to enforce the segregation and in order to install partitions.

Following the publication of the announcements, we met with Commissioner Niso Shaham, commander of the Jerusalem District Police, with the goal of preventing illegal segregation on the streets of Mea She'arim during the festival. At the meeting, we were informed that Toldot Aharon Yeshiva would only be permitted to install a partition fence in the area within 15 meters from the entrance to the yeshiva.

Jerusalem city councilor Rachel Azaria petitioned the Supreme Court against the imposition of segregation in the area around Toldot Aharon Yeshiva. Responding to the petition, the justices noted with displeasure that the previous ruling of the Supreme Court regarding segregated sidewalks had not been enforced. The district police commander undertook in court not to permit the installation of fences in the streets of Mea She'arim without permits; if fences were established, they would not be covered with jute. Segregation actions, including the presence of stewards, would be ended immediately, and a police liaison would be appointed to receive and coordinate public complaints on the subject. The justices noted the trend toward increasingly extreme patterns of gender segregation, and determined that this injures the residents of the neighborhood and constitutes the injurious domination of the residents by a minority in the neighborhood.[121]

According to the Israel Research Action Center Annual Report (2011):

In last year's report, (2010, ANG) we noted that almost all the demands for segregation are manifested in an effort to push women to the back, physically and figuratively. This underlines the origins of such demands in patriarchal approaches that seek to perpetuate a gender-based hierarchy. Last year, most of the demands for segregation involved situations where men occupied the front section of public space, while women were relegated to the rear. In this report, however, there are also many instances in which women are completely excluded from public space, or an entirely separate space is created for them, silencing their voice. The trend to silence women's public voice attracted considerable public attention, particularly in such contexts as the deliberate exclusion of women from public billboards in Jerusalem, and incidents when religious soldiers refused to participate in army events that included singing by women performers.

The trend toward the exclusion of women from public space is also manifested in efforts to conceal or subdue their visibility. The demand for modest dress, which was previously confined to the places of residence and meeting places of specific

---

[121] *Id.* at 35.

religious groups, is now spreading into the general public domain; where such demands were already present, they are becoming increasingly extreme. By way of example, it was recently reported that a special "modesty certificate" has been introduced for shops in the town of Sderot. The certificate is awarded to businesses that undertake to ensure that their employees are dressed modestly and that their advertisements maintain similar standards. In Beit Shemesh, which has become a benchmark for extremism in the exclusion of women, shops have been forbidden to display immodest clothes in their windows, red clothing has been outlawed, and numerous incidents have been reported in which violence has been used to enforce modesty rules and gender segregation.[122]

V. United Kingdom

Analyzing extremism in the United Kingdom requires determining whether the focus will be on "The Troubles" in Northern Ireland or examining more current tensions. A number of conversations led to my decision to focus on the latter and leave the former to others. To that end, a week-long visit to London focused on Islamic extremism and right-wing extremism. Meetings and interviews I conducted focused on both; discussions highlighted differences and similarities alike. Subject matter experts included academics, journalists, politicians, senior law enforcement and security officials, extremists, policy experts focusing on both forms of extremism, and practicing attorneys.

A previous visit to London[123] had been disconcerting; as I noted in *Freedom from Religion*:

> I ended the trip with the troubling impression that British lawmakers were deliberately ignoring a serious problem confronting not only their own country, but democracies around the globe....For one reason or another, the British government is not willing to acknowledge the reality of religious extremism in its country, and is often willing to go to great lengths to paint the problem in a different light...The attitude of an unwillingness to lay blame is similarly reflected in the British media...Some of the individuals I spoke to went even further, claiming that the true danger to the United Kingdom was not the threat posed by religious extremists, but the potential harm to British society that were to result were the government to emphasize the Islamic nature of religious terrorism.[124]

My trip coincided with intensive pre-Olympic planning by UK authorities; while I was in London the stunning incompetence of the private UK security company, G4S,

---

[122] *Available at* http://www.irac.org.il/UserFiles/File/%2005.pdf (in Hebrew) (last visited Aug. 17, 2013).

[123] December 2009 when researching *Freedom from Religion*.

[124] Amos Guiora, Freedom from Religion: *rights and national security* 2–3 (2009).

hired to provide security during the Olympics, was the subject of heated discussion in Parliament.[125] The suicide bombing in Burgas, Bulgaria (July 18, 2012) highlighted the vulnerability of tourist buses. In the aftermath of the attack, "MI5 and New Scotland Yard are reportedly thought to have raised their threat assessment in light of the terrorist attack in Bulgaria on Wednesday that killed 5 Israelis, the bus driver and a suicide bomber. In addition, the Sunday Times reports, the Israeli government has dispatched agents from the Shin Bet and Mossad to protect its 38-strong delegation."[126] Perhaps reflecting a confluence of the two events, particularly security concerns relevant to the Olympics, conversations with subject matter experts suggested somber and sober recognition of the threats posed by extremists.

An earlier assessment by Scotland Yard Deputy Assistant Commissioner that "'Islamic and terrorist are two words that do not go together'"[127] was replaced by analysis reflecting concern regarding homegrown terrorism, particularly acts committed by Islamic extremists. In addition, concern was expressed regarding the English Defense League, particularly with respect to an attack similar to Breivik's. In that vein, security officials and policy experts were largely unanimous in their assessment that the most pressing danger was posed by a "lone wolf," particularly an Islamic extremist. In discussing the threat posed by "lone wolves" unanimity was voiced regarding their intent, but questions were raised regarding their capability.[128]

With respect to dangers posed by lone wolves, security officials were candid in their assessment that significant deficiencies exist regarding intelligence monitoring, gathering, and surveillance. Subject matter experts, security officials, and policy analysts alike were unanimous in dismissing dangers posed by external threats. Although my predetermined emphasis was on extreme right-wing extremism, senior security officials with whom I met emphasized Islamic extremism poses the gravest threat facing the United Kingdom.

That is, although concern was expressed regarding extreme right-wing movements[129] the threat posed by such groups does not reach the level of Islamic extremism. British subject matter experts stressed that UK Moslem extremists are primarily interested in advancing a three-part agenda: creating an Islamic world government, establishing sharia in non-Moslem majority countries (such as the United Kingdom), and imposing

---

[125] Richard Allen Greene, *Olympics Security Failure Is "Humiliating Shambles," Boss Concedes*, CNN (July 17, 2012), http://edition.cnn.com/2012/07/17/sport/olympics-security/index.html.

[126] *Report: Israel Fears Iranian Terror Attack at London Olympics*, HAARETZ (July 22, 2012, 8:31 AM), http://www.haaretz.com/news/diplomacy-defense/report-israel-fears-iranian-terror-attack-at-london-2012-olympics-1.452699.

[127] GUIORA, *supra* note 124, at 2.

[128] For material on Lone Wolves, see http://www.lonewolfproject.org.uk/resources/LW-complete-final.pdf (last visited Aug. 12, 2012). Violent actions/terrorism: see [Lone Wolf report that lays out in documented fashion violent acts committed by far-right extremists *and* raises important question whether Lone Wolves] really are lone wolves.

[129] All the groups.

sanctions against Western armed forces in the Middle East. With respect to extreme right-wing groups, subject matter experts emphasized two points in particular: a powerful combination of xenophobic nationalism and support for the welfare state but not for immigrants.

In 1999 a young white man named David Copeland set off three nailbombs, in one week, in the heart of London's black community (Brixton), Bangladeshi community (Brick Lane), and gay community (Soho) killing 3 people and wounding 165. Copeland was a former member of the British National Party who migrated to a more extreme neo-Nazi organization that was an offshoot of a group calling itself Combat 18 (the 1 and 8 representing the numerical position of "A" and "H" for Adolf Hitler).[130]

According to experts I interviewed, the law enforcement and national security officials are allocating significant resources and energies to minimize the threat posed by both groups with the understanding that extreme right-wing groups have not committed acts of terrorism on the scale of Islamic extremists. Security officials and other subject matter experts repeatedly commented that terrorist acts in the United Kingdom were committed either by British citizens or individuals residing in the United Kingdom. Although the importance of external influence was recognized, outsiders did not commit the acts themselves. Subject matter experts, security officials, and policy analysts alike were unanimous in dismissing dangers posed by external threats.

A. RIGHT-WING EXTREMISM

The English Defense League (EDL) is a working class, blue-collar group largely comprised of adult white males opposed to immigration, as they are fearful of losing their jobs in the broader context of an economic downturn. Similar to other extreme right-wing groups in Europe, the EDL articulate three guiding principles: the recognition that Europe is under attack from immigrants; the need to reclaim our streets from immigrants, and the obligation to protect our values. With deep roots in the football hooliganism that previously plagued the United Kingdom, the EDL has engaged in violent behavior, particularly against Islamic women and at demonstrations.

The EDL was largely created in response to a march organized by the extremist Islamic group "Ahle Sunnah al Jamah—a splinter group from the banned extremist group

---

[130] He joined the far-right British National Party in May 1997, at the age of 21. He acted as a steward at a BNP meeting, in the course of which he came into contact with the BNP leadership and was photographed standing next to John Tyndall, then leader. It was during this period that Copeland read *The Turner Diaries*, and first learned how to make bombs using fireworks with alarm clocks as timers, after downloading a so-called terrorists' handbook from the Web. He left the BNP in 1998, regarding it as not hardline enough because it was not willing to engage in paramilitary action, and joined the smaller National Socialist Movement, becoming its regional leader for Hampshire just weeks before the start of his bombing campaign. It was around this time that he visited his family doctor and was prescribed antidepressants after telling the doctor he felt he was losing his mind.

al-Muhajiroun"[131] that demonstrated against British soldiers returning from Afghanistan at a homecoming parade in Luton.[132] In the aftermath of the Luton parade the group promised further marches against British soldiers returning from Afghanistan.

Unlike the BNP, the EDL is not a political party; rather it identifies itself as a movement that expresses working class anger. Furthermore, the EDL seeks to distinguish itself from the BNP that is perceived as racist, anti-Semitic, and fascist with clear Nazi undertones. Although the BNP does not enjoy electoral success in British parliamentary elections[133] the British right has performed well in European Parliament elections.[134] The EDL does not have an ideologue akin to Peder Are Nøstvold Jensen who writes under the penname "Fjordman" and was widely quoted in Breivik's manifesto.[135] Perhaps for that reason, the EDL is perceived as "negative" as it is not focused on building but rather restricts its activities to espousing English values and solidarity predicated on opposition to immigration.[136] To that end, the EDL advocates both limits on immigration and imposition of language requirements as a condition for receiving citizenship.

The sentiment that "England has been taken from me without my consent" is a powerful slogan for the extreme right wing; it was a refrain I heard in Holland and Norway expressing, in essence, dismay at and opposition to immigrants. In emphasizing the centrality of British values the EDL highlights dangers posed by the other strengthened by people in position of power enabling the taking of England. In that vein, working class antipathy for former UK prime minister Tony Blair was repeatedly mentioned as illustrative in understanding the resentment toward a public leader identified with multiculturalism.[137]

In opposing—perhaps resenting—expressions of Islamic identity, the EDL demands to know whether individuals are Moslems or Brits.[138] In asking this question the subtext

---

[131] Matthew Taylor, Jenny Percival & Vikram Dodd, *Muslim Group Pledges More Protests against UK Soldiers*, GUARDIAN (Mar. 11, 2009, 1:26 PM), http://www.guardian.co.uk/uk/2009/mar/11/muslim-group-anti-war-protests.

[132] Micheal Holden, *Anti-Islamist Protest Group to Form a Freedom Party in Britain*, REUTERS (Mar. 24, 2012), http://blogs.reuters.com/faithworld/2012/03/24/anti-islamist-protest-group-to-form-a-freedom-party-in-britain/. Luton is of particular importance and concern: it is a divided city between Moslems and white working class, and the possibility of further violence has been raised in the context of a tinderbox effect.

[133] For a UK Parliament Party breakdown see http://www.londonelects.org.uk/im-voter/results-and-past-elections/results-2012.

[134] With respect to poor election in UK elections, it was suggested that the cause is powerful antiracist movements/trends in the United Kingdom and because of a poor TV appearance by the party's then leader (Griffin).

[135] Breivik's Manifesto, *supra* note 30.

[136] As was repeatedly reinforced in conversations in Norway, Holland, and the United Kingdom the phrase "anti-immigrant" is code for "anti-Islam" as those opposed to immigration are, consistently, focused on Moslem immigrants whether from Turkey, Morocco, or Pakistan.

[137] With respect to multiculturalism a comment repeatedly mentioned was that the British government wasted resources without knowing the context of specific groups.

[138] DARREN MULLOY, AMERICAN EXTREMISM: HISTORY, POLITICS AND THE MILITIA MOVEMENT (2004). States that membership is typically of the lower educated.

is a loyalty check focusing on overt expressions of religiosity, particularly Islam. There is, of course, an additional implied subtext: immigrants, in the guise of extremism, are detrimental to society though their mere thoughts may not lead to terrorism. However, a public opinion poll indicated that British Moslems are the most patriotic British citizens as 81 percent feel themselves British first and Moslem second; this is in comparison to France where 46 percent of French Moslems feel themselves French first and Moslem second.[139]

B. THE ISLAMIC COMMUNITY

According to subject matter experts whose research focuses on the Islamic community,[140] Islamic extremists conduct their recruiting efforts away from the mainstream Islamic community. Unlike in the past, imams are not the focal point either of recruitment or radicalization. Imams are not engaged in recruitment extremists, and only a small minority is considered extremist. In conducting recruiting efforts outside the traditional mosque structure, extremists focus on the grassroots level outside the traditional community. Regarding imams, the working assumption among experts is that Western-educated imams will emphasize tolerance regarding Western culture and values, unlike those educated in North Africa or the Middle East.

Not dissimilar to recruiting efforts in other countries, recruiters focus their efforts on the following:

1) Individuals already involved in low-level street crime;
2) Individuals whose home-life is perceived to be dysfunctional;
3) Individuals with an understanding that religion provides redemption who are susceptible to conviction that violence is legitimate;
4) Individuals not previously involved in violence who are recruited to an idea rather than to action; unlike the three categories above this category focuses on individuals, particularly those exploring their identity, attracted to an idea;
5) Two convenient recruiting tools are the Rushdie affair[1] and the Srebrenica massacre;
6) Important to note the first three categories target individuals identified as having low self-esteem and therefore perceived as vulnerable, searching for a sense of identity, attracted to martyrdom; in all four categories above economic circumstances are deemed by subject matter experts as irrelevant to the recruiting process.

---

[139] Johnathan Paris, *Europe and Its Muslims*, FOREIGN AFFAIRS (Feb. 2007), http://www.foreignaffairs.com/articles/62281/jonathan-paris/europe-and-its-muslims.

[140] Conversations on this issue were conducted with law enforcement officials, politicians, and policy experts, including members of the Moslem community (all notes in author's records).

Young radicalized Moslems do not view their parents' Islam as legitimate primarily because it is rooted in Pakistani culture and therefore contaminated by the very culture they left. In that vein, the second and third generation challenges their parents through enhanced faith, with particular emphasis on the hijab[141] and niqab;[142] for the younger generation the niqab is viewed as manifesting extreme rejection of Western society. In that context, parents are perceived as having an ethnic, rather than religious, identity; the niqab is perceived as reflecting an extreme act of devotion that distinguishes the generations.

Subject matter experts repeatedly emphasized that recruiters, in focusing on action, engage in little instruction regarding faith-based issues (in contrast to the fourth category above), stressing rote learning not predicated on textual reasoning or analysis. In numerous conversations, the terrorist attack on July 7, 2005 was mentioned as a significant "wake-up" call for the British Moslem community. The coordinated attack targeting civilians using London's public transport system killed 52 individuals and wounded over 700.[143]

The challenge confronting UK law enforcement officials, similar to that faced by their counterparts elsewhere, is determining when does extremism become a risk; rearticulated: when does extremism in thought merge into extremism in action? To coin a phrase, determining when extremism violence replaces nonviolent radicalism is the challenge confronting law enforcement officials. That challenge is relevant to both right-wing extremists and Moslem extremists; although the two groups have distinct motivations, similarities are inevitable and reflect the commonality of extremists, regardless of their circumstances and conditions.

---

[141] *Hijab* in Arabic means "to cover" and is generally translated as "veil." Commonly worn today by Muslim women, the veil is a hair covering or scarf that covers the head, but *hijab* also refers to modest dress and seclusion—the system of separating women from men. *See* Michelle MacNeill, *The Practice of Veiling* 101 (June 5, 2009), http://suite101.com/article/the-practice-of-veiling-a123005.

[142] Supporters of banning the full face cover emphasize it is a public safety measure, citing that criminals and Islamic terrorists have taken advantage of wearing the burqa to conceal their identities. They wish to ban all face-covering masks in public places, including burqas. In 1975, a number of European towns banned the wearing of ski masks and motorcycle helmets in public, specifically because they covered the face, and so posed a security and crime risk. The same logic applies to the burqa. So, the ban on the burqa and niqab should be considered part of a broader ban on all face-covering masks in public, particularly in and around crowded areas and in public transportation. The niqab is the face veil worn by Islamic women.

[143] *See Report of the Official Account of the Bombings in London 7th July 2005*, HOUSE OF COMMONS, *available at* http://www.fas.org/irp/world/uk/7-july-report.pdf (last visited Jan. 12, 2013).

7

THE POWER OF "HATE SPEECH" AND WHAT, IF ANY, LIMITS SHOULD BE IMPOSED ON FREE SPEECH IN THE CONTEXT OF EXTREMISM

I. Israel

Approaching how to present this chapter to the reader weighed heavily on my mind at three different times: when developing the project proposal, when conducting in-country research, and when researching the specific topic of free speech. A word of background is essential to understanding the approach I ultimately chose: my introduction to the extraordinary tension between free speech and incitement was as an Israeli citizen, watching, deeply concerned, as the religious and political right-wing engaged in vitriolic incitement against Prime Minister Rabin.

It is for that reason, then, that I have chosen to begin this chapter with a practical discussion regarding the tension between free speech and the price paid for that right. In doing so, I hope to present the reader with the realities of the free speech dilemma; the discussion, with respect to Israel, is not abstract, for a terrible price was paid for tolerating incitement and intolerance. That is, both mainstream society and state agents—acting in accordance with the law but failing to either robustly enforce existing law or legislate laws in response to clear and present threats—respected the rights of those openly, constantly, and loudly inciting against Prime Minister Rabin, calling him "traitor" and "murderer."

The inciters were, primarily, right-wing rabbis deeply opposed to the Oslo Peace Process. The incitement was unrelenting and was clearly a clarion call for someone to do something. The rabbis were inciting with a keen understanding of their audience: right-wing religious nationalists deeply opposed to Rabin and his polices. The incitement against Rabin represents the danger posed when a perfect confluence exists between speaker and audience; the speaker (rabbis) knew his audience (right-wing religious nationalists) extremely well, and the audience (Amir) knew what the speakers expected of him. While the rabbis directly incited, politicians emboldened the vitriol against Rabin by participating in hate-filled demonstrations and rallies. Although those demonstrations and rallies were not illegal they, undoubtedly, directly contributed to the pre-assassination hate-filled environment. The participation by leading members of the opposition party (Likud) was in full accordance with the law. Nevertheless, the presence of highly respected politicians emboldened speakers and audience alike by lending the incitement credibility and legitimacy. In the free speech/incitement dilemma the importance of legitimizing unmitigated hate speech cannot be minimized.[1]

The Rabin assassination, then, represents a paradigm consisting of four actors: inciters (rabbis), audience-actors, emboldeners (politicians), and state agents (charged with legislating and enforcing legislation).

Could the assassination have occurred without politicians emboldening the incitement? Probably yes; nevertheless, by openly participating in hate-filled demonstrations the politicians legitimized rabbinical incitement. Although not a crime in accordance with the Israeli penal code, it raises profound questions regarding moral responsibility for the assassination.

Distinctions are critical: to that end, distinguishing between actions of the four politicians listed above and the rabbis who incited against Rabin is important.[2] That distinction is not intended to minimize the actions of the politicians but rather to distinguish between political discourse and words that directly contributed to Rabin's assassination.

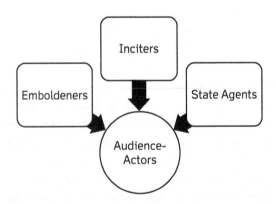

---

[1] Rabin's wife, Leah, refused to shake then Member of Knesset Netanyahu's hand at the funeral. *See* Naomi Segal, *Leah Rabin Dead at 72*, JTA (Nov. 13, 2000), http://www.jta.org/news/article/2000/11/13/6368/LeahRabindeadat7

[2] *See* Allan C. Brownfeld's review of *Murder in the Name of God: Where Religious Extremism Can Lead* by Michael Karpin and Ina Friedman, http://www.acjna.org/acjna/articles_detail.aspx?id=117 (last visited Jan. 10, 2013).

For two years prior to the assassination, extreme right-wing rabbis issued a variety of proclamations regarding him. Rabbi Shmuel Dvir, a teacher at the Har Etzion Yeshiva, told his students that it was "definitely permissible to kill Rabin under the provision of *din rodef.*"[3] *Din rodef* is the duty of a Jew to kill a Jew who imperils the life or property of another Jew.[4] Dvir even boasted to one of his students, "If Rabin comes to visit Gush Etzion, I myself will climb on a roof and shoot him with a rifle."[5]

The International Rabbinical Coalition for Israel, an organization of Orthodox rabbis, declared Rabin a *rodef,* a Jew who deserved to be killed because he imperiled the life or property of another Jew.[6] The ultra-Orthodox weekly paper, *Hashavna,* published a symposium issue addressing not only whether Rabin should be executed, but the most appropriate method to carry out the killing.[7] These are but a few of the examples of the extremist religious speech that directly encouraged violence against Rabin. In the run-up to Rabin's assassination, *pulsa denura* was issued against him—a call to kill the prime minister because of his decision to pursue the Oslo peace process.[8] The *pulsa denura,* translated as "lashes of fire," has long been a tradition of Kabbalah, a sect within Judaism. On the eve of Yom Kippur in 1995, rabbis gathered on the sidewalk in front of Rabin's home after midnight to recite the ancient execration of *pulsa denura.* These 10 rabbis were disciples of the late Rabbi Meir Kahane. Avigdor Eskin,[9] the group's leader, intoned, "I deliver to you, angel of wrath and ire, Yitzhak, the son of Rosa Rabin, that you may smother him and the specter of him, and cast him into bed, and dry up his wealth, and plague his thoughts, and scatter his mind that he may steadily diminish until he reaches his death."[10] As Eskin chanted, the other rabbis joined in, saying, "Put to death the cursed Yitzhak, son of Rosa Rabin, as quickly as possible because of his hatred for the Chosen People."[11] The ceremony came to an end with Eskin shouting, "May you be damned, damned, damned!"[12]

---

[3] Allan C. Brownfeld, *Israel: A Sharply Divided Society on the Brink of a Cultural Civil War,* WASH. REPORT ON Middle East Affairs, (July/August 1999), available at www.wrmea.com/backissues/0799/9907086.html.

[4] Allan C. Brownfeld, Growth of Religious Extremism in Israel Threatens the Peace Process, Wash. Report on Middle East Affairs (Aug./Sept. 2000), available at http://www.washington-report.org/archives/Aug_Sept_2000/0010072.html.

[5] Id.

[6] Brownfeld, supra note 2.

[7] Hashavna (The Weekly), Nov. 3, 1995.

[8] The former President (Chief Justice) of the Israeli Supreme Court, Aharon Barak, was also threatened with a pulsa denura; a police investigation determined that the threatening phone calls came from a yeshiva in the Haredi neighborhood, in Jerusalem, Mea She'arim; see Nachman Ben-Yehuda, Theocratic Democracy: The Social Construction of Religious and Secular Extremism 78 (2010).

[9] Eskin was subsequently convicted for violating Israel's terrorist law for organizing the pulsa denura ceremony. *See A Curse Is Ruled Terrorism,* N.Y. TIMES, July 21, 1997, http://www.nytimes.com/1997/07/21/world/a-curse-is-ruled-terrorism.html.

[10] MICHAEL KARPIN & INA FRIEDMAN, MURDER IN THE NAME OF GOD: THE PLOT TO KILL YITZHAK RABIN 90–91 (1998).

[11] *Id.*

[12] Zion Zohar, *Pulsa De-Nura: The Innovation of Modern Magic and Ritual,* 27 MODERN JUDAISM 1, 72 (2007).

The hatred in the streets culminating in the assassination on November 5, 1995, then, serves as a powerful background to free speech and incitement. Although I was critical of Rabin on occasion, his assassination has served, for me, as a powerful reminder of the power of the word; Rabin's murder dramatically manifests that words kill.

II. Background Information

Given the above, the question was how to address the question of free speech and incitement. I have chosen the following path: a brief recounting of the dramatic events of September 2012 in the Middle East in the aftermath (not necessarily in response) to the video *Innocence of Muslims* and the cartoon depiction of the Prophet Mohammed in the French magazine, *Charlie Hebdo*; brief analysis of the writings of Thomas Hobbes, John Locke, Voltaire, John Stuart Mill, Ronald Dworkin, Jeremy Waldron, and John Rawls; an in-depth discussion of the history of free speech in the United States; and a brief discussion of free speech in the United Kingdom, Holland, and Norway.

Much of the discussion regarding free speech/hate speech and what limits, if any, should be placed depends on the relationship between the speaker and the audience. Although there is nothing particularly original in highlighting this relationship the profound impact of social media and its extraordinary ability to disseminate speech at, literally, the sound of speed is a significant game changer. The traditional speech paradigm of major TV networks, newspaper dailies, and mainstream radio gave way to cable TV, largely replaced by the Internet, blogs, Twitter, and Facebook. As repeatedly demonstrated the power of YouTube significantly surpasses the impact of traditional media.

Accordingly, in analyzing the limits of free speech it is essential to appreciate a fundamental shift in the manner in which speech is expressed and received. The events of the Arab Spring[13] demonstrated the ability of social media to impact, if not facilitate, political developments of historic proportions. Decision-makers, clearly caught flatfooted, were remarkably disengaged from the challenges posed by this new reality. It is as if the New World had arrived under their noses, much to their total surprise.

This extraordinary shift in how speech is disseminated is essential to the discussion in the coming pages; the speed with which speech goes viral represents the future and must be understood in that vein. There is little doubt social media is essential to extremists; it significantly enhances the reach of their message and the manner in which target audiences (whether existing or future) receive the message. As has been repeatedly evident, extremists understand this new reality; the question is whether the learning curve of decision makers will reflect dexterity or clumsiness. With that, we turn our attention to the question of free speech and whether and when it should be limited when exercised by extremists. A caveat is

---

[13] For a general history and background on the Arab Spring, see *Arab Spring: A Research & Study Guide*, CORNELL UNIV. *available at* http://guides.library.cornell.edu/content.php?pid=259276&sid=2159754 (last visited Jan 11, 2013).

in order: focusing on the inciter of extremism is not intended to excuse the actor; it is, however, intended to highlight the power of speech and the repercussions of speech that falls on willing ears, resulting in harmful conduct.

III. September 2012

Free speech is an inherently complex topic whose intensity is, literally, breathtaking. The intensity is both in the abstract given the legal and philosophical nature of the discussion, and in the practical given violent responses, worldwide, to perceived insults to faith, based on videos and cartoons. The events in the Middle East (September 2012) in, *perhaps*, response to the video movie *Innocence of Muslims*[14] highlighted the tensions germane to hate speech and free speech.[15] The caveats are deliberate as it is unclear to what extent the video *actually* precipitated the demonstrations or whether the events reflected a coordinated terrorist attack. It is an open question whether those demonstrating actually viewed the video or were responding to calls by extremist inciters seizing an opportunity for political and other purposes.[16] As a result of the riots at least 30 people were killed.[17]

Shortly after the video came to public attention the French satire magazine, *Charlie Hebdo*, published cartoons mocking the Prophet Mohammed. In anticipation of violent responses, the French government ordered the closing of French embassies and schools.[18] Ironically, the same week that the cartoon was published, Salman Rushdie's autobiography, *Joseph Anton*, was also published.[19] Rushdie is, after all, the classic victim of the hate speech/free speech debate; although physical harm never befell him, the fatwa issued by the Ayatollah Khomeini drove Rushdie to living in hiding for over a decade. Similar to rioters in the Middle East ostensibly reacting to *Innocence of Muslims*, it is highly unlikely that Khomeini read *The Satanic Verses* before condemning Rushdie to death. Nevertheless, what is important—for our purposes—is the combustible confluence between hate speech, free speech, and incitement. Significantly complicating an already volatile convergence are two additional factors: opportunists seeking to take advantage,

---

[14] Sam Bacile, *Innocence of Muslims*, YouTube (Sept. 16, 2012), http://www.youtube.com/watch?v=6ySE-yYeelE.

[15] For discussion regarding the video see Kent Greenfield, *Is the Anti-Muhammad Film Constitutionally Unprotected "Fighting Words"?*, Huffington Post, Sept. 18, 2012, http://www.huffingtonpost.com/kent-greenfield/is-the-antimuhammad-film-_b_1891345.html?utm_hp_ref=politics.

[16] Bounty placed on video producer by Pakistani Minister of Railroads. *See Pakistan Condemns Bounty Offer on Film-Maker*, AlJazeera (Sept. 23, 2012), http://www.aljazeera.com/news/africa/2012/09/20129221691928921717.html.

[17] *French Cartoons Fuel Prophet Film Tensions*, Daily Star (Sept. 20, 2012, 1:42 AM), http://www.dailystar.com.lb/News/Middle-East/2012/Sep-20/188633-french-cartoons-fuel-prophet-film-tensions.ashx#axzz270UPOWfT.

[18] Kim Willsher, *Paris Magazine's Muhammad Cartoons Prompt Fears for French Embassies*, Guardian (Sept. 19, 2012, 6:21 AM), http://www.guardian.co.uk/world/2012/sep/19/paris-magazine-muhammad-cartoons-french.

[19] *Becoming "Anton," or, How Rushdie Survived a Fatwa*, NPR (Sept. 18, 2012, 3:35 AM), http://www.npr.org/2012/09/18/161172489/becoming-anton-or-how-rushdie-survived-a-fatwa.

in accordance with their agenda, of the film/cartoon/book and the quick-to-condemn tone adopted by policymakers whose response, seemingly not based on viewing or reading, is overprotectiveness of Islam.

The initial description of the film by Hilary Clinton, "disgusting and reprehensible,"[20] represents classic overreaction in the context of the overprotectiveness paradigm. The film, amateurish at best, depicts the Prophet Mohammed in an unflattering light; however, the gulf between that and "reprehensible" is broad and dangerous. After all, principles of free speech suggest the film, along with innumerable other artistic ventures,[21] reflect a broad range of opinions, some of them certainly causing "discomfort" if not "anger." However, to describe the video as "reprehensible" casts the video and its maker[22] in a vulnerable light in the face of those seeking to maximize, for their purposes, the repercussions of the video. In other words, Secretary of State Clinton fell into the not uncommon trap of articulating excessive mollification.[23] Clinton undoubtedly unintentionally provided "food for fodder"; it is for that reason that responses to inflammatory speech must be weighed carefully in the context of how particular audiences will interpret "mollifying speech."[24]

IV. Free Speech—From the Perspective of Philosophers

In analyzing the harm in hate speech Professor Jeremy Waldron makes the following cogent observation:

> Hate speech undermines this public good, or it makes the task of sustaining it much more difficult than it would otherwise be. It does this not only by intimating discrimination and violence, but by reawakening living nightmares of what this society was like—or what other societies have been like—in the past. In doing so, it creates something like an environmental threat to social peace, a sort of slow-acting poison,

---

[20] Brett LoGiurato, *HILLARY CLINTON: Anti-Muslim Film Is "Disgusting and Reprehensible,"* BUS. INSIDER (Sept. 13, 2012, 11:07 AM), http://www.businessinsider.com/hillary-clinton-innocence-of-muslims-disgusting-2012-9.

[21] With respect to the video, the word "artistic" is used generously, at best.

[22] The video creator was Nakoula Basseley Nakoula, an Egyptian-born US resident.

[23] For an example, see Brian Williams, NBC News, reporting on the French cartoon but noting that out of respect the cartoon will not be shown; see http://video.msnbc.msn.com/nightly-news/49095025#49095025. One wonders whether Mr. Williams appreciates his use of the word "respect" given the total lack of respect for free speech principles exhibited by the demonstrators. See Matthew Weaver, Haroon Siddique & Tom McCarthy, *Protests over Anti-Islam Film and Muhammad Cartoons—As It Happened*, GUARDIAN (Sept. 21 2012, 4:13 PM), http://www.guardian.co.uk/world/middle-east-live/2012/sep/21/tension-anti-islam-film-muhammad-cartoons. It is, obviously, an open question whether the demonstrators saw the cartoon while attacking Western facilities.

[24] For an example, see http://www.rightsidenews.com/2012092317088/editorial/rsn-pick-of-the-day/muslim-multiculturalism-and-western-post-nationalism.html (last visited Sept. 23, 2012).

accumulating here and there, word by word, so that eventually it becomes harder and less natural for even the good-hearted members of society to play their part in maintaining this public good.[25]

In advocating for restrictions on hate speech Waldron writes:

> I want to develop an affirmative characterization of hate speech laws that shows them in a favorable light—a characterization that makes good and interesting sense of the evils that might be averted by such laws and the values and principles that might plausibly motivate them."[26]

Waldron is right to highlight the need to engage in conversation regarding limiting speech and its inherent difficulty and controversy. However, given the power of speech the discussion is essential; the adage "words kill" is not an ephemeral concept devoid of content and painful history. Quite the opposite: examples of harm caused by words are bountiful and tragic. The harm is not only to specific individuals targeted by extremists or individuals who belong to particular ethnic and religious communities but to the larger society that tolerates hate speech in the name of free speech. However, as I argued in *Freedom from Religion*, religious extremist speech that potentially results in harm must not be granted immunity in the name of free speech. That is, free speech must not be understood to be a holy grail unencumbered by limits, principles of accountability, and restrictions imposed by legislators and the courts.

To suggest otherwise is to create, intentionally or unintentionally, a society at risk with respect to incitement. There is great danger in staking out this position for it raises the specter of government regulation of free speech subject to the vagaries of legislators, courts, and law enforcement. That concern is legitimate and with merit; many commentators advocate a "marketplace of ideas" approach rather than a heavy-handed regulation-based approach. Without doubt, the "marketplace of ideas" is compelling for it minimizes government intervention regarding speech while maximizing what Justice Holmes called "the free trade in ideas."[27]

John Stuart Mill in "On Liberty"[28] advanced a powerful argument favoring a "marketplace of ideas" paradigm regarding free speech. Mill's argument is predicated on the principle that limits on the power government can exercise over the individual are essential; according to Mill, the state can exercise power over the individual only to prevent harm to others: the "appropriate region of human liberty comprises.... the inward domain of consciousness; demanding liberty of conscience.... liberty of thought and feeling; absolute

---

[25] Jeremy Waldron, The Harm in Hate Speech 4 (2012).

[26] *Id.* at 15.

[27] *Id.* at 25.

[28] John Stuart Mill, On Liberty (Penguin Classics 1982) (1859).

freedom of opinion and sentiment on all subjects."[29] Mill highlights the two risks in limiting speech: for the state to suggest the falsity of particular speech implies state infallibility, and the risk that limiting opinion prevents others from hearing a particular opinion. In that context, Mill's argument suggests the danger of government excess with respect to restricting both the right to express an opinion and the right to hear one. In that spirit, Mill notes the danger of narrowing the diversity of opinions and, accordingly, highlights the advantages of the diversity of opinions. There are, according to Mill, four principle advantages to freedom of opinion: "if any opinion is compelled to silence, that opinion may, for aught we can certainly know, be true; though the silenced opinion be an error, it may, and very commonly does, contain a portion of truth; even if the received opinion be not only true, but the whole truth; the meaning of the doctrine itself will be in danger of being lost, or enfeebled, and deprived of its vital effect on the character and conduct."[30]

Mill advocates expression of unencumbered free speech conditioned on fair discussion and that the opinion be expressed in a temperate manner rather than unmeasured vituperation.[31] To that end, according to Mill, human beings must be free to form and express their opinions without reserve, but "opinions lose their immunity when circumstances in which they are expressed are such as to constitute their expression a positive instigation to some mischievous act."[32] In other words, the limit on liberty that Mill is willing to countenance depends on whether there is a nuisance to others: "The liberty of the individual must be thus far limited; he must not make himself a nuisance to other people."[33]

In that vein, Voltaire's letter, On the Liberty of the Press and of Theatres, to a First Commissioner (20 June 1733) is particularly insightful regarding harms emanating from government censorship.

> As you have it in your power, sir, to do some service to letters, I implore you not to clip the wings of our writers so closely, nor to turn into barn-door fowls those who, allowed a start, might become eagles; reasonable liberty permits the mind to soar— slavery makes it creep. Had there been a literary censorship in Rome, we should have had to-day neither Horace, Juvenal, nor the philosophical works of Cicero. If Milton, Dryden, Pope, and Locke had not been free, England would have had neither poets nor philosophers; there is something positively Turkish in proscribing printing; and hampering it is proscription. Be content with severely repressing diffamatory libels, for they are crimes: but so long as those infamous calottes are boldly published, and so many other unworthy and despicable productions, at least allow Bayle to circulate in France, and do not put him, who has been so great an honour to his country, among its contraband. You say that the magistrates who regulate

---

[29] *Id.* at 25.
[30] *Id.* at 89.
[31] *Id.* at 92.
[32] *Id.* at 94.
[33] *Id.*

the literary custom-house complain that there are too many books. That is just the same thing as if the provost of merchants complained there were too many provisions in Paris. People buy what they choose. A great library is like the City of Paris, in which there are about eight hundred thousand persons: you do not live with the whole crowd: you choose a certain society, and change it. So with books: you choose a few friends out of the many. There will be seven or eight thousand controversial books, and fifteen or sixteen thousand novels, which you will not read: a heap of pamphlets, which you will throw into the fire after you have read them. The man of taste will read only what is good; but the statesman will permit both bad and good. Men's thoughts have become an important article of commerce. The Dutch publishers make a million [francs] a year, because Frenchmen have brains. A feeble novel is, I know, among books what a fool, always striving after wit, is in the world. We laugh at him and tolerate him. Such a novel brings the means of life to the author who wrote it, the publisher who sells it, to the moulder, the printer, the paper-maker, the binder, the carrier—and finally to the bad wine-shop where they all take their money. Further, the book amuses for an hour or two a few women who like novelty in literature as in everything. Thus, despicable though it may be, it will have produced two important things—profit and pleasure.[34]

In *Leviathan*, Thomas Hobbes mentioned four categories of abuses of speech:

First, when men register their thoughts wrong....Secondly, when they use words metaphorically; that is, in other sense than that they are ordained for; and thereby deceiving others. Thirdly, when by words they declare that to be their will; which is not. Fourthly, when they use them to grieve one another...it is but an abuse of Speech, to grieve him with the tongue, unless it be one who wee are obliged to govern; and then it is not to grieve, but to correct and amend.[35]

Our concern is with Hobbes's fourth category; speech, whether predicated on religion or secular extremism, that incites to harmful conduct.

While this chapter highlights danger emanating from speech it is worth noting the distinction between religious and secular violence as Hector Avalos suggests:

Unlike many non-religious sources of conflict, religious conflict relies solely on resources whose scarcity is wholly manufactured by, or reliant on, unverifiable premises. When the truth or falsity of opposing propositions cannot be verified,

---

[34] *On the Liberty of the Press and of Theatres, to a First Commissioner*, WHITMAN UNIV., http://www.whitman.edu/VSA/letters/20.6.1733.html (last visited Jan 10, 2013).

[35] THOMAS HOBBES, LEVIATHAN 20–21 (2009).

then violence becomes a common resort in adjudicating disputes. That is the differentia that makes religious violence even more tragic than nonreligious violence.[36]

Whether Avalos's interpretation regarding the primacy of religious violence accurately reflects the reality of religious and secular violence is a matter of discussion and controversy. As this book proposes both religious and secular extremism pose significant danger to society; it is in that context that the proposal to limit free speech is offered. In an important article, "The Rise of Settler Terrorism,"[37] Daniel Byman and Dr. Natan Sachs correctly argue: "to slow the tide of radicalism, Israeli leaders must denounce extremists and shun their representatives, placing particular pressure on religious leaders who incite violence."[38] Bynam and Sach's analysis regarding rabbis who incite violence is applicable to secular extremists who incite violence; to distinguish between the two categories potentially minimizes the danger posed by both groups. In that vein, limiting the free speech of extremists who incite, whether predicated in religious or non-religious context, is essential to protecting society and members (external and internal communities) potentially at risk from extremist speech. With respect to the free speech discussion the focus is on limiting the impact of extremists who incite; Waldron's concise categories are particularly helpful:

> ...opponents of hate speech legislation go out of their way to denigrate the terms in which claims about harm are phrased...they proceed on the basis that the harm is most likely nonexistent or overblown; and that in any case it is appropriate to denigrate claims of harm in terms that would be quite fatal if they were applied to the vague and airy considerations with which, on the other side of the balance, the principle of free speech is defended. The idea seems to be that we should give the supposed advantages of free speech the benefit of the doubt because free speech is a well-established liberal principle.[39]

That said, Waldron correctly cautions regarding limits on free speech:

> Defenders of hate speech regulation need to face up honestly to the moral costs of their proposals....The restrictions I have been talking about have a direct bearing on freedom to publish, sometimes on freedom of the press, very likely on freedom of the Internet. The point is to stop these messages from taking a publicly visible part of the landscape, part of the evident stock of a people's ideas circulating in a society and looming over the environment in which people live their lives.[40]

---

[36] HECTOR AVALOS, FIGHTING WORDS: THE ORIGINS OF RELIGIOUS VIOLENCE 18 (2005).

[37] Daniel Byman & Natan Sachs, *The Rise of Settler Terrorism, Foreign Affairs* (Sept./Oct. 2012).

[38] *Id.* at 75.

[39] WALDRON, *supra* note 25, at 147–48.

[40] *Id.* at 148–49.

In the ideal, the tone and tenor of public debate—whether religious or secular—would not require imposing limits on free speech. However, as the discussion in this book highlights, the harm posed by extremist incitement warrants government regulation and restriction. The burden lies in careful line drawing that avoids over-regulation while providing sufficient protection to distinct at risk members of society. Line drawing is essential for it enables creation of a paradigm that facilitates determining whose speech is to be protected. Whose speech do we protect: Salman Rushdie, or those who issued the fatwa in response to publication of *The Satanic Verses*; Kurt Westergaard,[41] or those who incited riots resulting in numerous deaths?

The answer, from the perspective of Western civil society, is clear: the free speech of Rushdie and Westergaard must be protected and the speech of those who incite to violence in response to their ideas must be restricted. That is the essence of Professor Minow's tolerance/intolerance thesis and the basis for John Locke's "A Letter Concerning Toleration": "The toleration of those that differ from others in matters of religion is so agreeable to the Gospel of Jesus Christ, and to the genuine reason of mankind, that it seems monstrous for men to be so blind as not to perceive the necessity and advantage of it in so clear a light."[42]

The speech we are protecting is that of voices engaged in public debate and discussion; the speech that must be subject to regulation and restriction incites extremists to violence whether against specific voices or against particular ethnic, religious, and gender groups. The difficulty is twofold: recognition that speech need be limited, and then determination of where the line best be drawn. It is, then, a two-step process requiring a linear progression; devoid of step one, there is no step two. Step one poses a double risk: acknowledging that speech need be limited beyond existing parameters raises profound concerns; ignoring the threat posed by extremists imposes unnecessary risks on innocent individuals, whether belonging to a specific group or members of society at large, who are in harm's way. Advocating free speech be limited beyond present parameters is not, naturally, risk-free; however, the risk in not placing limits is similarly great, if not greater. The requisite line drawing poses significant legal, political, cultural, and practical obstacles; however, as proposed below in the Brandenburg[43] discussion, limits can be both articulated and implemented.

In that context, Ronald Dworkin's comments on the First Amendment are particularly important:

The First Amendment, like many of the Constitution's most important provisions, is drafted in the abstract language of political morality: it guarantees a "right" of

---

[41] Westergaard is the Danish cartoonist who created the controversial cartoon of the Prophet Mohammed depicted with a bomb in his turban; Westergaard hid in his home (along with his granddaughter) when an axe- and knife-wielding assailant attacked his home.

[42] John Locke, *A Letter Concerning Toleration*, CONSTITUTION.ORG, http://www.constitution.org/jl/tolerati. htm (last visited Jan 10, 2013).

[43] Brandenburg v. Ohio, 395 U.S. 444 (1969).

free speech but does not specify the dimensions of that right—whether it includes a right of cigarette manufacturers to advertise their product on television, for instance, or a right of a Ku Klux Klan chapter publicly to insult and defame blacks or Jews, or a right of foreign governments to broadcast political advice in American elections. Decisions on these and a hundred other issues require interpretation and if any justice's interpretation is not to be arbitrary or purely partisan, it must be guided by principle—by some theory of why speech deserves exemption from government regulation in principle. Otherwise the Constitution's language becomes only a meaningless mantra to be incanted whenever a judge wants for any reason to protect some form of communication. Precedent—how the First Amendment has been interpreted and applied by the Supreme Court in the past—must also be respected. But since the meaning of past decisions is also a matter of interpretation, that, too, must be guided by a principled account of the First Amendment's point.

Freedom of political speech is an essential condition of an effective democracy because it ensures that voters have access to as wide and diverse a range of information and political opinion as possible. Oliver Wendell Holmes Jr., Learned Hand, and other great judges and scholars argued that citizens are more likely to reach good decisions if no ideas, however radical, are censored. But even if that is not so, the basic justification of majoritarian democracy—that it gives power to the informed and settled opinions of the largest number of people—nevertheless requires what Holmes called a "free marketplace of ideas."[44]

Although Dworkin's analysis is correct, it does not fully address the question of when free speech can be limited. While noting, correctly, "freedom of political speech is an essential condition of an effective democracy," left unsaid is the fate of political speech when it nears or crosses the line of incitement. Much like John Stuart Mill and Justice Oliver Wendell Holmes, Dworkin emphasizes the importance of the "marketplace of ideas." That argument was proposed to me both by a leading Dutch academic and a senior Israeli Ministry of Justice official; although, obviously, the "marketplace of ideas" is an argument widely accepted in the free speech discussion, I share Waldron's concern regarding "the marketplace of ideas" with respect to free speech. That is, the effort to protect society from extremism and extremists—whether religious or secular—cannot rely on the "marketplace" to sufficiently discriminate and distinguish between speech and incitement.

The danger, naturally, is that government will engage in a paradigm of excessive limiting of free speech in an effort to minimize the reach and impact of problematic speakers. That is, of course, a natural and justified concern; nevertheless, that concern must not deter us from inquiring whether individuals and society are sufficiently protected

---

[44] Ronald Dworkin, *The Decision That Threatens Democracy*, N.Y. BOOKS (May 13, 2010), http://www.nybooks.com/articles/archives/2010/may/13/decision-threatens-democracy/?pagination=false.

from speakers whose speech dangerously morphs into incitement. In that vein, I suggest Dworkin's assessment, although reflective of case law and widely held opinions, does not satisfactorily protect potential victims of hate speech and incitement.

V. Free Speech in the United States

Congress shall make no law respecting an establishment of religion, or prohibiting the free exercise thereof; or abridging the freedom of speech, or of the press; or the right of the people peaceably to assemble, and to petition the Government for a redress of grievances.

—*The First Amendment to the U.S. Constitution*

The First Amendment protects the freedom of speech, press, religion, assembly, and petition; it is the great protector of individual rights, clearly articulating limits of government power. Despite uniform support for the amorphous term "free speech," Americans vigorously dispute both what it actually means and what it is intended to protect.[45] For example, 73 percent of Americans say the First Amendment does not go too far in protecting free speech,[46] yet 31 percent say musicians should *not* be allowed to sing songs with lyrics that others might find offensive, while 35 percent would support an amendment banning flag burning.[47]

Freedom of speech is much revered as a clear symbol of American democracy; nevertheless as the historical survey below indicates, it has had clear ups and downs. US presidents, Congress, and courts have struggled to define the boundaries of free speech; arguably, nowhere is this struggle more evident than during wartime. Although the liberal, democratic ethos advocates maximum rights of and for the individual, dangers posed by extremism requires reexamining that premise. Membership and participation in civil democratic society explicitly demand the citizen understand and respect that the rule of law is supreme. If we follow the logic of Rousseau, as citizens we are all signatories to the grand social contract.[48] In essence, we have given up any truly absolute rights in exchange for the safety and comfort that a government and village can provide to the individual and family; simply stated, in creating society we have agreed to be subject to laws and regulations.

Beginning with the Sedition Act of 1798 and continuing to present-day tensions and conflicts, successive presidents have struggled to balance civil liberties with national security; line drawing with respect to free speech has been the subject of robust debate.

---

[45] First Amendment Center, *State of the First Amendment 2009* (2009), *available at* http://s111617.gridserver.com/madison/wp-content/uploads/2011/03/SOFA2009.analysis.tables.pdf.

[46] *Id.* at 2.

[47] *Id.* at 6.

[48] Christopher Bertram, Routledge Philosophy Guidebook to Rousseau and the Social Contract 74–75 (2004).

A. SEDITION ACT OF 1798

Shortly after the First Amendment was ratified, Congress enacted the Sedition Act (1798)[49] restricting freedom of speech, in response to the possible outbreak of war between the United States and France.[50] Acting out of concern that sympathizers to France would "stir up trouble," Congress passed the Sedition Act imposing criminal penalties for saying or publishing anything "false, scandalous, or malicious" against the federal government, Congress, or the president.[51] Twenty-five American citizens were arrested under the Act,[52] including a congressman imprisoned for calling President Adams a man who had "a continual grasp for power."[53] The Act was particularly controversial; Virginia threatened to secede over this issue.[54]

In one of his first official acts as president, Thomas Jefferson, a bitter political opponent of President Adams and the Sedition Act, pardoned all those convicted under this law.[55] The Act was never challenged before the Supreme Court; forty years later, however, Congress repaid all of the fines exacted under the Sedition Act, with interest, to the legal representatives of those who had been convicted.[56] The congressional committee report declared that the Sedition Act had been passed under a "mistaken exercise" of power and was "null and void."[57] In 1964, the Supreme Court echoed this sentiment, stating "although the Sedition Act was never tested in this Court, the attack upon its validity has carried the day in the court of history."[58]

B. CIVIL WAR—THE ARREST OF CLEMENT VALLANDIGHAM

Upon taking office, President Lincoln was faced with a difficult choice between the lesser of two evils: permit dissenting voices to exercise their rights and risk losing states such as Maryland, or suppress dissent in an effort to hold the nation together.

Despite being a strong advocate for civil liberties, President Lincoln was greatly concerned with maintaining the fragile Union. In an effort to suppress pro-secessionist groups in border states Lincoln took several measures, including declaring martial law, suspending the writ of habeas corpus, and arresting individuals suspected of disloyalty in those areas. Lincoln explained that harsh measures were necessary in the early days of the rebellion because "every department of the Government [had been] paralyzed by

---

[49] Sedition Act of 1798, ch. 74, 1 Stat. 596.

[50] Constitutional Rights Foundation, *A Clear and Present Danger*, http://www.crf-usa.org/america-responds-to-terrorism/a-clear-and-present-danger.html (last visited Jan. 11, 2013).

[51] *Id.*

[52] *Id.*

[53] *Id.*

[54] *Id.*

[55] GEOFFREY R. STONE, PERILOUS TIMES: FREE SPEECH IN WARTIME 73 (2004).

[56] *Id.*

[57] *Id.*

[58] *Id.*

treason."[59] He analogized that a limb must sometimes be amputated to save a life, but that a life must never be given to save a limb.[60]

In March 1863, Lincoln appointed General Ambrose Burnside the Union commander of the Department of Ohio, a state where substantial protests regarding the war had been held. After discovering that newspapers in Ohio were openly critical of the president and the war efforts, Burnside issued General Order no. 38, which announced (among other things) that "the habit of declaring sympathies for the enemy will not be allowed in this Department."[61] Burnside, without Lincoln's knowledge, established himself as the ultimate arbiter of such charges.[62]

In May 1863, Burnside arrested an outspoken critic of the war, Clement Vallandigham. Vallandigham was charged and convicted by a military commission, holding that his speeches "could but induce in his hearers a distrust of their own government and sympathy for those in arms against it."[63] Vallandigham argued, to no avail, that his speeches were merely an appeal to the people to change public policy by lawful means.

Vallandigham immediately petitioned for a writ of habeas corpus in federal court. In response to his petition, Judge Humphrey Leavitt applied a balancing test between Vallandigham's civil liberty interest and the government's national security interest; as discussed below, this test continues to be applied today. Judge Leavitt held that General Burnside had acted reasonably given the circumstances, reasoning that during wartime, self-preservation was "paramount law," even rising above the Constitution. Leavitt concluded it is not the judiciary's place to overrule the Commander in Chief during wartime as a sufficient check on the president's power already existed in Congress's impeachment power.[64]

In response to pleas for the release of Vallandigham, Lincoln justified the arrest with the following statement:

> It is asserted... that Mr. Vallandigham was... seized and tried "for no other reason than world addressed to a public meeting, in criticism of the... Administration, and in condemnation of the Military orders of the General." Now, if there be no mistake about this; if this assertion is the truth and the whole truth; if there was no other reason for the arrest, then I concede that the arrest was wrong...
>
> But the arrest, as I understand, was made for a very different reason... his arrest was made because he was laboring with some effect, to prevent the raising of troops;

---

[59] Executive Order no. 1, Relating to Political Prisoners, Feb. 14, 1862, in 2:2 *The War of the Rebellion: A Compilation of the Official Records of the Union and Confederate Armies* 222 (Government Printing Office 1902).

[60] *See* SHELBY FOOTE, THE CIVIL WAR: A NARRATIVE 630 (1963).

[61] STONE, *supra* note 55, at 96.

[62] *Id.* at 97.

[63] *Id.* at 101.

[64] *Ex Parte* Vallandigham, 28 F. Cases 874, 921–24 (Cir. Ct. Ohio 1863).

to encourage desertions from the army; and to leave the Rebellion without an adequate military force to suppress it ... [65]

The case raised the question that is as relevant today as it was then: in times of war, should some civil liberties, otherwise protected under the Constitution, be suspended?

C. WORLD WAR I—THE ESPIONAGE ACT OF 1917

The Espionage Act of 1917 was the first legislation since the Sedition Act (1798) to limit free speech. Passed on June 15, 1917, shortly after the United States entered World War I and against the backdrop of fear and uncertainty, it represents a low point for free speech in American history.

The Wilson administration was deeply concerned about the effect that disloyalty would have on the war effort. To that end, President Wilson asked Congress to give him authority with respect to individuals who might undermine national unity. The president wanted, among other things, the power of censorship of the media, but Congress refused.[66] According to the legislation the following acts were subject to criminal prosecution:

> To convey information with intent to interfere with the operation or success of the armed forces of the United States or to promote the success of its enemies.
>
> To cause or attempt to cause insubordination, disloyalty, mutiny, refusal of duty, in the military or naval forces of the United States, or to willfully obstruct the recruiting or enlistment service of the United States.[67]

The Act also gave the Postmaster General authority to refuse to mail or to impound publications that he determined to be in violation of its prohibitions.[68]

In *Schenck v. United States*[69] the US Supreme Court considered the constitutionality of the Espionage Act. Charles Schenck, the Secretary of the Socialist Party of America, distributed leaflets that advocated opposition to the draft; Schenck was indicted and subsequently convicted for conspiracy to violate the Espionage Act for having caused and attempting to cause insubordination in the military and to obstructing the recruiting process. The Court in a unanimous opinion written by Justice Oliver Wendell Holmes, Jr. ruled Schenck's criminal conviction constitutional.

---

[65] Letter from Abraham Lincoln to Erastus Corning and Others, June 12, 1863, *in* STONE, *supra* note 55, at 110–11.

[66] STONE, *supra* note 55, at 147–49.

[67] Espionage Act of 1917, 40 Stat 217, 219.

[68] *Id.* at 230–31.

[69] Schenck v. United States, 249 U.S. 47 (1919).

According to Holmes, the First Amendment did not protect speech encouraging insubordination, as "when a nation is at war many things that might be said in time of peace are such a hindrance to its effort that their utterance will not be endured so long as men fight, and that no Court could regard them as protected by any constitutional right."[70] In other words, the circumstances of wartime permit greater restrictions on free speech than would be allowable during peacetime.

In the opinion's most famous passage, Justice Holmes sets out the "clear and present danger" test:

> The most stringent protection of free speech would not protect a man in falsely shouting fire in a theatre and causing a panic...The question in every case is whether the words used are used in such circumstances and are of such a nature as to create a clear and present danger that they will bring about the substantive evils that Congress has a right to prevent.[71]

Holmes was quick to defer to the government during wartime; his analysis focuses more on the government's ability to restrict speech during wartime as opposed to First Amendment protections. Though Holmes used the term "clear and present danger" it is unclear whether the circumstances truly satisfied such a burden. Schenck, after all, was printing and distributing anti-draft materials; whether that is akin to "shouting fire in a crowded theater" is arguable, if not doubtful. The core question is the proximity between the speech and the imminent danger arising from that speech; the facts and circumstances in *Schenck* suggest, from a historical perspective, a greatly removed nexus.

One week after *Schenck*, the Supreme Court decided two additional free speech cases. Jacob Frowherk was a copy editor who helped prepare and publish a series of antiwar articles in the *Missouri Staats Zeitung*, a German-language newspaper. Like Schenck, Frowherk was convicted under the Espionage Act, and the Supreme Court in a unanimous decision upheld his conviction.[72] Again Holmes gave short shrift to the First Amendment issue; though interestingly, he makes no reference in *Frowherk* or *Debs*[73] to the clear and present danger test.

Eugene V. Debs was an American labor and political leader and five-time Socialist Party of America candidate for the American presidency. On June 16, 1918, Debs made an antiwar speech in Canton, Ohio, protesting US involvement in World War I; Debs was subsequently arrested under the Espionage Act, convicted, and sentenced to ten years in prison and loss of his citizenship. The Supreme Court found Debs had shown the

---

[70] *Id.* at 52.
[71] *Id.*
[72] Frowherk v. United States, 249 U.S. 204 (1919).
[73] Debs v. United States, 249 U.S. 211 (1919).

"intention and effect of obstructing the draft and recruitment for the war";[74] in affirming his conviction the Court cited Debs's praise for those imprisoned for obstructing the draft.

This period marked a low point in free speech in America; the test articulated by Holmes in these three decisions raised great concerns regarding the limits of free speech in the United States. However, when the Court reconvened for its next session, Justice Holmes apparently had a change of heart; it has been suggested by some this was a result of his friendship and correspondence with US District Court Judge Learned Hand. Hand, much revered for his intellect, would become one of the most prominent voices in American jurisprudence. In 1917, Hand was considered a likely nominee for the US Court of Appeals; however that (temporarily) changed in the aftermath of his opinion in *Masses Publishing Co. v. Patten*.[75]

At issue in *Masses* was a provision in the Espionage Act granting the Postmaster General authority both to refuse to mail and to impound publications he determined to be in violation of the Act. Hand held the New York postmaster's refusal to allow circulation of an antiwar journal violated the First Amendment. In his opinion, Hand held that if a citizen "stops short of urging upon others that it is their duty or their interest to resist the law,"[76] then he or she is protected by the First Amendment. Hand's opinion was reversed by the Court of Appeals; in addition, Hand—perhaps in a reflection of the tenor of the times—was not nominated to the Court of Appeals. Hand, who would ultimately sit on the Appeals Court, reflected that the case "cost me something, at least at the time," but added, "I have been very happy to do what I believe was some service to temperateness and sanity."[77]

Hand, according to many observers, had a profound impact on his friend Justice Holmes. In *United States v. Abrams*,[78] Holmes joined Justice Brandeis in dissent, taking a strong pro-speech position. In *Abrams*, the defendants were convicted for printing and subsequently throwing from windows of a New York City building two antiwar leaflets. The Supreme Court ruled 7–2 that the Espionage Act did not violate the freedom of speech protected by the First Amendment. In his dissent, Holmes wrote that although the defendant's pamphlet called for a cease in weapons production, it had not violated the act because the defendants did not have the requisite intent to cripple or hinder the United States in the prosecution of the war.[79] Holmes's dissent set the stage for what would ultimately become the modern-day clear and present danger test.

---

[74] *Id.*

[75] Masses Publishing Co. v. Patten, 244 F. 535 (S.D.N.Y. 1917).

[76] *Id.* at 540.

[77] Letter from Learned Hand to Charles Burlingham, Oct. 6, 1917, *excerpted in* STONE, *supra* note 55, at 170.

[78] United States v. Abrams, 250 U.S. 616 (1919).

[79] *Id.* at 628.

D. COLD WAR—COMMUNISM

In the aftermath of World War II there was grave concern in the United States regarding both the rising influence of the Soviet Union and penetration of Communism and Communists into the United States. In 1940, Congress passed the Smith Act,[80] which criminalized the advocating of the overthrow of the US government by force or violence. In 1950 Senator Joseph McCarthy (R-WI) began a nationwide witch-hunt to root out Communist sympathizers; virtually the entire nation was swept up in anti-communist fever, if not panic. Judge Hand, now sitting on the Second Circuit Court of Appeals, was critical of Senator McCarthy's efforts. In a public address, Hand stated that "risk for risk," he would rather take chance that some traitors will escape detection than risk spreading across the land "a spirit of general suspicion and distrust."[81] Now in 1950, would the great mind behind the decision in *Masses*[82] stand up for the First Amendment against the tidal wave of fear?

Eugene Dennis, the secretary of the Communist Party of America, was an outspoken advocate of Communism. Dennis, along with several other party members, was indicted (July 1948) in accordance with the Smith Act for conspiring and organizing the overthrow and destruction of the US government by force and violence. Smith and his co-defendants upon conviction by the trial court appealed to the Second Circuit. Though Hand was a strong advocate for free speech, as an Appeals Court judge he was bound by Supreme Court precedent. In analyzing previous Supreme Court holdings Hand concluded that the Court had been applying a version of the clear and present danger test. As he eloquently put it, "In each case [courts] must ask whether the gravity of the 'evil,' discounted by its improbability, justifies such invasion of free speech as necessary to avoid the danger."[83]

The question before the court, according to Hand, was one of imminence. How long must the government, having discovered such a conspiracy, wait before acting? When does the conspiracy become a "present danger"? According to Hand, "the jury found that the conspirators will 'strike as soon as success seems possible.' "[84] The government is not required to wait till the actual eve of hostilities; rather at the point when the danger becomes clear and present.[85] Hand's analysis balances the clear and present danger test with national security concerns; as the level of danger increases, the imminence government must demonstrate before it can act decreases. Essentially, Hand proposed a cost–benefit analysis weighing costs of suppression with the cost of the potential harm were the speech not restricted. The Supreme Court adopted Hand's balancing test, holding the threat of Communism justified

---

[80] Smith Act, 18 U.S.C. § 2385 (1940).
[81] STONE, *supra* note 55, at 399.
[82] 244 F. 535 (S.D.N.Y. 1917).
[83] United States v. Dennis, 183 F.2d 201, 212 (1950).
[84] *Id.* at 212–13.
[85] *Id.*

a broader interpretation of imminence. Regarding the defendants, Judge Hand later stated he would "never have prosecuted those birds";[86] in his view, the prosecution would do nothing but "encourage the faithful and maybe help the Committee on Propaganda."[87] But, he added, this "has nothing to do with my job,"[88] which was to faithfully apply the law. In upholding the convictions, the Supreme Court in *Dennis*[89] appeared to give the green light to government officials to aggressively target Communist supporters. Between 1951 and 1957, the government arrested and prosecuted 145 members and leaders of the Communist Party; 108 were convicted, 10 were acquitted, and the rest were awaiting trial when *Yates*[90] was decided in June 1957.[91] In none of the prosecutions was evidence presented suggestive of concrete plans to use force or violence to overthrow the government.

But between *Dennis* and *Yates*, the political climate in America changed significantly: Stalin, the Soviet leader, passed away; an armistice had been declared in Korea; the Senate had condemned Senator McCarthy; and the public attitude toward the "red scare" had relaxed. In addition, significant changes occurred on the Supreme Court as Justices Harlan, Brennan, Whittaker, and Chief Justice Warren replaced justices Vinson, Reed, Minton, and Jackson; this change in the Court's makeup led to a significant shift in the Court's judicial philosophy. In *Yates*,[92] the Court drew a distinction between actual advocacy to action and mere advocacy in the abstract. Justice Harlan stated that the Smith Act did not prohibit "advocacy of forcible overthrow of the government as an abstract doctrine" even "if engaged in with the intent to accomplish overthrow." Such advocacy was simply "too remote from concrete action."[93]

Although Harlan did not require that the unlawful action be imminent, he did insist that, to be punishable, the advocacy must include a call for specific, concrete action. Thus, a speaker who teaches the general principles of Marxism, even with the intent to promote a revolution, will not cross the line drawn in *Yates*; the Court recognized that actual "advocacy to action" circumstances would be "few and far between."[94] Indeed, following *Yates*, the government filed no further prosecutions under the Smith Act.

E. INCITEMENT—CLEAR AND PRESENT DANGER TODAY

Brandenburg[95] is the seminal speech protection case in American jurisprudence. The US Supreme Court reversed the conviction of a Ku Klux Klan leader who had advocated

---

[86] Letter from Learned Hand to Irving Dilliard, Apr. 3, 1952, excerpted in STONE, *supra* note 55, at 401.
[87] *Id.*
[88] *Id.*
[89] Dennis v. United States, 341 U.S. 494 (1951).
[90] Yates v. United States, 354 U.S. 298 (1957).
[91] STONE, *supra* note 55, at 411.
[92] 354 U.S. 298 (1957).
[93] *Id.* at 318, 321.
[94] *Id.* at 327.
[95] 395 U.S. 444 (1969) (per curiam).

violence, holding that the government cannot, under the First Amendment, punish the abstract advocacy of violence.[96] Under *Brandenburg*, the government can limit speech only if: (1) the speech promotes imminent harm; (2) there is a high likelihood that the speech will result in listeners participating in illegal action; and (3) the speaker intended to cause such illegality.[97]

In an age where religious and non-religious violence threaten civil society, should this speech-protective case be reexamined, or even overruled? The question is one of line drawing; the challenge is in clearly, and concisely drawing that line, not in a "case by case" analysis but, rather, by developing and recommending criteria for limiting freedom of speech that does not unduly trammel on otherwise guaranteed rights. As noted above, the difficulty is compounded as means of communication undergo radical transformation posing extraordinary challenges, particularly when balancing broader societal interests while preserving guaranteed individual rights.

In 1964, Clarence Brandenburg, a KKK leader, was charged and convicted for advocating violence under the State of Ohio's criminal syndicalism statute for his participation in a rally and for the speeches he made. In particular, Brandenburg stated at one point: "Personally, I believe the nigger should be returned to Africa, the Jew returned to Israel."[98] In an additional speech among several Klan members who were carrying firearms, Brandenburg claimed, "We're not a revengent organization, but if our President, our Congress, our Supreme Court, continues to suppress the white, Caucasian race, it's possible that there might have to be some revengeance taken."[99] Brandenburg appealed his conviction to the Supreme Court, claiming the statute violated his First Amendment rights; the Court, in its most speech-protective holding, sided with Brandenburg, holding the statute violated his First Amendment rights.

However, the question is whether this holding sufficiently protects society; rearticulated: does *Brandenburg* grant the speaker too much wiggle room thereby posing a danger to individuals in particular and society at large? That question, widely asked, has no wrong or right answer. The answer depends on a wide range of circumstances including the respondent's political, economic cultural, social, and religious background and milieu. It also depends on current events; that is, the answer cannot be separated from particular developments that directly affect individuals and society alike. For that reason it is essential that discussion regarding limits of free speech be conducted dispassionately, divorced from the hurly-burly of particular events.

Although the Supreme Court articulated a three-part test in Brandenburg the question is its efficacy in protecting individuals and society. In asking this question the intent is to not only protect the speaker's rights, but also to ensure that potential targets are

---

[96] *Id.* at 448.

[97] *See id.* at 447–48.

[98] Brandenburg v. Ohio, 385 U.S. 444 (1969).

[99] *Id.* at 446.

sufficiently protected. Herein lies the rub: how do we satisfactorily determine there is a potential target rather than casting too broad a net, thereby unjustifiably and unnecessarily limiting speech that does not meet the incitement test? To that end, I propose the following standard of determining whether the relevant speech morphs into incitement. My proposal is based on an analysis of *Brandenburg* that suggests its test is overly protective of freedom of speech and does not, for instance, adequately address the *potential* danger posed by a pastor who weekly preaches fire and brimstone against abortion-performing physicians.

How, after all, is a police officer supposed to know that such a sermon is meant only rhetorically and therefore fails the third element? How is a police officer to know whether there is a high likelihood that a congregant will act in the spirit of such a sermon? Furthermore, as the sermons are given weekly, does that mean the harm they promote is "imminent"? Audiences and commentators alike expressed repeated concern regarding these dilemmas; question-and-answer sessions resulted in little agreement, perhaps because this is where the proverbial "rubber hits the road." These questions caused discomfort among many; "operationalizing" limits on free speech, after all, challenges the essence of democratic values. The question is one of line drawing; the challenge is to clearly draw that line.

If *Brandenburg* is to be rearticulated, an alternative clear, workable test must be established. States cannot engage in a case-by-case—rather than principled—approach in determining whether religious liberties can be limited. Amorphous criteria both invite government excess and create significant due process concerns whereby both speaker and law enforcement will not be equipped to consistently predict whether the speech conforms to the law. Therefore, I propose three possibilities:

1. Unprotected Speech

Categorizing religious extremist speech that promotes hatred or violence of others as wholly unprotected incitement, without the need for determining intent or for ascertaining whether the speech likely resulted in illegality. In other words, this approach would apply only the first element of the *Brandenburg* test and remove the last two;

2. Lower Intent

Lowering the bar for the intent element of the *Brandenburg* test whenever the speaker in question is a figure of religious authority; or

3. Intermediate Scrutiny

Leaving the three *Brandenburg* elements as they are, but lowering the standard from traditional strict scrutiny to intermediate scrutiny in the case of extremist religious speech.

F. PRIOR RESTRAINT—PENTAGON PAPERS

The First Amendment was intended to protect against prior restraints on speech; Blackstone declared that "the liberty of the press is, indeed, essential to the nature of a free state; but this consists in laying no previous restraints upon publication, and not in freedom from censure for criminal matter when published."[100] A prior restraint prevents speech from occurring, as opposed to punishing it after the fact. It typically takes the form of a license or injunction; it has been said that although a criminal statute "chills," an injunction "freezes."[101]

As the Supreme Court held in the Pentagon Papers case "[a]ny system of prior restraints of expression comes to this Court bearing a heavy presumption against its constitutional validity."[102] This is because "prior restraints on speech and publication are the most serious and least tolerable infringement on First Amendment rights."[103]

The Supreme Court's initial foray into prior restraint was *Near v. Minnesota;*[104] the Court held prior restraints to be unconstitutional, except in extremely limited circumstances such as national security issues. That was not the case in *Near;* quite the opposite for the ruling was in reaction to a prior restraint order issued against a newspaper, owned by Near, after it published exposés of Minneapolis's elected officials' alleged illicit activities. The Court held that the state had no power to enjoin publication of the paper, as this was prior restraint reflective of censorship.

The most famous prior restraint case is known as the *Pentagon Papers.* In 1967, Secretary of Defense McNamara commissioned compilation of a "History of U.S. Decision-Making Process on Vietnam Policy, 1945–1967," otherwise known as the Pentagon Papers. The Papers took two years to complete and resulted in over 7000 pages of classified documents; McNamara later commented, "[Y]ou know, they could hang people for what's in there."[105]

In 1971, Daniel Ellsburg, a one-time consultant and supporter of US policy in Vietnam turned antiwar activist leaked the papers to the *New York Times* (*NYT*). The Justice Department immediately sought an injunction in federal court, claiming both that publication was a violation of the Espionage Act of 1917 and that it presented a serious threat to national security because the papers contained critical intelligence information relevant to the ongoing war effort. Pending the District Court's decision, Ellsburg released the papers to the *Washington Post*; the Justice Department sought an injunction against the *Post.* Judge Gesell of the Federal District Court in Washington, DC, ruled

---

[100] WILLIAM BLACKSTONE, COMMENTARIES 151–52 (1769).

[101] *See* ALEXANDER M. BICKEL, THE MORALITY OF CONSENT 61 (1975), referenced in STONE, *supra* note 55, at 506.

[102] New York Times v. United States, 403 U.S. 713, 714 (1971).

[103] Neb. Press Ass'n v. Stuart, 427 U.S. 539, 559 (1976).

[104] Near v Minnesota, 283 U.S. 697 (1931).

[105] *See* DAVID HALBERSTAM, THE BEST AND THE BRIGHTEST 663 (1972).

the government failed to present evidence that the Papers posed a serious danger to the nation. Thereafter, Judge Gurfein of the Southern District of New York also denied the government's request for an injunction against the *NYT*; the government immediately appealed both rulings to the Supreme Court.

The government based its appeal on the "national security" exception discussed in *Near*;[106] however, in a brief per curiam decision the Supreme Court agreed with the lower court, holding the government had not met its "heavy burden" of showing a justification for a prior restraint, and ordered the injunction be lifted immediately.[107]

Several of the justices wrote their own opinions in this critical free speech case. Justice Hugo Black wrote "every moment's continuance of the injunctions against these newspapers amounts to a flagrant, indefensible, and continuing violation of the First Amendment."[108] Justice Brennan insisted that even in wartime a prior restraint on the press could be constitutional *only* if the government proved that "publication must inevitably, directly, and immediately cause the occurrence of an event kindred to imperiling the safety of a transport already at sea."[109]

G. FIGHTING WORDS

Fighting words, like incitement, are not protected by the First Amendment and can be punishable. The difference between incitement and fighting words is subtle, focusing on the intent of the speaker. Inciting speech is characterized by the speaker's intent to make someone else the instrument of her unlawful will, whereas fighting words, by contrast, are intended to cause the hearer to react to the speaker.

The Supreme Court first developed the fighting words doctrine in *Chaplinsky*[110] in 1942. Chaplinsky was arrested for disturbing the peace after uttering to the local marshal: "You are a God damned racketeer" and "a damned Fascist and the whole government of Rochester are Fascists or agents of Fascists."[111] The Supreme Court upheld the conviction in a unanimous opinion, holding:

> There are certain well-defined and narrowly limited classes of speech, the prevention and punishment of which has never been thought to raise any Constitutional problem. These include… "fighting" words—those, which by their very utterance inflict injury or tend to incite an immediate breach of the peace.[112]

---

[106] 283 U.S. 697 (1931).
[107] *New York Times*, 403 U.S. at 714.
[108] *Id.* at 715.
[109] *Id.* at 726–27.
[110] Chaplinsky v. State of New Hampshire, 315 U.S. 568 (1942).
[111] *Id.* at 569.
[112] *Id.* at 571–72.

Since *Chaplinsky*, the Court has continued to uphold the doctrine but has also steadily narrowed the grounds on which the fighting words test applies. In *Street v. New York*[113] the Court overturned a statute prohibiting flag burning, holding that mere offensiveness does not qualify as "fighting words." Consistent with *Street*, in *Cohen v. California*,[114] the Court held that Cohen's jacket with the words "fuck the draft" did not constitute fighting words because the words on the jacket were not a "direct personal insult" and no one had reacted violently to the jacket. This ruling established that fighting words should be confined to direct personal insults.

In 1992, in *R.A.V. v. City of St. Paul*[115] the Supreme Court overturned a city ordinance that made it a crime to burn a cross on public or private property with the intent to arouse anger, alarm, or resentment in others based on race, color creed, etc. According to the Court:

> The ordinance, even as narrowly construed by the State Supreme Court, is facially unconstitutional, because it imposes special prohibitions on those speakers who express views on the disfavored subjects of race, color, creed, religion or gender…Moreover, in its practical operation, the ordinance goes beyond mere content, to actual viewpoint, discrimination…St. Paul's desire to communicate to minority groups that it does not condone the group hatred of bias-motivated speech does not justify selectively silencing speech on the basis of its content.

In addition, the ordinance's content discrimination is not justified on the ground that the ordinance is narrowly tailored to serve a compelling state interest in ensuring the basic human rights of groups historically discriminated against, because an ordinance not limited to the favored topics would have precisely the same beneficial effect.[116]

H. TRUE THREATS

Similar to "incitement" and "fighting words," a "true threat" is another area of speech that is not protected by the First Amendment. A true threat exists where a speaker directs a threat to a person or group of persons with the *intent* of placing the victim in fear of bodily harm or death. Yet the line between protected expression and an unprotected true threat is often hazy and uncertain, often turning on the determination of intent.

---

[113] Street v. New York, 394 U.S. 576 (1969).
[114] Cohen v. California, 403 U.S. 15 (1971).
[115] R.A.V. v. City of St. Paul, 505 U.S. 377 (1992).
[116] *Id.* at 393–96.

For example, in *Watts v. United States,*[117] Watts, a young African American man, was arrested for saying the following during an antiwar protest in Washington DC: "If they ever make me carry a rifle the first man I want to get in my sights is L.B.J. They are not going to make me kill my black brothers." In overturning his conviction, the Supreme Court ruled that Watts's statement was political hyperbole rather than a true threat. "We agree with [Watts] that his only offense here was 'a kind of very crude offensive method of stating a political opposition to the President.'"[118]

In *Virginia v. Black,*[119] the Supreme Court decided a case similar to *R.A.V.*[120] under the true threats doctrine. The Court held that cross burning could constitute a true threat, and thereby be proscribed by law, *if* it is done with the intent to intimidate or place the victim in fear of bodily harm or death. It may not, however, be used as prima facie evidence of intent to intimidate, because cross burning may serve other intentions, such as a show of solidarity.

I. HATE SPEECH

Hate speech is a hotly contested area of First Amendment debate. Unlike fighting words, or true threats, hate speech is a broad category of speech that encompasses both protected and unprotected speech. To the extent that hate speech constitutes a true threat or fighting words, it is unprotected; to the extent it does not reach the level of a true threat or fighting words it is protected.

During the 1980s and early 1990s more than 350 public colleges and universities sought to combat discrimination and harassment on campuses through the use of so-called speech codes.[121] Proponents of the codes contend that existing First Amendment jurisprudence must be changed because the marketplace of ideas does not adequately protect minorities. They charge that hate speech subjugates minority voices and prevents them from exercising their First Amendment rights. Similarly, proponents posit that hate speech is akin to fighting words, a category of expression that should not receive First Amendment protection, because as the Court held in *Chaplinsky* they "are no essential part of any exposition of ideas, and are of such slight social value as a step to the truth that any benefit that may be derived from them is clearly outweighed by the social interest in order and morality."[122]

However, speech codes that have been challenged in court have not fared well; though no case has been brought before the Supreme Court on this question, lower courts have

---

[117] Watts v. United States, 394 U.S. 705 (1969).

[118] *Id.* at 707–08.

[119] Virginia v. Black, 538 U.S. 343 (2003).

[120] 505 U.S. 377 (1992).

[121] David L. Hudson Jr., *Hate Speech and Campus Speech Codes*, FIRST AMEND. CENTER (Sept. 13, 2002), http://www.firstamendmentcenter.org/hate-speech-campus-speech-codes.

[122] Chaplinsky v. State of New Hampshire, 315 U.S. 568, 572 (1942).

struck these policies down as either overbroad or vague. The District Court for the Eastern District of Wisconsin in the University of Wisconsin school code case articulated the reasoning behind the codes' lack of constitutional muster:

> This commitment to free expression must be unwavering, because there exist many situations where, in the short run, it appears advantageous to limit speech to solve pressing social problems, such as discriminatory harassment. If a balancing approach is applied, these pressing and tangible short run concerns are likely to outweigh the more amorphous and long run benefits of free speech. However, the suppression of speech, even where the speech's content appears to have little value and great costs, amounts to governmental thought control.[123]

VII. Analysis of American Free Speech Jurisprudence

Although a literal interpretation of the First Amendment forbids any law abridging speech in any form, the Supreme Court has taken a more nuanced approach recognizing legitimate competing interests that must be considered. For example, although free speech is a guaranteed right according to the First Amendment, the executive branch is similarly charged with protecting the safety and security of the nation's citizens. As Justice Holmes articulated, "the most stringent protection of free speech would not protect a man in falsely shouting fire in a theater, and causing a panic."[124]

Although some would argue that the "marketplace of ideas" should take precedence over efforts to limit free speech protections the reality is, arguably, more complicated. As I have argued elsewhere,[125] the danger posed by religious extremist incitement should give serious pause as incitement occurring in houses of worship meets the tests articulated by the Supreme Court. In that vein, although the Supreme Court begins its analysis of free speech questions with the presumption that *all* speech is protected, unless it falls within one of two exceptions, it is not an absolute right.

The analysis must determine whether the proposed restriction is content-based or content-neutral; the former refers to restrictions that apply to particular viewpoints; in these situations the proposed restriction carries a heavy presumption that it violates the First Amendment. In such a paradigm, the Court applies a strict scrutiny standard in evaluating the restriction's lawfulness; to survive strict scrutiny, the restriction must be *narrowly tailored* to achieve *an important governmental interest*. That means that it cannot be, among other things, over-inclusive, under-inclusive, or vague. This standard effectively places a heavy burden on the government in defending the restriction.

---

[123] UWM Post, Inc. v. Bd. of Regents of Univ. of Wisconsin Sys., 774 F. Supp. 1163, 1174 (E.D. Wisc. 1991).

[124] Schenck v. United States, 249 U.S. 47, 52 (1919).

[125] *See* AMOS GUIORA, FREEDOM FROM RELIGION: *RIGHTS AND NATIONAL SECURITY* (2009).

However, if the restriction is content-neutral, whereby the concern is not with the speech itself but rather pertains to the details surrounding the speech, then the government is allowed to set certain parameters involving time, place, and manner. Content-neutral restrictions on speech are reviewed under intermediate scrutiny rather than strict scrutiny because the speech is restricted solely in the manner in which the information is communicated rather than content itself.

In *United States v. O'Brien*,[126] the Supreme Court established a four-part test to determine whether a content-neutral restriction on speech is constitutional: (1) Is the restriction within the constitutional power of government, (2) Does the restriction further an important or substantial governmental interest, (3) Is the governmental interest unrelated to the suppression of free expression, and (4) Is the restriction narrowly tailored (i.e., no greater than necessary). Subsequently, a fifth factor was added in *City of Ladue v. Gilleo*[127] inquiring whether the restriction leaves open ample opportunities of communication.

Finally, there is an exception to the content-based rule that requires an analysis of the value of the speech in question. Certain forms of speech, such as political speech, are thought to be at the very core of the First Amendment's protection, and therefore, merit the greatest protection under the law. The freedom to openly challenge the government is essential to a democracy. However, that principle has been fungible; witness Supreme Court holdings particularly during World War I and somewhat in the aftermath of World War II.

Though American society has significantly matured over the past 200 years the responses when under threat are surprisingly uniform and consistent in accepting a rights minimization paradigm imposed by government and upheld by the Court. A careful reading of American history, executive decision-making, and judicial holdings suggests this possibility must not be discounted in the free speech discussion. The question, in a nutshell, is whether national security and public order justify minimizing free speech. In some ways, American history has demonstrated a ready willingness to answer in the affirmative. The costs, as repeatedly demonstrated, are significant both with respect to the principles articulated in the First Amendment and on a human, individual basis. A quick perusal of the World War I and post–WWII prosecutions offers ready proof. The dilemma is determining how serious is the threat to national security and public order and whether limiting free speech will mitigate that threat and at what cost to individual liberty.

VIII. United Kingdom

The United Kingdom, historically, has practiced extraordinary tolerance for free speech. In the context of the freedom of religious speech, that tolerance is based in part on the historically limited influence of the Anglican Church[128] in English life. Great Britain's

---

[126] United States v. O'Brien, 391 U.S. 367 (1968).

[127] City of LaDue v. Gilleo, 512 U.S. 43 (1994).

[128] *See* U.S. Department of State, http://www.state.gov/g/drl/rls/irf/2006/71416.htm. *See generally* Peter Cumper, *The United Kingdom and the UN Declaration on the Elimination of Intolerance,* 21 EMORY INTL L. REV. 13.

commitment to freedom of speech predates modern international conventions. British writer and philosopher John Milton was one of the earliest proponents of freedom of expression, and Sir Thomas More helped establish the parliamentary privilege of free speech during the 1500s.[129] In the 1600s, Milton argued that censorship acts to the detriment of a nation's progress, as truth will always defeat falsehood; but a single individual cannot be trusted to tell the two apart, and therefore no individual can be trusted to act as censor for all individuals.[130] John Stuart Mill furthered Milton's arguments in the 1800s by promoting the principle of the "marketplace of ideas", where objectionable speech has a place because truth will prevail, and even hateful speech has a value in that it provides an opportunity for others to confront opposition, examine their assumptions, and ultimately refine their own thoughts and arguments.[131]

In recent years, homegrown Islamic terrorist attacks, influenced by al Qaeda but ultimately separate from the organization, have rocked the social fabric in Great Britain. On July 7, 2005, 56 people were killed in a series of bombings in the London subway.[132] In August 2006, a plot to simultaneously destroy US-bound commercial airlines departing from London was uncovered;[133] on June 30, 2007, Glasgow Airport was attacked;[134] and, in December 2010, 12 men with links to Pakistan and Bangladesh were arrested in London on suspicion of plotting large-scale terror attacks in the United Kingdom.[135] In the aftermath of the attacks, the British Parliament passed counterterrorism-related legislation.

However, as one British academic has noted:

It has also been difficult to know where to draw the line between statements at Friday prayers that are allowed and those that are not. There is now a case of a suspect imam who the public and the police think is preaching incitement but who has been released by the High Court on very strict bail because the police have been unable to produce evidence for a specific charge.[136]

---

[129] *The Life of Sir Thomas More, available at* http://www.luminarium.org/renlit/morebio.htm (last visited, Feb. 6, 2013). *See also Parliamentary Privilege and Free Speech: MPs' Privileges and Citizens' Freedom from Oppression,* Mar. 9, 2006, *available at* www.adls.org.nz/filedownload?id=b3e74fd4-6cb8-4276-9029-a15a59247246.

[130] JOHN MILTON, AREOPAGITICA (1643).

[131] MILL, *supra* note 28.

[132] *Bombers Target London,* CNN, *available at* http://www.cnn.com/SPECIALS/2005/london.bombing/ (last visited July 7, 2012).

[133] Statement by Homeland Security Secretary Michael Chertoff announcing a change to the Nation's Threat Level for the Aviation Sector, *available at* http://www.dhs.gov/xnews/releases/pr_1158349923199.shtm (last visited July 9, 2013).

[134] *Flaming SUV Rams U.K. Airport; 2 Arrests, Newsmax.com* (June 30, 2007), *available at* http://archive.newsmax.com/archives/articles/2007/6/30/144208.shtml.

[135] *12 Men Arrested in Suspected UK Terrorism Plot,* FOXNEWS (Dec. 20, 2010), http://www.foxnews.com/world/2010/12/20/men-arrested-suspected-uk-terrorism-plot/.

[136] Email exchange with author.

Under the Serious Crime Act 2007, the common law offense of inciting the commission of another offense was abolished and replaced by three statutory inchoate offenses under ss.44-46. The three offenses are:

(A) Intentionally encouraging or assisting an offence (s. 44);
(B) Encouraging or assisting an offence believing it will be committed (s.45); and
(C) Encouraging or assisting offences believing one or more will be committed (s. 46).
  (i) A person commits an offence under s.44 if:
    (1) He does an act capable of encouraging or assisting the commission of an offence; and
    (2) He intends to encourage or assist its commission.
But he is not to be taken to have intended to encourage or assist the commission of an offence merely because such encouragement or assistance was a foreseeable consequence of his act. But it is sufficient to prove that he intended to encourage or assist the doing of an act which would amount to the commission of that offence. There is a defence of acting reasonably.
  (ii) A person commits an offence under s.45 if:
    (1) He does an act capable of encouraging or assisting the commission of an offence; and
    (2) He believes: (a) that the offence will be committed; and (b) that his act will encourage or assist its commission
Where it is alleged that a person believed that an offence would be committed and that his act would encourage or assist its commission, it is sufficient to prove that he believed that an act would be done which would amount to the commission of that offence and that his act would encourage or assist in the doing of that act. A defence of acting reasonably is provided.
  (iii) A person commits an offence under s.46 if:
    (1) He does an act capable of encouraging or assisting the commission of one or more of a number of offences; and
    (2) He believes: (a) that one or more of those offences will be committed (but has no belief as to which); and (b) that his act will encourage or assist the commission of one or more of them.
A defence of acting reasonably is provided.
As regards whether an act is one which if done would amount to the commission of an offence, if the offence requires proof of fault it must be proved the defendant believed or was reckless as to whether it would be done with that fault or his state of mind was such that were he to do it, it would be done with that fault. If the offence requires proof of particular circumstances and or consequences, it must be proved that the defendant intended or believed or was reckless that, were the act to be done, it would be done in those circumstances or with those consequences.

The question is "where to draw the line" *and* whether the line is to be drawn differently if the speech is religious. Although England has traditionally not imposed restrictions on free speech, does the reality of a specific threat to society require Parliament, the courts, and the police to reconsider how to effectively respond to religiously inspired terrorism? The cases of Samina Malik and Mohammed Siddique potentially suggest that the United Kingdom has abandoned its historical roots of respecting free speech—particularly religious speech—in the wake of Islamic-based terrorist attacks. In 2007, 23-year-old Samina Malik was convicted of "possessing records likely to be used for terrorist purposes" under the 2006 Terrorism Act. In June 2008, her conviction was overturned on appeal, and the Crown Prosecution Service decided not to seek a retrial.[137]

In high school, Malik began writing love poems and other poetry inspired by the rap music of Americans 50 Cent and Tupac Shakur. At age 20, she became more religious and began wearing a hijab and calling herself the "Lyrical Terrorist," later claiming that she picked the name because it "sounded cool." The documents Malik possessed included a library of books on firearms, poisons, hand-to-hand combat, and terrorism techniques. Malik was convicted for possessing documents that included her poetry, in which she expressed a desire to be a martyr, an approval of beheadings, respect for Osama bin Laden, and contempt for non-Muslims. Malik has claimed that the poetry was meaningless and taken out of context, insisting that she was not a terrorist.[138] The judge termed her a "complete enigma."[139]

Mohammed Siddique was arrested on April 13, 2006, after accompanying his uncle to the Glasgow Airport. There, the two were told they would not be allowed to fly, and Siddique's cell phone and laptop were confiscated. Siddique was charged with collecting information that would "likely be useful" to a terrorist under Section 58 (1b) of the Terrorism Act 2000. He was found guilty of "collecting terrorist-related information, setting up websites...and circulating inflammatory terrorist publications." Siddique was sentenced to eight years imprisonment. His defense has consistently been that he was a merely a 20-year-old "looking for answers," a model student who still lived with his parents. His attorneys have pointed out that there was never any evidence to support the allegation that Siddique intended to join a terrorist group.

An analyst who summarized the images, documents, and videos that Siddique had downloaded said after the conviction that Siddique "lacked the skills, sophistication, lengthy credentials and cold-blooded professionalism" associated with actual terrorists, describing him as "undoubtedly naïve."[140] The danger posed by these prosecutions

---

[137] *CPS Response to Samina Malika Appeal, Crown Prosecution Service* (June 17, 2008), http://www.cps.gov.uk/news/pressreleases/143_08.html.

[138] *Lyrical Terrorist Found Guilty*, BBCNEWS (Nov. 8, 2007), http://news.bbc.co.uk/2/hi/uk_news/7084801.stm.

[139] *Id.*

[140] *Man Convicted of Terror Offenses*, BBCNEWS (Sept. 17, 2007), http://news.bbc.co.uk/2/hi/uk_news/scotland/tayside_and_central/6997830.stm; *Terror Trial Hears Al-Qaeda Praise Claim*, STV, http://www.stv.tv/content/news/main/display.html?id=opencms:/news/Terror_trial_hears_AlQaeda_praise_clai.

is obvious. Neither Malik nor Siddique killed, much less attacked anyone, nor is there evidence that they attempted to commit such acts. Yet both were convicted of serious crimes. Suppose Malik and Siddique are both telling the truth—that they were simply exploring the concepts of terrorism intellectually; however, juries convicted both.

Great Britain is obligated to respect freedom of speech under Article 19 of the Universal Declaration of Human Rights, Article 19 of the ICCPR, and Article 10 of the European Convention of Human Rights (ECHR). Furthermore, Great Britain has gone so far as to expressly incorporate the ECHR into domestic law. Article 10 states, "Everyone has the right to freedom of expression. This right shall include freedom to hold opinions and to receive and impart information and ideas without interference by public authority and regardless of frontiers."[141] This Article does, however, impose some limitations on the right:

> The exercise of these freedoms, since it carries with it duties and responsibilities, may be subject to such formalities, conditions, restrictions or penalties as are prescribed by law and are necessary in a democratic society, in the interests of national security, territorial integrity or public safety, for the prevention of disorder or crime, for the protection of health or morals, for the protection of the reputation or the rights of others, for preventing the disclosure of information received in confidence, or for maintaining the authority and impartiality of the judiciary.[142]

Going beyond the enumerated limitations of Article 10, the United Kingdom imposes a number of additional limitations on freedom of speech for it recognizes incitement to racial hatred and incitement to religious hatred as crimes.[143] The UK's laws on defamation are also extremely strict, imposing a high burden of proof on the defendant—one reason many public figures who would never sue a publication in the United States regularly file suit in the United Kingdom.

IX. The Netherlands

Theo van Gogh was a filmmaker, actor, and columnist well-known for his very public criticism of Islam; he was murdered after the release of his anti-Islam film, *Submission*. The two most striking descriptions of him are that he was a provocateur and gadfly. There is little doubt that van Gogh irritated, enraged, and offended a wide array of people from different ethnic and religious groups, particularly Muslims. It is also fair to say, based

---

[141] Charter of Fundamental Rights, Article 10, *available at* http://ec.europa.eu/justice_home/unit/charte/en/charter-freedoms.html.

[142] Human Rights Act, Article 8, *available at* http://news.bbc.co.uk/1/low/uk/946400.stm.

[143] §§ 17–29 of the Public Order Act 1986. The Criminal Justice and Public Order Act 1994 made a criminal offense publication of material that incited racial hatred.

on interviews with people who knew him, that he was unconcerned by the fact that he offended others. Though clearly offensive to many and irritating to others, van Gogh represented an important aspect of liberal democracy—the right to speak, the right to create, and the right to express opinions, even opinions considered outrageous. It was this quality that led to his brutal murder.

On November 2, 2004, Mohammed Bouyeri shot van Gogh eight times, slit his throat, nearly decapitating him, and stabbed him in the chest. Two knives were left in van Gogh's corpse, one attaching a five-page "open letter to Hirshi [*sic*] Ali" to his body that threatened Western governments, Jews, and van Gogh's collaborator, Ayaan Hirsi Ali. Bouyeri was convicted and sentenced to life in prison with no chance of parole. Bouyeri was a member of the Hofstad Network, which the Dutch government characterizes as a terrorist organization.[144] The Hofstad Network is influenced by the ideology of Takfir wal-Hijra, a Muslim extremist group that advocates armed battle against Jews, Christians, and apostate Muslims in order to restore an Islamic world order. Takfir wal-Hijra's ideology instructs that the ends justify the means; group members adopt non-Islamic appearances and practices (shaving their beards, wearing ties, drinking alcohol, eating pork) in order to blend in with non-Muslims.[145] The Hofstad Network has been suspected of planning to kill several members of the Dutch government and parliament.

What differentiates the Hofstad Network from Theo van Gogh, who openly espoused highly controversial views in the media? If both Hofstad and van Gogh have the potential to incite, if they both have the potential to persuade people to act on their behalf, should not they both be subject to similar limitations? After all, it is a matter of perspective in determining whose ideas are more offensive when in theoretical form only. The difference is that extremist religious speech more readily instigates violence than secular speech does. Theo van Gogh was a powerful voice to some, a gadfly to others, dismissed in some quarters as a racist not to be taken seriously, and considered by some to be an unrepentant Islam basher who needed to be silenced.

But, if the ultimate strength of liberal democracy is the voice that makes us uncomfortable—right or left, religious or secular—then van Gogh manifests that strength. Was he extreme in his views? According to many with whom I met, the answer is *yes*. But, those views, in the context of the right to free speech, did not fall into the category of words that need to be silenced. The right to free speech was, in some ways, designed for a Theo van Gogh. He was not a spiritual leader; he had no army of followers who were going to endanger either national security or public order. Though offensive to some, he was not a danger to society at large or to specific elements of society.

---

[144] On January 23, 2008, a Dutch appeals court ruled that the government did not meet its burden of proving that the Hofstad Network is a terrorist organization as defined by Dutch law.

[145] Transcript, *Al Qaeda's New Front,* produced and directed by Neil Docherty, FRONTLINE, *available at* http://www.pbs.org/wgbh/pages/frontline/shows/front/etc/script.html (last visited Aug. 17, 2013).

That is why limits on free speech do not pertain to a Theo van Gogh, but do apply to rabbis, pastors, and imams who espouse extreme views that threaten specific individuals (internal communities) and larger (external) communities alike. After all, van Gogh did not advocate violence.

X. Norway

Conversations with Norwegian subject matter experts regarding free speech dilemmas in Norway highlighted how distinct the Norwegian paradigm and experiences are from the other surveyed countries. The lack of significant free speech cases in Norway, reflects, according to Norwegian academics, law enforcement officials, and public policy commentators a culture that has, largely, not been confronted with free speech dilemmas. As one thoughtful commentator noted: "we are largely a homogenous country, comprised of traditional Norwegians, and therefore have never had free speech challenges and debates."[146] That homogeneity largely ensured a consensus among the "traditional" population that, seemingly, contributed to a conflict-free culture and dialogue among those who have roots of deep commonality.

That is not, however, to suggest that Norwegians have inherently agreed on critical issues confronting Norwegian society. The sharp, and painful, divide between those who collaborated with Nazi Germany and those who did not reflects a homogenous culture choosing two distinct sides. Although this reflects a profound lack of consensus on an issue of extraordinary national importance, the core homogeneity that defines Norway was, ultimately, not impacted. Therefore, the tensions that define other societies and nations regarding philosophical, legal, and practical free speech dilemmas have, in the main, not been a part of Norwegian culture.

A homogenous population sharing deep cultural, religious, and societal values and roots is, in the main, an unchallenged society from within. That is, threats to individuals and society are largely missing from the Norwegian experience. Although that is not intended to minimize the horror of Breivik's murderous attack on July 22, 2011, it does highlight an important reality of Norwegian culture and history: profound shared values among the traditional Norwegian population. The challenges posed to the other countries are, largely, not faced by Norway either practically or existentially. The caveat, obviously, is Breivik and whether his act is an aberration in the Norwegian ethos or indicative of deeper trends and sentiments shared by others, who are also capable of action. In that vein, the Norwegian free speech discussion is different from the countries previously surveyed: a homogenous population rarely challenged internally presently forced to confront uncomfortable questions in the face of a terrible domestic terrorist attack.

---

[146] Phone conversation (notes in author's records).

Conversations with Norwegian subject matter experts reflect a general consensus that Breivik was the action of a lone individual, whose actions were motivated by the blogger Fjordman but not the result of deliberate, consistent incitement reflective of the Rabin assassination. In that context, the distinction between Yigal Amir and Breivik is significant; what is, obviously, unclear is the possibility of an additional Breivik motivated by the July 22, 2011 attack. As previously referenced, interviews with Norwegian security and law enforcement officials reflect a powerful wake-up call on two distinct fronts: the presence in their midst of a Norwegian right-wing extremist whose targets are fellow, traditional Norwegians and the need to address both intelligence and security failures.

The second lesson learned is directly related to the larger theme this book addresses: the willingness of Western societies to engage in honest discussion and reflection regarding the presence of extremists in their midst. Much like the "conception" among Israeli security officials that an Israeli Jew was incapable of assassinating a prime minister, Norwegian security officials were overwhelmingly surprised by the actions of a traditional Norwegian. That surprise is very much relevant to the free speech discussion: the pre-assassination incitement tested the outer limits of free speech. In direct contrast, prior to July 22, 2011, Norwegian public debate, under no circumstances, reflected or mirrored the pre–November 4, 1995 Israeli atmosphere. The question is whether the public and decision-makers recognize the clear dangers posed by extremist actors and more importantly by extremist inciters. That is, what are the lessons learned from Amir and Breivik and whether applying those lessons results in minimizing individual rights and liberties, particularly with respect to free speech. As was made clear by Israeli Ministry of Justice officials with whom I met the answer is, largely, "free speech privileges" and the "marketplace of ideas." With respect to Norway, the response reflected a conviction that Breivik was a lone wolf and belief (perhaps hope is a better term) that another Breivik is all but unlikely. Perhaps, perhaps not; the question is whether—and to what extent— Norwegian society will engage in a free speech discussion should extremist inciters (religious and secular alike) push the limits of tolerable speech.

On that note, it is important to recall—as previously discussed—that the homogenous, traditional Norwegian population essential to understanding the consensus culture is undergoing change. How that impacts the extremist/incitement/free speech discussion remains to be seen; nevertheless as noted by an Oslo cab driver "the Norway of tomorrow is not the Norway of yesterday." With that comment as a springboard we turn our attention to Norwegian legislation and constitution and two cases that directly address free speech.

According to Article 100 of the Norwegian constitution (May 17, 1814 and subsequently amended):

There shall be freedom of expression.

No person may be held liable in law for having imparted or received information, ideas or messages unless this can be justified in relation to the grounds for freedom of expression, which are the seeking of truth, the promotion of democracy and the individual's freedom to form opinions. Such legal liability shall be prescribed by law.

Everyone shall be free to speak his mind frankly on the administration of the State and on any other subject whatsoever. Clearly defined limitations to this right may only be imposed when particularly weighty considerations so justify in relation to the grounds for freedom of expression.

Prior censorship and other preventive measures may not be applied unless so required in order to protect children and young persons from the harmful influence of moving pictures. Censorship of letters may only be imposed in institutions.[147]

According to Article 135 (A) of the Norwegian General Civil Penal Code:

Section 135 a. Any person who willfully or through gross negligence publicly utters a discriminatory or hateful expression shall be a liable to fines or imprisonment for a term not exceeding three years. An expression that is uttered in such a way that is likely to reach a large number of persons shall be deemed equivalent to a publicly uttered expression. An person who aids and abets such an offence shall be liable to the same penalty.

A discriminatory or hateful expression here means threatening or insulting anyone, or inciting hatred or persecution of or contempt for anyone because of his or her

a) skin colour or national or ethnic origin,
b) religion or life stance, or
c) homosexuality, lifestyle or orientation

Section 140. Any person who publicity urges or instigates the commission of a criminal act or extols such an act or offers to commit or to assist in the commission of it, or who aids and abets such urging, instigation, extolling, or offer, shall be liable to fines or to detention or imprisonment for a term no exceeding eight ears, but in no case to a custodial penalty exceeding two-thirds of the maximum applicable to the act itself. [148]

---

[147] *See The Constitution*, STORTINGET, *available at* http://www.stortinget.no/en/In-English/About-the-Storting/The-Constitution/The-Constitution/ (last visited Jan 11, 2013); although a number of amendments have been enacted since the constitution was originally drafted, Article 100 was not amended until 2004; for a brief description (English) of the Freedom of Speech Commission conclusion that led up to the constitutional amendment of 2004—including the text of the new provision—see http://www.regjeringen.no/nb/dep/jd/dok/nouer/1999/nou-1999-27/13.html?id=142132 (last visited Jan. 11, 2013).

[148] *See* the General Civil Penal Code, Act of May 22, 1902, *available at* www.ub.uio.no/ujur/ulovdata/lov-19020522-010-eng.pdf (last visited Aug. 17, 2013).

The Human Rights Act of 1999[149] incorporated the European Convention on Human Rights (ECHR), the International Covenant of Civil and Political Rights (ICCPR), and other international human rights instruments into Norwegian law giving both the ECHR and ICCPR "semi-constitutional effect."[150] According to Article 10 of the ECHR:

1. Everyone has the right to freedom of expression. This right shall include freedom to hold opinions and to receive and impart in- formation and ideas without interference by public authority and regardless of frontiers. This Article shall not prevent States from requiring the licensing of broadcasting, television or cinema enterprises.
2. The exercise of these freedoms, since it carries with it duties and responsibilities, may be subject to such formalities, conditions restrictions or penalties as are prescribed by law and are necessary in a democratic society, in the interests of national security, territorial integrity or public safety, for the prevention of disorder or crime, for the protection of health or morals, for the protection of the reputation or rights of others, for preventing the disclosure of information received in confidence, or for maintaining the authority and impartiality of the judiciary.[151]

An analysis of the Norwegian constitution reflects a culture deeply respectful of the individual's right to free speech and expression; the ECHR is in full accordance with that principle and right. Although Norwegian law and ECHR articulate limits on the freedom of speech, the provisions are in accordance with free speech traditions and values of Western civil political culture and society. In addition, the traditional Norwegian culture of homogeneity and consensus imply a deep tolerance of free speech precisely because of the paucity of internal challenges to culture and society. That is, the traditional culture of consensus largely minimized dangers posed by free speech; in a society defined as "traditional Norwegian," limits on free speech beyond the provisions of Article 100 (Constitution) and Article 135 A (Penal Code) would be deemed superfluous and not reflective of societal concerns, given the paucity of domestic threats and risks.

In accordance with across-the-board advice generously and graciously provided by Norwegian subject matter experts, two cases stand out as particularly helpful in understanding the practical ramifications of Norwegian free speech provisions. In analyzing and considering both cases it is important to recall the previous discussion regarding both the core tradition of Norwegian society and the terrible events of July 22, 2011.

---

[149] *See generally* http://www.gender.no/Topics/19/sub_topics?path=5/964, which discusses the Human Rights Act of 1999.

[150] Email in author's private records.

[151] *The European Convention on Human Rights*, Coun. of Europe, *available at* http://www.hri.org/docs/ECHR50.html.

A. MULLAH KREKAR[152]

"Krekar has voiced support for Islamic terrorists, encourages holy war and, after years of controversy, was ultimately declared a threat to national security in Norway. Local authorities have been unable to deport him, however, because they lack guarantees he won't be executed back home in Iraq."[153] To that end, Krekar was protected by Norwegian respect for international law obligations regarding harm that may befall an individual post-deportation. Although Krekar pushed the limits of free speech—with full confidence that international law provided him extraordinary protections—a valid argument suggests his support for Islamic terrorists falls within the definition of protected speech.

Krekar's support for Islamic terrorists can be described as troubling and possibly incendiary; however, it does not morph into the realm of violating the Norwegian penal code. In the same vein that the range of opinions expressed daily in the public sphere represent a wide range of perspectives, Krekar's comments reflect his position. The wide gulf between "support for terrorists" and incitement to violence suggests statements of support fall within free speech protections premised on a weak nexus between his words and the actions of Islam terrorists. However, were terrorists to claim that Krekar's words of encouragement were the basis for an attack, then a direct link could be drawn between the words and resulting conduct.

However, the basis for Krekar's trial and conviction were comments made to members of the foreign press (in Norway) regarding harm that would befall Norwegian officials were he to be deported or harmed. After claiming that "it's Norway's responsibility" to find him a secure country to live, he said that if he dies, whoever is responsible for his death will suffer the same fate. "Norway will pay a price," he told the foreign journalists assembled. "My death will cost the Norwegian society. If a leader like Erna Solberg [a former government minister now in opposition as leader of the Conservative Party] sends me out, and I die, she will suffer the same fate." Similar remarks led to police protection for Solberg a few years ago. Krekar stated firmly that he has not "laid a plan" to carry out any assassination, "but my followers will."[154]

Krekar was convicted in accordance with Articles 140, 147 (a-2), and 227 (1) in the General Penal Code, which address the content of his speech, in particular direct threats made against Norwegian officials in positions of authority, particularly Conservative Party chair Erna Solberg.

Article 140. Any person who publicly urges or instigates the commission of a criminal act or extols such an act or offers to commit or to assist in the commission of it, or who

---

[152] *See You Deserve a Brick Today*, GATES OF VIENNA (Kar. 28, 2012), http://gatesofvienna.blogspot.com/2012/03/you-deserve-brick-today.html#more (last visited Sept. 26, 2012).

[153] *Judge Sentences Mullah Krekar to Five Years in Prison for Making Threats*, VIEWS AND NEWS FROM NORWAY (Mar. 26, 2012), http://www.newsinenglish.no/2012/03/26/judge-sentences-mullah-krekar-to-five-years-in-prison/.

[154] *Mullah Krekar Meets the Press*, VIEWS AND NEWS FROM NORWAY (June 10, 2010), http://www.newsinenglish.no/2010/06/10/mullah-krekar-meets-the-press/.

aids and abets such urging, instigation, extolling, or offer, shall be liable to fines or to detention or imprisonment for a term not exceeding eight years, but in no case to a custodial penalty exceeding two-thirds of the maximum applicable to the act itself. Criminal acts shall here include acts the commission of which it is criminal to induce or instigate.[155]

Article 147 a. A criminal act…is considered to be a terrorist act and is punishable by imprisonment for a term not exceeding 21 years when such act has been committed with the intention of…(2) seriously intimidating a population…[156]

Article 227. Any person who by word or deed threatens to commit a criminal act that is subject to a more severe penalty than detention for one year or imprisonment for six months, under such circumstances that the threat is likely to cause serious fear, or who aids and abets such threat, shall be liable to fines or imprisonment for a term not exceeding three years…[157]

That is, Krekar was not prosecuted/convicted because of the support expressed for Islamic terrorists, but instead for direct threats against specific individuals. Rather than perceiving the speech as hate or racist speech the emphasis was on incitement regarding officials in positions of authority. To that end, Krekar's conviction is predicated on incitement to personal harm of specific individuals.[158] As suggested by a subject matter expert, the "Norwegian legal tradition reflects a pragmatic legal approach rather than formalistic which implies a test of context; conviction is possible only if threats and words are viable"[159]

Important for our purposes is the decision to prosecute Krekar in accordance with Article 147 rather than Article 135; the decision reflects a position that supporting Islamic terrorism does not run afoul of the law, whereas incitement to harm specific individuals violates Norwegian law. The prosecutorial decision suggests both enormous respect for the right to express an opinion and little tolerance for speech that potentially harms a specific individual. In the Krekar case, then, the line drawing is, indeed, reflective of a pragmatic (as suggested by a subject matter expert) rather than a formalistic approach. In that context, a pragmatic approach emphasizes potential harm to a specific individual rather than potential harm for which Krekar may bear no responsibility. Obviously that analysis would require rearticulation were an Islamic terrorist to state Krekar's comments motivated and propelled a specific terrorist attack.

---

[155] *See General Civil Penal Code*, UN, http://www.un.org/Depts/los/LEGISLATIONANDTREATIES/PDFFILES/NOR_penal_code.pdf (last visited Jan 11, 2013).

[156] *Id.*

[157] *Id.*

[158] *Norway: Cleric Sentenced for Threats*, N.Y. TIMES, Mar. 27, 2012, http://www.nytimes.com/2012/03/27/world/europe/norway-cleric-sentenced-for-threats.html?_r=3&scp=8&sq=Norwegian&s.

[159] Email in author's records.

B. SUMMARY OF DECISIONS

1. Norwegian Review

The speaker in the Boots Boy Speech[160] charged with violation of § 135a of the Norwegian Penal Code (NPC) was acquitted by the Norwegian Supreme Court. Justice Stabel writing for the majority underlined that the hate speech prohibition had to be interpreted in light of the protection of free speech in NC (Norwegian constitution, ANG) § 100, and that it covered only manifestly offensive speech.

Although finding the speech in question to be "fundamentally derogatory and offensive,"[161] the majority held that it was not offensive enough to constitute a breach of § 135a. In reaching this conclusion, Justice Stabel considered the statement "every day our people and country are being plundered and destroyed by the Jews, who suck our country empty of wealth and replace it with immoral and un-Norwegian thoughts" to be "absurd" and "spurning rational interpretation."

Justice Stabel, to support her conclusion that the statements were nevertheless to be regarded as protected speech, emphasized that no actual threats were made, and that the speech did not amount to any encouragement to carry out particular actions.

Justice Flock for the dissent agreed to the majority construction of the legal foundations found in NPC § 135a read in light of NC § 100 and the international obligations. He underlined, however, that the speech could neither be interpreted purely linguistically, but rather with the aim of establishing how it might reasonably have been perceived by the people present. To do this, he maintained that in addition to the speech, the situation and the actions of the speaker and his crowd had to be taken into consideration.[162]

2. International Review

Following the Norwegian Supreme Court acquittal, a communication was filed before the U.N. Committee on the Elimination of Racial Discrimination.[163] The Committee reaffirmed that the prohibition of all ideas based upon racial superiority or hatred is compatible with the right to freedom of opinion and expression and concluded that the statements in question, given that they were of exceptionally/manifestly offensive character, were not protected by the due regard clause.

The Committee employed a similar interpretive approach as that of the Norwegian Supreme Court's minority. In doing so, the Committee coupled the statement about Norway being "plundered and destroyed by Jews, who suck our country empty of wealth

---

[160] See Chapter Six.

[161] *Id.*

[162] *Id.*

[163] *See generally the International Convention on Elimination of All Forms of Racial Discrimination*, UN, http://www.regjeringen.no/upload/kilde/jd/prm/2005/0059/ddd/pdfv/255370-cerd_communication_30_2003.pdf (last visited Jan. 12, 2013).

and replace it with immoral and un-Norwegian thoughts" with the reference to Rudolf Hess and Adolf Hitler and their principles. The Committee's conclusion was that the Boot Boys expression that they "follow in their footsteps and fight for what (we) believe in" expresses racial superiority or hatred, given "the deference to Hitler and his principles and 'footstep' to be taken as incitement at least to racial discrimination, if not to violence".[164]

The Committee emphasized that the prohibition of all ideas based upon racial superiority or hatred is compatible with the right to freedom of opinion and expression. It emphasized that the "due regard" clause relates generally to all principles embodied in the Universal Declaration of Human Rights, not only freedom of speech, and that all international instruments that guarantee free speech also provide for the possibility, under certain circumstances, of limiting the exercise of this right. It thus concluded that the "due regard" clause did not protect the manifestly offensive speech by the Boot Boys leader.

XI. Final Word

This is a long chapter, covering a wide swath of territory; its length was dictated by the need to incorporate significant amounts of material in order to fully address the question that is, in many ways, at this book's core. In inquiring whether free speech should be limited it is necessary to include the writings of philosophers and to engage in country-specific discussion. Otherwise, the question remains in the realm of the abstract, devoid of concreteness and practicality. Although the ephemeral is intellectually interesting and important it does not facilitate achieving what this book seeks to do: engage in robust discussion regarding free speech in the context of free speech. To that end, analyzing case law, legislation, and constitutional provisions of the surveyed countries is intended to enhance the concreteness of the discussion.

The question whether to limit free speech in the face of extremist incitement is not posed casually. It is an issue that cuts to the heart of Western democracy both because of the danger in limiting speech and the commensurate risk in not limiting speech when the speaker poses a threat. The dilemma is visceral and complicated for it forces the public and decision-makers alike to determine the extent to which society can tolerate intolerant speech. The theme brilliantly articulated by Professor Minow articulates the tension; in many ways, it "sets the table" for the limits of the free speech dilemma.

For final thoughts we turn to John Rawls regarding the freedom of speech:

Never in our history has there been a time when free political speech, and in particular subversive advocacy, could be restricted or suppressed. And this suggests that in a country with a vigorous tradition of democratic institutions, a constitutional

---

[164] CERD/C/67/D/30/2003, 10.4.

crisis need never arise unless its people and institutions are simply overwhelmed from the outside. For practical purposes, then in a well-governed democratic society under reasonably favorable conditions, the free public use of our reason in questions of political and social justice would seem to be absolute.[165]

The question, as highlighted in the Israeli paradigm and relevant to the other surveyed countries, is whether advocacy should be restricted when—in the Rawls analysis—"people and institutions are simply overwhelmed" not from the outside, but as discussed in this chapter, from the inside.

---

[165] JOHN RAWLS, POLITICAL LIBERALISM 355 (2005).

8

LOOKING FORWARD

WHEN I UNDERTOOK this book project, *Freedom from Religion: Rights and National Security* and the comments, reactions, and criticisms it elicited were very much on my mind. As mentioned in the Introduction, my hesitation in writing this book was whether it was sufficiently distinguishable and distinct from *Freedom from Religion*. After intensive meetings with subject matter experts in the surveyed countries I concluded that the two books, although sharing a similar theme, are clearly dissimilar. As one reader noted the two books complement each other in addressing extremism through the lens of free speech, individual rights, and the state's obligation to protect both the larger society and the particular, endangered individual.

The operative word is "balance"; there is no perfect mathematical formula that will satisfy all interested parties. To suggest otherwise is to engage in wishful thinking. As the excerpt (below) from an email I received while writing this book makes clear, the danger posed by extremism is neither amorphous nor imagined:

> Because of your interest in this subject, here is some of the background to the current situation in Colorado City/Hildale. [Name and title redacted] has been down there, and is very aware of the tendency to exaggerated rumors in the community, but says that the theme of children being removed is a consistent one. Based on what has happened in Texas, and knowing what the FLDS are capable of, it seems a legitimate concern. These are some of the things that have been reported to [name of organization redacted].

As you know, Warren Jeffs is still dictating from prison what his followers are to do. He is convinced that if they "purify" themselves then he will be miraculously freed from his prison cell. He has created a group called the United Order (UO) that are those that follow his edicts and are deemed holy/righteous enough to be called "worthy". Only those in the UO are allowed to eat from the storehouses, attend meetings, etc. Those in the UO are not allowed to speak to or even be in presence of those deemed not worthy. Which means those found unworthy are being quarantined in lower parts of the home or rooms by themselves, or worse. Over the past year hundreds have been asked to leave the community and "repent from afar" so they can someday return and be holy enough to be part of the UO. Parents sent to repent are instructed to leave their children as the parent truly believes that if they just repent enough Warren will allow them to come back. He is splitting families and reassigning them to new families. Children without parents present are being told their father is now Warren Jeffs, they are no longer the children of their biological fathers. As a result we are estimating that there are several hundred groups of children from infant to early 20's in households without parents or with one parent caring for several families children (groups of up to 20–30 at a time). From our experience, and the stories of the young adults we are serving, we know that this is a backdrop for extreme physical and sexual abuse (which is rampant in the community—up to 70% of our clients were abused at some point). As Warren's control and commands have continued to increase, the stories we are hearing and the numbers contacting us are escalating.

This week has been by far the worst though. Here are just the stories we have recently heard:

- 11 yr old boy committed suicide because he was told he was no longer worthy to be part of UO and therefore no longer worthy to eat
- 18 yr old boy committed suicide because no longer worthy to eat
- little girl was placed in a chicken coop behind her home because she was no longer worthy and therefore could not have contact with the rest of the family—she was later allowed back in the home, but no one knows what is happening to her now
- A mother had her 3 children removed from her care and supposedly placed in Lyle Jeffs (brother of Warren Jeffs) home as she was not worthy, but they were
- 3 mothers with children have called for assistance this week as they are fleeing with their kids
- Some are saying the UO has ordered buses and are taking all of the children that have been deemed worthy out of the community by December 23 (birthday of Joseph Smith). Over the past year we have heard reports of vanloads of girls being taken away, but parents have not been willing to file police reports. This is huge. Hundreds of children could disappear and never be seen again.

With many parents absent from the homes, the removal of many of these children would be uncontested.

- Numerous accounts of children not being fed because they were not deemed worthy, and even those found worthy not having much because the storehouse is low on supplies. They are a closed society though—so any contact with us is enough to get them kicked out, so they won't let us help them.

    That this is going on in Utah and Arizona without the intervention or at least the close scrutiny of the law seems inconceivable.[1]

Whether all the above are precisely accurate is literally beside the point; it is sufficient that some, perhaps even only one claim, be correct for the extraordinary danger to be fully appreciated. What is particularly disconcerting, actually troubling, is the impression that state agents are, once again, failing in their duty to protect the vulnerable. This was a recurring theme throughout many of my travels; whether "willful malfeasance" is too strong a phrase is a matter of debate. What is clear is a consistent pattern of ignoring threats, vulnerabilities, and harm. As discussed in previous chapters, different reasons have been proffered for this unfortunate and troubling reality. I have found none of them compelling. In rejecting various explanations I harken back to Professor Minow's law review article discussed in earlier chapters: to what extent should society tolerate intolerance?

This is, obviously, a complicated question, fraught with danger. There is, obviously, great danger in casting too broad a swath in creating a paradigm where intolerance is not tolerated. After all, the essence of democracy is a mosaic of voices, opinions, and beliefs. To prevent dialogue and debate is enormously risky for it raises obvious questions regarding standards, criteria, and "who decides." These are, clearly, weighty issues not easily dismissible; however, given the dangers posed by extremism, state leaders cannot sit idly by while vulnerable individuals are endangered. The themes of vulnerability and endangerment are essential to understanding extremism; emphasizing both highlights the clear danger extremists pose. This was made clear to me in the following context:

Over a number of weeks (Fall 2012–Winter 2013) I conducted personal interviews with former FLDS members; those with whom I met had recently left the Church and relocated to the Salt Lake City area. Their ages ranged from late teens to mid-40s; I met with men and women alike. Our conversations, which took place over the course of many hours, were painful, revealing, deeply emotional, and immensely important in understanding the regime of fear imposed by Jeffs, regardless of his physical location. The individuals with whom I met were remarkably forthcoming in their descriptions of the FLDS culture and how they had, prior to leaving, been deeply committed to the faith and its "way of life." In our meetings, I guaranteed anonymity; in their presence I took handwritten notes (which I did not share with them) in an effort to capture both the

---

[1] Private email (in author's records).

specific point the individual was making and its relationship to previous comments made by other interviewees. All the notes are in my personal records.

With one exception, all those interviewed indicated that they would never, under any condition return to the FLDS community; one, in remarkable candor, stated that under the correct circumstance she would weigh with the utmost seriousness the possibility of returning. This, in spite of knowing—in her words—that Warren Jeffs is akin to Hitler and that friends with whom she is in contact have described the current atmosphere as resembling "terrorism." The motivation for this person's willingness to consider returning is a direct result of Jeff's directives that cause unmitigated harm to individuals and families alike: this woman's husband was ordered to leave the community (and obviously, his family) in order to repent for unspecified sins he committed.

As part of the repentance process the husband (a polygamist with two other wives and multiple children and grandchildren) is not allowed to have any contact with any family members. Important to note: in spite of the fact that Jeffs is incarcerated in Texas and the husband is, according to his wife, probably in Idaho, he refuses to have any contact with her, so great is the "regime of fear" created by Jeffs. Nevertheless, in spite of her clearly expressed anger at her husband, the woman was adamant she cannot conclusively reject return to the FLDS culture were that his condition for reconciliation. Restated: in spite of her clear understanding of the harm FLDS has caused her and her children, the possibility of return was not discounted.

Her commitment to FLDS (not to Jeffs) was unwavering, regardless of known dangers. At first blush her willingness was surprising; upon further conversation with her, other former FLDS members, and outside experts her response now "makes sense" to me. In contrast to those who suffer from "Stockholm Syndrome" FLDS members do not have a normative previous worldview as a distinct point of reference. As suggested by a thoughtful non-FLDS member who has long studied the community, members know only the FLDS culture and do not have a suitable comparison paradigm.

That is essential to the harm discussion: the inherent danger of insularity is that conduct deemed harmful by "outside" society has been presented to the group as necessary and essential to please the leader acting on behalf of the divine. In creating a paradigm predicated on "glory to God" or "honoring the leader," the leader ensures loyalty, subservience, and unquestioning obedience. Those who have the temerity to question the leader, or are perceived as questioning, are subject to punishment as they are viewed as apostates who must be educated.

In the FLDS culture, the punishment meted out by Jeffs for questioning—whether the person *actually* questioned Jeffs's leadership is irrelevant—is forced exile for an unlimited period of time, to be determined exclusively by Jeffs. The social, personal, and familial damage is extraordinary; nevertheless, in the "absolute" model Jeffs has created the individual designated for "exile" accepts his or her "sentence" without question, in spite of the unimaginable pain.

Nevertheless, scenes of pain of families torn apart by fiat are not powerful enough to convince FLDS members to reject the "unworthy" label and refuse the order to separate. Other faith requirements in clear violation of the law are fully executed regardless of the damage caused to children and adults alike. Rearticulated: FLDS beliefs result in violations of the law and direct harm to its members alike. Individual members and the community at large are incapable of protecting themselves from the harmful conduct inherent to the FLDS faith as demanded by Jeffs. Therefore, the state is required to intercede on behalf of those incapable of protecting themselves, abandoned by those responsible for their protection.

Restated: in the name of obedience to Jeffs's dictates, parents are violating their obligation to protect their children and are engaged in behavior that directly harms them. Parents may suggest their conduct is not intended to harm their children, emphasizing their actions are predicated on devotion to faith and respect for the dictates of the faith leader; however, the result is harmful conduct that endangers their children. FLDS beliefs include the practice of polygamy defined by the Supreme Court of British Columbia as a "crime of harm." In its seminal decision the Court wrote: "I have concluded that this case is essentially about harm; more specifically, Parliament's reasoned apprehension of harm arising out of the practice of polygamy. This includes harm to women, to children, to society and to the institution of monogamous marriage."[2]

There are, then, three distinct harms pervading modern-day FLDS culture: child brides, Lost Boys, and polygamy. In addition to causing harm to members, all three are in direct violation of the law, yet all three are practiced with impunity on a regular basis in accordance with FLDS beliefs; Jeffs's instructions; imposition of the instructions by enforcers; the willingness of community members to engage in this conduct; and the state's failure, in an institutionalized manner, to protect the vulnerable. Extensive interviews with former FLDS members highlighted the powerful convergence between the three distinct harms/crimes and the five steps required for their occurrence. It is this convergence between the two forces (crimes) and facilitation that we will focus on in the pages to come.

The perfect convergence between the three crimes—underage marriage, abandoned sons, polygamy—and the five facilitators pose a clear and present danger to the vulnerable members of a closed group. The primary responsibility of a parent is to provide for and protect his or her children; that is codified in child endangerment laws in numerous states. The laws make clear parental responsibility and the penalties associated with endangering one's child. The laws were codified in legislative recognition of the failure of many parents to adequately, competently, and consistently provide for their children. There is, of course, risk in penalizing parents: as evidenced by the Texas raid, evidence is problematic, and the state is not necessarily equipped to "step into the shoes" of parents who endanger their children.

---

[2] *Reference re: Section 293 of the Criminal Code of Canada*, 2011 BCSC 1588, para. 5 (Can.).

What the interviews made clear is the extraordinary control exercised by Jeffs over the community: remarkable given the lack of actual physical contact with the incarcerated Jeffs. In addressing this issue, one interviewee commented that for many community members hearing his voice was sufficient cause for acting in accordance with his demands and acceding to new Revelations.

Rebellion is, necessarily, highly secretive, furtive, and modest; one married couple engaged in sexual relations in spite of Jeffs's edict that only the 12 males he has personally chosen are allowed to impregnate FLDS women (sexual relations, according to FLDS dictates, are exclusively for the purpose of impregnating women); another couple engaged in foreplay that did not culminate in full sexual relations; others surfed the Internet (this is strictly forbidden); and others used birth control measures (this is strictly forbidden) and one male (in his words) partied (i.e., consumed alcohol, flirted with non-FLDS girls). Although the couple (married) felt comfortable telling me they had full sexual relations using birth control (condoms), they chose not to answer my question regarding how and where they acquired them, whether purchased or provided by someone else. The interviewees commented other members with whom they were acquainted also engaged in "illicit" conduct. Although their conduct was not indicative of widespread opposition to Jeffs, they clearly relished engaging in rebellious acts, however minor they might seem to an outsider.

That observation is of particular importance because it highlights, unintentionally, the reality of Jeffs's control, enforcement by his handpicked "trusted" bishops and fear other community members might "report" conduct that contradicts revelations and orders. That triangle ensures obedience and control; the methodology harkens to "reporting" mechanisms implemented by Mao Tse-Tung whereby children were expected to report parental misdeeds to the authorities. Those interviewed repeatedly emphasized fear predicated on the all-knowing/all seeing Warren Jeffs, the constant state of uncertainty regarding correct/incorrect conduct, and the powerful consequences if Jeffs determined the individual "unworthy."

These interviews, then, highlight the practical consequence of extremism; the conversations, difficult as they may have been, were extraordinarily insightful for they articulated the daily and existential lives of individuals living in an extremist paradigm. The FLDS culture is a vivid demonstration of harm caused by extremism; the interviews poignantly highlighted how an extremist leader controls members of his community. Although some are able to leave, the overwhelming majority is either incapable or unwilling to do so. To what extent those who do not leave understand the harm to which they are subjected is an open question; what is not an open question is the harm caused and the failure of state agents to sufficiently protect the vulnerable and endangered.

However, as the proceeding chapters highlighted, determining who is endangered and vulnerable is far from clear-cut; the trial of Geert Wilders makes that perfectly clear. Rather than protecting Wilders's right to free speech, the Amsterdam court ordered his trial on the grounds that his speech was offensive to Islam and Moslems. It would be hard to argue that Wilders's speech endangered Moslems or heightened their vulnerability.

Intended to cause discomfort and force public debate, the movie *Fitna* accurately depicts events and religious text. Nevertheless the decision was made to order Wilders's prosecution; this is particularly troubling given that imams who issue fatwas targeting specific individuals are not subject to prosecution.

This paradox is highlighted in the chapter addressing multiculturalism; rather than limiting the free speech of an extremist faith leader who deliberately endangered an individual (Marcoush) the decision (by the court, not the prosecutor) was to limit the free speech of an individual who does not have the intent, much less capability, to harm others. Akin to Theo van Gogh who was a provocateur, Geert Wilders seeks to impact public opinion on a particular issue. That is the essence of democracy; devoid of vigorous public debate, competing voices and opinions are not heard. However, there is an important question, addressed in depth[3] that is directly related to extremism and tolerance: what are the limits of free speech? The follow-up question, as highlighted by the Wilders discussion, is whose free speech should be limited.

The extremism discussion on both questions for the relationship between extremism and free speech is of extraordinary importance. The numerous conversations with subject matter experts in the six surveyed countries consistently reinforced the inexorable link between the two. Although other factors are important in the extremism paradigm, the role of the inciter is paramount. Whether the inciter is a faith leader or a secular voice the relationship between the actions of the extremist and the speech that propelled him is powerful.

In innumerable conversations in Norway, Israel, the United Kingdom, and Holland the question of how to minimize the impact of extremism was posed to my interlocutors. The common refrain among the overwhelming majority of discussants was that extremism cannot be eradicated but can be minimized. The working assumption from the perspective of academics, law enforcement and national security officials, policy analysts, former extremists, and members of the media was the extraordinary staying power of extremism. To that somber analysis was added widespread concern regarding an increase in extremist tendencies and sympathies. In large part this increase was particularly attributable to three distinct factors that have overlapping characteristics: the current European economic crisis; a heightened sense of antagonism with respect to the "other," particularly immigrants predicated on sentiment that "our way of life is threatened and they don't share our values"; and the ability and ease with which extremists can communicate through the Internet.

Additional factors mentioned include tensions between different extremist groups that contribute to increased manifestations of extremism, whether in actual actions or threats; the failure of state agents to directly and consistently confront extremists; and closed communities that accentuate parallel societies and minimize external (state) influence.

---

[3] See Chapter Seven.

The theme of "tolerating intolerance" is essential to this discussion; efforts to minimize extremism must confront two questions: to what extent is society willing to tolerate extremism, and to what extent is society willing to actively combat extremists? The two questions, although similar, are not the same; there is a difference between tolerating (passive) and engaging (active). Resolving this dilemma requires policymakers to acknowledge that extremism *both* exists *and* poses a danger to society and specific individuals alike.

In other words, if policymakers determine that extremism and extremist pose a threat, then the point of departure is how to minimize its impact. "Minimize" is the operative word given the unanimous assessment by subject matter experts in different countries that extremism cannot be erased. That is the dilemma confronting policymakers, law enforcement officials, and government leaders: how to minimize the impact of extremism in a manner that neither backfires by enhancing the public image of extremists nor violates otherwise guaranteed rights. Obviously this is a fine balance; nevertheless, as made clear by events in Norway, Holland, Israel, the United States, the United Kingdom, and Germany, action must be taken.

Extremists can be divided into different categories of commitment and fervor; although some members are fully engaged to a particular cause, others are swayable and therefore receptive to de-radicalization.

Dan Ben-David writes in the forward to "State of the Nation Report"[4]:

> In 1970 Israel was much poorer and its production needs could be supplied by a very large number of workers with low education levels. At that time, over 90 percent of workers in all education level groups were employed—whether they had less than four years of schooling or more than 16 years of schooling…in 21st century Israel, the lower the educational level of prime working age men, the more rapid the decline in their employment rates and the lower the level to which those rates have dropped. If, 40 years ago, over 90 percent of those with 1-4 years of schooling were employed, that rate now approaches 50 percent. Employment among those with 5-8 years of schooling no longer exceeds 60 percent. As the level of education rises, so do employment rates.[5]

Similarly, Haya Stier argues that:

> Industrialized labor markets are currently characterized by economic instability that is expressed both in significant fluctuations in unemployment rates and in the employment difficulties of workers who, while they may succeed in finding

---

[4] STATE OF THE NATION REPORT, SOCIETY, ECONOMY AND POLICY IN ISRAEL (Taub Center for Social Policy Studies in Israel 2010).

[5] *Id.* at 12–13.

employment, often earn wages too low to maintain a decent standard of living, or who are employed only part-time despite their desire to invest more of their time in the labor market...markets are characterized by increasing competitiveness due to the opening up of international markets and to an influx of migrant workers as well as technological developments that have changed the labor configuration and distribution of opportunities within the labor market. These changes have increased opportunities for the highly skilled and narrowed those for workers lacking the appropriate skills and educational background.[6]

Professor Ben-David's and Professor Stier's analysis are relevant across the board and are not, therefore, symptomatic only of Israel. Both commentaries note the growth in international markets, an increase in numbers of migrant workers, and dwindling employment opportunities for uneducated workers. The result is the creation of a category of individuals, largely male, best described as "left behind."

For extremist groups this category provides large numbers of potential members, oftentimes united by powerful commonalities: low education, minimal job opportunities, anger at the immigrant, and powerful sense of despair. As Europe's history has compellingly demonstrated, this is not a unique development; European leaders have either been forced to respond to working class anger or been the beneficiaries of that anger. With respect to the latter, one must only examine the rise of Hitler in the aftermath of the reparations forced on Germany by the Treaty of Versailles.

Although the commentary below by Nachum Blass is specific to Israel the issues it raises regarding educational levels and values are also generic:

[S]ince ultra-Orthodox curricula stress religious studies over Hebrew, mathematics, English, computer literacy and civics, growth in the relative size of the ultra-Orthodox pupil population is tantamount to an increasing percentage of Israeli pupils whose educational experience fails to respond to the needs and values of Western democracies or to meet the demands of developed modern economies. Second, since the ultra-Orthodox population is largely poor, growth in the relative size of the ultra-Orthodox pupil population is as good as an increasing percentage of pupils whose socioeconomic background is likely to have adverse effects on academic achievements.[7]

Blass's commentary regarding educational levels is of the utmost importance in developing, or at least proposing, mechanisms to minimize the dangers posed by extremists. The analysis is as relevant to countering extremism in Europe as it is in Israel. The three commentaries above, based on research findings of the Center for Social Policy Studies in

---

[6] *Id.* at 155–56.
[7] *Id.* at 238.

Israel, reflect the overwhelming importance of both education and employment opportunities in creating a vibrant, economically sound society that minimizes the impact of extremism. There is, of course, nothing new in this analysis; what is important, however, is recognizing two important developments in contemporary Europe.

In many ways, the two are deeply intertwined: the downturn in the European economy combined with immigration, particularly from North Africa, Turkey, and Pakistan, has a significant impact on enhancing extremism. The term "other" was repeatedly mentioned in the course of my conversations with subject matter experts; the reference, without doubt, was to immigrants, and in particular to nonwhite immigrants.

As Jamie Bartlett, Jonathan Birdwell and Mark Littler write:

> Over the last decade, populist parties have been growing in strength across Western Europe. These parties are defined by their opposition to immigration and concern for protecting national and European culture, sometimes using the language of human rights and freedom. On economic policy, they are often critical of globalization and the effects of international capitalism on workers rights.... (T)he growth of these movements is mirrored online.... (T)his nascent, messy and more ephemeral form of politics is becoming the norm for a younger, digital generation.[8]

What unites these disparate groups, then, are high unemployment, low education levels, and enormous resentment. That said, important to recall an important observation suggested by a Norwegian scholar:

> Well, the argument only holds true in part. If we are talking about right-wing extremism in Europe, the finding of recent research is that material deprivation alone can not explain it fully (summarized in political scientist Cas Mudde's dictum: "It's not the economy, stupid!"). It most certainly cannot account for the case of ABB (the reference is to Breivik, ANG), who could have lived an ordinary life with a reasonable regular income had he so chosen.[9]

The Islamic extremists responsible for the terrorist attack committed in London on July 7, 2007, and at Glasgow Airport on September 30, 2007, were middle- to upper- middle class UK citizens; Breivik was a member of Norwegian upper middle class society. Economic circumstances, then, must not be used as a convenient hook to explain the actions of extremists. After all, those responsible for 9/11, primarily including Bin Laden, were neither financially destitute nor unemployable. Given that economic circumstances and education levels were neither the cause for Breivik's actions nor Bin Laden's, measures recommended to minimize extremism do not apply across the board.

---

[8] Jamie Bartlett, Jonathan Birdwell & Mark Littler, The New Face of Digital Populism 15 (2011).

[9] Email exchange (in author's files).

It is for that reason, then, that the impact of the triangle of economic conditions, educational level, and influx of immigrants applies to a *particular* category of extremism rather than broadly to all extremists. This particular category is comprised of those whose anger at the "other" is fueled by a lack of education that directly contributes to unemployability. A caveat is warranted: anger at the "other" whose importance cannot be sufficiently emphasized is not solely the result of education and employment opportunities. As innumerable studies have shown, the causes of racism and hatred are varied, complex, and dependent on both internal and external circumstances.[10]

In exploring both groups—right-wing extremists and radical Moslems—it is important to recall their similarities and distinctions; understanding and appreciating both significantly facilitates implementing measures that reduce their impact. With respect to Islamic extremism, the possible influence of moderate Moslems in the context of de-radicalization must be considered. Case in point: the Brixton Mosque "is an ideal hunting ground for terrorist talent spotters since it attracts mainly young worshipers, including ex-convicts it helps rehabilitate. A criminal background is a useful indication that the candidate is not afraid to break the law. Recruiters often approach their targets at small, private Islamic study groups that meet outside the mosques."[11]

> According to a report in Time Magazine, in an effort to protect the mosque from the increasing attempts of extremist protagonists and their followers to destabilise the mosque and provide an alternative violently radical narrative, the administration took some of the following steps:
> - Changed the charitable status of the mosque into a trust with a set quorum of trustees who had the sole responsibility of electing and deselecting new or fellow trustees.
> - Purchased the mosque premises, placing it under the direct ownership of holding trustees.
> - Prevented the distribution of any publication or leaflets outside the immediate vicinity of the mosque. This included its own material which would, in the event, be distributed from within the mosque premises.
> - Prevented any unofficial classes or study circles taking place.
> - Provided more access to renowned scholars and their students from the Muslim world.
> - Addressed the violent extremists and their ideologies publicly in sermons, conferences and publications.

---

[10] *See generally* Scott Atran, *God and the Ivory Tower*, FOREIGN POLICY (Aug. 6, 2012), http://www.foreign-policy.com/articles/2012/08/06/god_and_the_ivory_tower.

[11] Helen Gibson, *Looking for Trouble*, TIME, Jan. 21, 2002, http://www.time.com/time/world/article/0,8599,193661,00.html.

- Physical preventative measures were adopted for those physically threatening the security of the mosque and its attendees.[12]

A word of caution: not all extremists are driven to action by inciters; Breivik is a prime example of a largely self-motivated lone-wolf actor. Although influenced by the blogger Fjordman, Breivik's decision to attack was unrelated to the incitement discussion. A lone-wolf actor poses extraordinary challenges for the law enforcement and national security communities because of the paucity of "links" to like-minded individuals or leaders and inciters. Although the danger posed by lone-wolf actors must not be minimized, the danger posed by inciters must, similarly, be recognized. In that context, the dilemma is how to more effectively balance free speech protections with protection of individuals and society alike.

The challenge is enormously compounded by the Internet and the resulting cyber incitement. As discussed in Chapter Five, the Internet is an extraordinarily important instrument for extremists. The anonymity, reach, and unrestricted tone and content that is the essence of the Internet is low-hanging fruit for extremists. It enables, literally, unlimited access to believers and provides fertile ground for unhindered, broad-scale recruiting. My conversations with website administrators highlighted the built-in advantage enjoyed by cyber-inciters: the websites are easily accessible, and administrators are deeply opposed to limiting content, regardless of its tone and tenor. Nevertheless, cyber-incitement deserves our attention; there is great danger in the reflexive response of administrators whose unwillingness to engage in discussion regarding content restriction ensures unfettered ability to incite.

Our collective failure to directly address, much less recognize, dangers arising from the link between extremism and speech is an ongoing reality. The discussion is complicated primarily because of the extraordinary hesitation to restrict free speech. The common rejoinder of thoughtful readers of earlier drafts of this manuscript was "marketplace of ideas." In other words, the strength of democracy is the spirit of rigorous debate and discussion; limiting discourse is an anathema to democracy and ultimately weakens it. That is a valid and important argument that Mill and others brilliantly and compellingly articulated. It is a thesis that powerfully resonates with me, particularly when efforts are made to limit voices considered "outside the mainstream."

By example: in December, 2012 the Israeli Knesset Election Committee voted to bar Hanin Zoabi, an Israeli-Arab, from participating in the January 2013 election.[13] The decision, largely based on MP Zoabi's involvement in the May 2010 Freedom Flotilla from Turkey to the Gaza Strip,[14] is expected to be overturned by the Israel Supreme

---

[12] Abdul Haqq Baker, *A View from the Inside*, 73 CRIM. JUSTICE MATTERS 24–25 (2008).

[13] *See* Johnathan Lis, *Israel Election Committee Disqualifies MK Hanin Zabi from Running for Knesset*, HAARETZ (Dec. 19, 2012, 5:30 PM), http://www.haaretz.com/news/national/israel-election-committee-disqualifies-mk-hanin-zuabi-from-running-for-knesset-1.485895.

[14] *See Gaza Flotilla*, HAARETZ, http://www.haaretz.com/misc/tags/Tag/Second%2525252525252520Lebanon%2525252525252520War-1.477718/Gaza%20flotilla-1.476996 (last visited Jan. 17, 2013).

Court.[15] The decision to bar Zoabi's participation in the election reflects disturbing trends in the Israeli extreme political right; although Zoabi's involvement in the Flotilla was a matter of intense public debate it would be an exaggeration to suggest her actions endangered the state. The dilemma is concisely described below:

> The Coalition Against Racism in Israel, opposing the decision, said it was based on political calculations. A strong democracy is tested by its ability to contain opinions, even if they are different or hurtful," said coalition director Nadal Othomann. "Even if we do not all agree with Zoabi's words, we shall fight for her right to express them," he said.[16]

However, there is a flip side to that coin; the one that asks, as Professor Minow posed, what are the limits that intolerance is to be tolerated. The proverbial clear lines in the sand do not exist; to suggest otherwise is to engage in either political demagoguery or intellectual dishonesty. One of the great challenges confronting Western democracy is, indeed, determining the limits of tolerating intolerance. To answer that question requires acknowledging that individual rights are not absolute and are subject to minimization in response to particular threats and circumstances. However, that two-step process demands recognition that extremists endanger society and that the state's primary obligation is to protect the vulnerable. It is for that reason that defining extremism is essential, for otherwise the paradigm is akin to round up the usual suspects.

In the journey that is this book the tension was in identifying in each culture extremists and then determining whether they posed a danger to specific individuals or the larger society. The premise, and conclusion, is that extremists pose a danger to both categories; however, the analysis cannot stop there for attention must be paid to distinct categories.

As discussed in Chapters Three and Six there is a palpable tension in Europe between multiculturalism and immigration: the former preaches acceptance of the "other"; the latter raises deep concerns regarding parallel communities and a willingness to truly be acculturated into a new society. Research and conversations in the United Kingdom, Norway, and Holland raised significant questions regarding the context to which immigrants become members of mainstream society and similarly the degree to which traditional society accepts them. Rearticulated: the distinctions between traditional society and recent immigrants are significant; enhancing the differentiation is concern that newcomers do not "adopt" to the norms and mores of their new society, preferring instead the language, customs, and ways of their home culture.

---

[15] This is not the first time a political party has been banned in Israel: in 1988 Kach (founded by Rabbi Meir Kahane) was banned by the Israel Election Commission, a decision upheld by the Israel Supreme Court. The basis for the ban was the IEC's position that the party was "racist" and "undemocratic."

[16] *See* Lis, *supra* note 13.

Terminology is important; the semantics in Norway unequivocally suggested that society is divided between traditional Norwegians and immigrants; the former are white, the latter Moslems. Obviously, not all immigrants are Moslems; after all, Danes and Poles have moved to Norway and are, therefore, immigrants. However, it would be an exaggeration to suggest that my Danish waiter at an Oslo restaurant would be referred to as an immigrant akin to a Moslem from Turkey or Morocco. That was made clear in meetings with immigration experts who emphasized Moslem immigration even though non-Moslems are also immigrants. Conversations with taxi drivers reinforced the sharp distinction between traditional Norwegians and Moslem immigrants; this distinction was never made between traditional Norwegians and white immigrants. Similar sentiments were expressed in the United Kingdom and Holland.

Why is this important? For the simple reason that distinctions and differentiations become self-fulfilling prophecies whereby "outsider" status is reinforced; that status can also reflect an unwillingness to join the new culture. This is extraordinarily important with respect to the issues discussed in this book; simply put, "outsider" status enormously facilitates recruitment by extremist organizations able to magnify the "in–out" distinction. The consequences are dangerous: failure to successfully integrate immigrant communities into mainstream society directly contributes to marginalization, compounded by high unemployment, low education, and religious extremism. The statistics suggested by scholars in Israel, Norway, and the Netherlands suggest powerful similarity in distinct paradigms: the lack of education directly leads to unemployment[17] with its inevitable and troubling consequences.

Do extremists manipulate this paradigm to their advantage? The unfortunate response is *yes*. In Israel, for example, the high unemployment of adult males compounded by broad-scale exemption from service in the Israel Defense Forces directly contributes to distinct societal categories. This is particularly troubling when the distinction implies delegitimization of state institutions. How else to explain attacks on IDF soldiers by nationalist right-wing settlers, articulation by orthodox rabbis that religious law supersedes state law, and incitement against Arabs and left-wing Jews by right-wing Israelis, religious and secular alike? More troubling than the attacks—physical and verbal—is the deafening silence of state authorities tasked with enforcing the law. Although various reasons have been offered to explain this, the most telling, and arguably accurate, was suggested by a former cabinet minister. His explanation for the failure to question or prosecute rabbis who incited against Rabin: fear of the response of right-wing rabbis and their supporters.

Initially I was surprised by this analysis (2008); however, subsequent research in Israel and elsewhere has tragically re-enforced and reaffirmed this theory. The failure to directly

---

[17] As the Taub Center in Israel suggests, the more troubling issue is "unemployability" of profoundly undereducated adult males (Orthodox Jews) whose English language and mathematical skills are, at best, equivalent to a grade-school level.

confront extremists reflects disturbing weakness by the general public and state officials, with particular blame attributed to the latter. There is, after all, only so much the public can do if law enforcement, prosecutors, and courts are recalcitrant in their efforts and deleterious in their responsibilities. There is no substitute for a firm commitment by those entrusted to protecting the public in general and specific individuals in particular; just like those responsible for inciting Rabin's assassin were never prosecuted, state officials in Utah have consistently failed to protect underage brides and Lost Boys. In both cases, terrible crimes are committed: the assassination of an Israeli prime minister and institutionalized statutory rape and child endangerment.

It is for that very reason that the discussion regarding extremism must move from the abstract to the concrete: the harm is real, not abstract, the consequences visceral, not ephemeral. To that end, the discussion has been threefold: descriptive, philosophical, and legal. The descriptive is essential to recognizing the scope, nature, and danger of extremism; the philosophical necessary to understanding its deeper meanings and causes; the legal inherent to addressing the question of how to minimize the dangers posed by extremists. There are, however, two distinct dangers with respect to imposing legal restrictions on extremism: limiting free speech is a dangerous road to travel, and relying exclusively on the law to limit dangers is, similarly, a problematic path to traverse.

It is to Martin Niemoller's[18] famous poem that we turn our attention:

First they came for the Socialists, and I did not speak out— Because I was not a Socialist.
Then they came for the Trade Unionists, and I did not speak out— Because I was not a Trade Unionist.
Then they came for the Jews, and I did not speak out— Because I was not a Jew.
Then they came for me—and there was no one left to speak for me.[19]

On the assumption society cannot afford to turn a blind eye, there are two recommended avenues in minimizing the threats posed by extremists. Failure to choose either option all but ensures realization of the horrifying paradigm Niemoller's powerful poem compellingly depicts. The failure to understand the ramifications both of extremism itself and silence in the face of extremism has extraordinary consequences. Those consequences are relevant both to the fate of particular individuals and to the larger society.

---

[18] Niemoller was a prominent Protestant pastor who emerged as an outspoken public foe of Adolf Hitler and spent the last seven years of Nazi rule in concentration camps; *see generally, Martin Niemoller: First They Came for the Socialists*, U.S. Holocaust Memorial Museum, http://www.ushmm.org/wlc/en/article.php?ModuleId=10007392 (last visited Jan 17, 2013).

[19] *Id.*

Perhaps that is what led both UK prime minister Cameroon and German chancellor Merkel to conclude that multiculturalism has failed. Although different cultures are important for a broad mosaic, there is an important "but": dangers posed to specific individuals and the broader society if an insular group refuses to adapt to the laws and mores of the home society. Although Western democratic societies are predicated on freedom of speech and belief, there is no justification for that tolerance to be become a weapon for extremists within insular communities. That, more than anything, articulates the great danger posed by an undiscriminating embrace of multiculturalism.

A simple examination of the horrors resulting from honor killings and female genital mutilation sufficiently highlights the dangers to which Moslem females are subjected. Under no condition can either practice be tolerated or understood in the context of respect for other cultures; both acts are a crime that must be met with the full force of the law. Unfortunately, as widely documented and discussed in previous chapters, that is not the case. To that end, *even* if a particular practice is presented in accordance with the tenets and mores of a faith, society has the obligation to proactively prevent it if deemed to harm individuals. The harm test, then, is essential to this conversation.

As I wrote elsewhere:

In a recent Great Britain honor killing case, Justice Roderick Evans commented regarding a young woman killed: "She was being squeezed between two cultures—the culture and way of life that she saw around her and wanted to embrace, and the culture and way of life you wanted to impose on her.' "[20]

In that vein, Gila Stopler sheds important light on the relationship between religion and women:

The symbolic devaluing of women in relation to the divine is achieved in the Hebrew monotheist religion through the establishment of a supreme, male God who makes a covenant exclusively with men that excludes women from the religious ritual and from the religious symbol systems. Through the portrayal of woman, especially her sexuality, as the source of all weakness and evil, this symbolic devaluation becomes one of the two founding metaphors of western civilization.

Women are incomplete and damaged human beings of an entirely different order than men. Whereas male is active female is passive; whereas male is soul female is matter. Whereas the male is a complete human being comprised of both matter and soul, the female is a mutilated male who lacks soul and is only matter.

Men's monopoly over defining, determining, and interpreting truth and knowledge perpetuates the hegemony of patriarchy and maintains men's control over women. Nowhere is the structure of patriarchy more evident than in patriarchal religions, which are built on two pillars of control—men's control over truth and

---

[20] Julia Ann Chamberlin & Amos N. Guiora, *Polygamy: Not "Big Love" but Significant Harm*, 35 WOMEN'S RTS. L. REP. (forthcoming 2014).

knowledge, which ensures their control over women, and men's control over women's sexuality and reproductive capacity.[21]

Where do we go from here? There are, I suggest, three viable alternatives to combating the dangers posed by extremism. There is also a fourth that I find morally unconscionable and legally deeply troubling: ignoring the threat and hoping for the best. Martin Niemoller brilliantly articulated why that option endangers society and individual alike and is, therefore, not an option.

The viable three options I propose as viable are: limiting the free speech of extremist inciters, enhancing and broadening educational opportunities for those living in extremist cultures, and engaging in dialogue with extremists. Before addressing the three, it is important to recall the presumption in this discussion is that extremism does, indeed, pose a threat to society and individuals alike, and turning a blind eye is simply not a viable approach.

With respect to dialogue: perhaps this is reflective of and influenced by my experience in operational counterterrorism, but an approach exclusively predicated on dialogue will not persuade extremist leaders to embrace "de-extremism." The pages of history are filled with examples of efforts to reach out to extremists; the dialogue is effective only if coupled with inducements commensurate with self-interest. Herein lies a troubling weakness with this option: self-interest whereby society recognizes the validity and legitimacy of extremist actions is akin to the multiculturalism efforts that both Cameroon and Merkel identified as "failed." In other words, the concept of understanding other cultures is not unlimited for there is a price paid if limits are not imposed on beliefs expressed and practiced. The results of not imposing limits are tragic; society must overcome hesitation in directly confronting cultures that engage in clear harm-based conduct.

Otherwise, how can we explain the troubling paucity of criminal actions against parents and other family members who participate in female genital mutilation and honor killings? Both are direct attacks on females; both are violent, reprehensible, and must not be understood in the context of dialogue. In this same way, Orthodox Jewry's efforts to relegate women to second-class status—forcing women to sit on the back of buses or preventing women from praying at the Western Wall—is reflective of actions incommensurate with Western democracies. In the same spirit, political calculations have led successive Israeli governments to extend deferments from IDF obligation to Orthodox males; although reflective of the price of ensuring electoral support by the Orthodox community, the larger questions regarding the nature and ethos of society are, largely, ignored. This is not, then, dialogue; it is, for lack of a better term, capitulation predicated on narrow and political calculations. Rearticulated: the failure to directly address the crimes committed in the name of Islam, and the decision to enable sexual discrimination and profound imbalance among Israeli citizens suggests a one-way dialogue in which

---

[21] *Id.* at 25.

society is enabling extremism at the cost of imposing harm on individuals. This is not true dialogue; true dialogue would require the extremists to adopt their ways to that of the larger society. However, as discussed in the proceeding chapters, adopting is antithetical to extremism for it reflects failure to adhere to rigid codes and tenets.

Although the physician described in the Introduction was not an extremist, for he was not, I believe, a person of violence, his rigidity was overwhelming. While professing love for his children as paramount, greater value was attached to religious scripture. I am deeply doubtful that his son, whose hypothetical same-sex marriage was the basis for our conversation, could persuade my seatmate to attend the hypothetical wedding. This was vividly reinforced in a dialogue I had with an orthodox Jew who was adamant that he would not attend the wedding of *his* son were he to marry a Gentile. I pressed, suggesting his son's happiness in finding a partner was to be celebrated; the response was clear: "marrying a Gentile is a rejection and repudiation of everything I [the father] believe in." This individual, who by all accounts is gracious, thoughtful, and generous, was as uncompromising as my plane seatmate.

Both conversations cast, for me, deep skepticism regarding the efficacy of dialogue not accompanied by significant self-interest. That is, the very essence of extremism—whether accompanied by violence or not—is the absolute commitment to a particular belief or set of principles. Although dialogue is, understandably, a compelling alternative, the essence of dialogue is an interaction, by at least two individuals open to an exchange of ideas that implies the possibility of changing opinions and viewpoints. That is, in many ways, the existential opposite of extremism, which, in the dialogue/monologue paradigm, is far more reflective of monologue in the echo chamber, as previously discussed.

Accordingly, I am skeptical of the willingness of the extremist to engage in conversation intended to persuade him to change his ways as that counters the essence of extremism. The more appropriate question is whether dialogue in conjunction with other means can be effective in countering extremism. To that end, of the other two measures suggested as relevant to effectively minimizing extremism the most relevant—in the dialogue context—is education. As discussed in proceeding chapters, research by the Taub Center (Israel) compelling and convincingly highlights the power of education and its extraordinarily positive impact. Conversely, findings demonstrate the dangers, harms, and negative repercussions resulting from a failure to educate young people. To clarify: education in this context refers to a broad education extending far beyond rote memorization of religious scripture—Christian, Jewish, and Muslim—whereby the individual's worldview is extraordinarily limited, and devoid of curiosity and engagement with the outside world. The religious "education" preferred by religious extremists insures perpetuation of ignorance, compliance, and rigidity. The interviews with former FLDS members powerfully highlighted the extraordinarily limited nature of their "education"; that model is as applicable to the FLDS culture as it is to Orthodox Jewry as it is to madrassas where Moslem children learn. The model is the same, only the text differs; divorced from critical thinking, reliance on strict discipline, and ensurance of perpetual ignorance is the essence of strict religious education. In essence, this is not education for it is indoctrination with one powerful goal: ensuring the continuation of closed, insular worlds devoid of external influence. As history has repeatedly demonstrated the consequences are deeply distressing; today's newspapers reflect the dangers posed by indoctrination, rather than education, to individuals and society alike.

However, creating an infrastructure whereby individuals of deep religious faith can study subjects more commonly associated with liberal Western society would represent a dramatic paradigm shift. Whether the impetus would reflect economic reality, internal pressure, or other factors is a matter of debate. What is clear, and need not be a matter of debate, are the extraordinarily positive ramifications of such a development. Unlike the dangers of cyber-incitement discussed in Chapter Five, the positive power of the Internet in opening up new vistas and horizons is unparalleled. It is not by chance that religious extremists deny their followers Internet access; conversations with FLDS members powerfully articulated the extent to which Warren Jeffs is deeply concerned about the Internet's impact on his community. In that same vein, the manner in which Orthodox Jewish women use Facebook to communicate with the outside world, expressing their distress, suggests understanding of the world beyond their immediate cloistered walls.

Similarly, economic reality increasingly forces Orthodox women to join contemporary society's workplace, as compared to the traditional role of schoolteacher. Whether this will have an impact on forcing the larger Orthodox community to engage with modern Israeli society remains to be seen; nevertheless, it suggests an important shift whose importance need not be minimized.

Dialogue (not echo chamber) and education are, then, the carrots in minimizing extremism; limiting the free speech of extremist inciters is the stick. It is to that we turn our attention. We are at a crossroads: my travels over the past few years have forced me to confront the dangers posed by not aggressively confronting inciters. I have been extremely fortunate that a broad range of individuals have graciously agreed to engage me in discussion on this issue. Obviously, not all agree with the core recommendation to limit free speech; some find this proposal deeply troubling, suggesting it violates the very ethos of liberal Western society. They are right. However, I respectfully disagree with them for there are limits to which the "marketplace of ideas" is the most effective mechanism to minimize the reach of an inciter, particularly when the Internet makes that reach, literally, unlimited. Mill's argument, on which I was raised and educated, may well not be relevant to a world where an inciter has the world, literally, at his fingertips. Whether Breivik ever met Fjordman is not important; what is relevant for our purposes is that Fjordman's writings were available to Breivik and millions of others through the Internet. The same is true with respect to Major Hassan, who was propelled to kill fellow US military personnel because of cyber-incitement.

However, my recommendation goes beyond the computer: the FBI's failure to directly address the radical imam in Minneapolis who radicalized second-generation Somali youth to become suicide bombers is a mistake that we cannot allow to occur again. That is also true with respect to the stunning failure of Israeli authorities regarding right-wing rabbis. In the ultimate paradox, MP Wilders was brought to trial for offending Moslems; his acquittal need not detract from the enormity of the decision to prosecute him. A careful review of *Fitna* and Wilders's public comments reflect an individual raising powerful flags of caution with respect to clear threats to Dutch society. However, rather than prosecute the imam who issued a fatwa against Marcoush, the decision was made to prosecute the warner.

Although Wilders's commentary and methods, understandably, cause discomfort, that is neither existentially, legally, or practically akin to the clear physical harm Marcoush expressed to me the evening we had dinner. He well understood the very direct threat under which he had been placed. The same is true with respect to Rabin. In that spirit, the same is true with respect to underage girls subject to statutory rape, honor killings, and female genital mutilation as I write these lines.

It is to *them* that we owe a duty and it is for their protection that we *must* seriously consider limiting the free speech of those directly responsible for the harm and danger in which they live. Western society's obligation to protect the vulnerable is no less sacred than Western society's obligation to ensure freedom of speech.

Somehow, somewhere that balancing requirement must be adjusted before an inciter causes further harm. In that spirit, we cannot take our collective and individual eye off the ball that is the harm posed by extremism.

Index

Debs, Eugene V., 138, 139
de Gouttes, Régis, 103, 104
Demant, Froukje, 92
democracy/democracies
    free speech and, xviii, 72, 163–64, 176, 180
    limits of tolerating intolerance and, 177
    religion and state law in, 55
    religious freedom and, xviii
    religious tolerance, 56
    threats and, 45
Denmark, 39, 102
Dennis, Eugene, 141
Dennis v. United States (1951), 142
Diskin, Yuval, 25
Doe, Normon, 90
Druze, IDF and, 25
Dryden, John, 130
Dutch Party of Freedom, 22
Dvir, Shmuel, 125
Dworkin, Ronald, 133–35

East Germany, 75
ECHR (European Convention on Human
    Rights), 90, 154, 159
economic crisis in Europe, 85, 171
EDL (English Defense League), 117, 118–19
Edmunds Act (1882), 62
education levels and extremism, xxi, 46, 47, 88,
    172–75, 178, 181, 182–83
Eisenhower, Dwight D., 30, 31
Ellsburg, Daniel, 145
el-Moumni affair, 89
employment
    assimilation and, 33, 88
    immigration for, 36
    in Israel, 106, 109, 172–73, 174, 178
    minimizing extremism with, xxi, 175, 178
    rates in European countries, 86, 91
    unemployment, 38, 72, 174, 178
*Employment Division, Department of Human
    Resources of Oregon v. Smith* (1988), 32–33
English Defense League (EDL), 117, 118–19
Eriksen, Jens-Martin, 44
Eskin, Avigdor, 125, 125n9
Espionage Act (1917), 138–40
Europe
    economic crisis in, 85, 171

education levels and extremism, 174–75
extremists use of the Internet/social media
    and the, 75–76
honor killings in, 50
immigrants in, 23
individual rights vs. national security in, 2,
    177–78
right-wing extremists in, 93–94
terrorist attacks in, 51
terrorist organizations in, 79
working class anger in, 173
See also multiculturalism; *Specific countries*
European Commission's Expert Group on
    Radicalization, 93
European Convention on Human Rights
    (ECHR), 90, 154, 159
European Court of Human Rights, 90
Evans, Roderick, 180
extremism
    alternatives for combating, 181–84
    defined, xix, xxii–xxiii, 1–7, 6nn14–15
    education levels and extremism, xxi, 46, 47,
        88, 172–75, 178, 181, 182–83
    Internet and social media use for, 74, 75–83
    overview, xv–xxiv
    right-wing actions, xvii, 93–104, 116, 117–20,
        118n130, 156–57, 174
    See also religious extremism; secular extremism;
        society, dangers extremism poses to

Facebook, 71, 72, 74, 126, 183
Fascism, 57, 57n4
Fatah, Tarek, 44
Fatherland Party, 100
fatwa, 33, 33n57
FBI (Federal Bureau of Investigation), 8–9,
    9nn25, 27, 12, 183
female genital mutilation (FGM), 48–49,
    48n55, 180, 181, 184
50 Cent (rapper), 153
fighting words, 13, 146–47
First Amendment
    as applied, 135–50
    Dworkin on, 133–35
    limiting Internet speech and the, 77
    limiting speech and the, 13–17
    religious freedom and medical treatments, 69